ROUTLEDGE LIBRARY EDITIONS:
FAMILY

Volume 17

CAPTIVE CLIENTS

CAPTIVE CLIENTS

Social Work with Families of Children Home on Trial

JUNE THOBURN

LONDON AND NEW YORK

First published in 1980 by Routledge & Kegan Paul Ltd

This edition first published in 2023
by Routledge
4 Park Square, Milton Park, Abingdon, Oxon OX14 4RN

and by Routledge
605 Third Avenue, New York, NY 10158

Routledge is an imprint of the Taylor & Francis Group, an informa business

© 1980 June Thoburn

All rights reserved. No part of this book may be reprinted or reproduced or utilised in any form or by any electronic, mechanical, or other means, now known or hereafter invented, including photocopying and recording, or in any information storage or retrieval system, without permission in writing from the publishers.

Trademark notice: Product or corporate names may be trademarks or registered trademarks, and are used only for identification and explanation without intent to infringe.

British Library Cataloguing in Publication Data
A catalogue record for this book is available from the British Library

ISBN: 978-1-032-51072-9 (Set)
ISBN: 978-1-032-53031-4 (Volume 17) (hbk)
ISBN: 978-1-032-53038-3 (Volume 17) (pbk)
ISBN: 978-1-003-40984-7 (Volume 17) (ebk)

DOI: 10.4324/9781003409847

Publisher's Note
The publisher has gone to great lengths to ensure the quality of this reprint but points out that some imperfections in the original copies may be apparent.

Disclaimer
The publisher has made every effort to trace copyright holders and would welcome correspondence from those they have been unable to trace.

CAPTIVE CLIENTS
Social Work with Families of Children Home on Trial

JUNE THOBURN

ROUTLEDGE DIRECT EDITIONS

ROUTLEDGE & KEGAN PAUL
London, Boston and Henley

First published in 1980
by Routledge & Kegan Paul Ltd
39 Store Street,
London WC1E 7DD,
9 Park Street,
Boston, Mass. 02108, USA, and
Broadway House,
Newtown Road,
Henley-on-Thames,
Oxon RG9 1EN
and printed in Great Britain by
Redwood Burn Limited
Trowbridge and Esher
© June Thoburn 1980
No part of this book may be reproduced in
any form without permission from the
publisher, except for the quotation of brief
passages in criticism

British Library Cataloguing in Publication Data

Thoburn, June
  Captive clients.
  1. Family social work - Great Britain
  2. Children - Institutional care -
Great Britain
  I. Title
  362.8'2   HV700.G7   80-40389

  ISBN 0 7100 0528 8

For John, Nicky and Alan

CONTENTS

PREFACE	ix
ACKNOWLEDGMENTS	xi
1 THE THEORETICAL FRAMEWORK	1
Introduction	1
'Beyond the best interests of the child'	2
The 'cycle of deprivation'	4
Studies of child placement	7
Studies of social work intervention	9
2 OUTLINE OF THE STUDY AND METHODS USED	13
Finding the families	14
The interviews with the parents	17
The interviews with the social workers	18
The report	19
3 SOME ILLUSTRATIVE CASE STUDIES	20
Infants: often actual or suspected cases of non-accidental injury	20
Younger children whose home conditions were unsatisfactory	25
Older children with behaviour, delinquency, or school problems	29
4 PARENTS AND CHILDREN	32
Material circumstances of the families	32
Physical health of parents and children	36
Mental health and emotional problems of parents	37
Childhood experiences of parents, and contact with the extended family	39
Friends and neighbours	40
Delinquency of parents	40
Attitudes to marriage, and marital problems	41
Single-parent families	42
Attitudes to children	43
Parental behaviour leading to statutory action	45
Emotional and behaviour difficulties of children	47

5 THE PROCESS OF CARE: ITS IMPACT ON PARENTS AND CHILDREN	51
The children in the study	51
The children in care	52
The children when away from home	53
Reactions of parents when children went away	59
The return home of the children	61
The children when at home	64
6 THE SOCIAL WORKERS AND THE HELP THEY OFFERED	70
The social workers	71
The social work help offered	74
Conclusions	110
7 DECISION-MAKING AND PLACEMENT POLICY	118
Attitudes and the way these affected service offered and decisions made	119
Resources	131
Visiting	142
Some administrative and legal factors which affected decisions	150
8 WHO GOES HOME? SOME CONCLUSIONS AND SUGGESTIONS FOR AN IMPROVED SERVICE	169
Who goes home?	169
Some suggestions for an improved service	171
Some comments on the debate about the least detrimental alternative for children in care	175
Appendix I THE LEGAL FRAMEWORK	181
Appendix II INTRODUCTORY LETTER FROM THE DIRECTOR OF SOCIAL SERVICES	185
NOTES	187
BIBLIOGRAPHY	190
INDEX	197

PREFACE

This study was made possible by a grant from the Central Council for Education and Training in Social Work under a Fellowship Scheme which aims to encourage research by social workers into the practical problems which they encounter. It starts with the problems facing the social worker when a care order is made. Should he work towards preserving the original family unit, or should he aim to provide the child with substitute parents? How does he decide how 'the welfare of the child throughout his childhood' (Children Act, 1975) can best be promoted? If he decides that the child's future lies with the family which has been judged to be failing him in some respect, how does he work towards his goal? Where does he place the child? How do the parents react to having the care of their child transferred to the state, and to the state's attempts, through the social worker, to help them?

Much has been written about children who are adopted, in foster care or in residential care, but there has been no study which looks specifically at that group of children who remain the responsibility of the local authority but are actually living in their own homes. Yet in 1976 Department of Health and Social Security statistics show that of 100,600 children in care in England and Wales, 18,000 were 'under the charge of parent, guardian, relative or friend', usually referred to as 'home on trial'. This book is not a statistical study from which quantitative conclusions can be drawn. It is essentially descriptive, and sets out to examine in some depth twenty-five families, thirty-four of whose children are, or have been, 'home on trial', and the social work help they have been offered, through their own and their social workers' eyes. Other studies of consumer opinion of the child and family care services, (notably Mayer and Timms' (1970) and Sainsbury's (1975) studies) have concentrated on clients who had some element of choice about whether they wished to receive the service, and Sainsbury (p.59) suggests that 'it would be instructive to explore what happens to process and relationships in social work when dissatisfied clients are, in one sense or another, captive'. The families in this study, even when compared with most of the clients of statutory agencies, had little room for choice, in that they saw themselves as having to accept the visits of the social worker, or risk losing their children. However delicately the social worker went about his job, they were 'captive clients'. As one parent put it: 'Me. I'm in a position where I cannot put a foot wrong. I have to go along with the welfare.' It is this strong element of authority, and the vulnerability of the children concerned, which makes working with these families particularly difficult and demanding, and which means that they take up social workers' time out of all proportion with the numbers involved.

ACKNOWLEDGMENTS

In acknowledging the help I have received with the preparation of this book, I must first express my deepest gratitude to the parents and children who shared with me their past unhappiness and their hopes for the future. The need for confidentiality precludes my mentioning by name the social workers who gave generously of their time and expertise, both at the planning stages and during the lengthy interviews. I would particularly like to thank Sue B. and Sue G., who discussed the project at various stages, and provided encouragement throughout. I also want to thank the managers and administrators of the social services department who made it possible for me to identify and contact the families, and especially the research officer for stimulating discussions, practical help, and detailed comments.

The research was financed by a CCETSW Fellowship for Advanced Studies, for which I am most grateful. I should like to thank Joy Guy and those other members of the CCETSW staff who took part in the research seminars, and showed continued interest in the progress of the project. Dennis Marsden of the University of Essex acted as academic supervisor for the research, and his help, especially at the planning stage, was invaluable.

Amongst those who have influenced my thinking on the subject of children at risk, I single out for warmest thanks Olive Stevenson and Bob Holman. Both have been generous with their time and ideas from the early stages to the completion of the book. I am also grateful to Victor George and Michael Rutter for help at the planning stage; to Jane Aldgate, Lydia Lambert, and Rosamund Thorpe for stimulating discussions on the problems of research on children in care; and to Juliet Berry, Martin Davies, and Nancy Drucker for comments on the manuscript.

Marie Munn and Sylvia Walker typed the manuscript, and I thank them for their speed and efficiency.

Finally I thank my husband John for his encouragement and Nicholas and Alan for tolerating my inadequacies as a frequently preoccupied mother.

Chapter 1

THE THEORETICAL FRAMEWORK

INTRODUCTION

This study was planned and carried out at a time when theories of child care were under intense scrutiny, and some which had formed the basis of child care policy for the previous twenty years were being challenged. The deaths of Maria Colwell, John Auckland, Steven Meurs and others, and the subsequent reports on the role of the social services in these cases, intensified the debate about child care policies in academic and professional circles, and at the same time brought politicians and the general public into the arena. The climate of opinion was on the whole hostile to parents who were shown to have neglected their children. Some of the experts, notably Mia Kellmer-Pringle and John Howells, expressed the view that too much emphasis has been placed on prevention and rehabilitation, and that it should be made easier for links between parents and children to be severed in some cases. Others, especially Bob Holman, members of the Child and Family Care Committee of the British Association of Social Workers, and organisations for single parent families, maintained that a great deal more could and should be done in the community to help parents.

At the time of the interviews the 1975 Children Act (see Appendix I) was on the statute books, but had not been fully implemented. The concern of society about child abuse and neglect was evident not only in the Children Act, but also in the government memoranda on cases of 'non-accidental injury' and 'failure to thrive', and in the fact that, at a time when resources were scarce, social services departments were giving high priority to cases of children at risk. This debate about child care policy, the tragedies which led to the debate, and the administrative and policy implications, were either explicit or lurking below the surface in many of the interviews with parents as well as social workers which form the basis of this study.

In planning the research I was influenced by three distinct but interlocking bodies of work: 1 theoretical work based on psychological and sociological research into child development, and the causes and effects of deprivation, and often making recommendations about how the best interest of the child can be secured; 2 social policy studies of child placement; and 3 studies examining the

nature and effectiveness of social work, including those which
examine the views of the consumers.

'BEYOND THE BEST INTERESTS OF THE CHILD' (1)

About one principle in child care there is no disagreement: that
the welfare of the child should be the prime consideration for those
who make decisions about children. The problem of deciding how the
child's welfare can best be ensured is one which social workers face
daily. The 1948 Children Act requires them to be satisfied before
receiving a child into voluntary care that 'the intervention of the
local authority ... is necessary in the interests of the welfare of
the child'. The 1963 Children and Young Persons Act makes it 'the
duty of every local authority to make available such advice, guidance
and assistance as may promote the welfare of children by diminishing
the need to receive children into or keep them in care', and the 1975
Children Act states: 'In reaching any decision relating to a child
in their care a local authority shall give first consideration to the
need to safeguard and promote the welfare of the child throughout
his childhood.' It is of some significance that this clause replaces
a requirement in the 1948 Act for the authority to 'exercise their
powers with respect to the child so as to further his best interest'.
It has been realised in the period since 1948 that, for children in
care, as Goldstein puts it, 'the child in question is already a
victim of his environmental circumstances, that he is greatly at risk,
and that speedy action is necessary to avoid further harm being done
to his chances of healthy psychological development' (Goldstein et al.,
1973, p.54). For children in care, or where the family is not able
unaided to meet the child's needs, what is 'best' is not available,
and Goldstein suggests that a more realistic aim would be that
'placements should provide the least detrimental available alternative
for safeguarding the child's proper growth and development'.

It is at this point that writers begin to differ. Families vary
greatly in the way they meet their children's needs and in their
capacity to do so (see J. and E. Newson, 1963; 1968). At what stage
does the care offered by parents (or for that matter foster parents,
daily minders or residential workers) cease to be 'good enough' (2)
to ensure the child's proper growth and development? How much help
should the state provide so that parents who cannot meet their
children's needs unaided can be helped to do so? If it is clear that
some parents are at a given time, or perhaps even permanently, unable
to meet their children's needs, should they be able to maintain links
with those children, or should such links be broken so that the
children can be free to form new attachments with substitute parents?
To what extent, and in which cases, should a parent's right to be in
contact with his child be terminated to facilitate the growth of new
attachments? Some have argued that continued contact with the
natural family leads to a better adjustment in adult life (Weinstein,
1960); others (Goldstein et al., 1973) that a child can have an
attachment to only one set of parents. The most recent examination
of this subject is contained in 'Good Enough Parenting', a series of
papers published by the Central Council for Education and Training in
Social Work (1978).

Chapter 1

Although psychologists and psychiatrists have been the principal formulators of theories of child development and have made recommendations about placement policy, it is the social workers who make the majority of decisions and have built up guidelines for practice, based on the theories available and their own experience. These guidelines have been greatly influenced by the work of John Bowlby (1951; 1971) and by those who, like him, stress the vital importance of a child's early relationship with his mother for future personality development. These include Donald Winnicott (1965; 1971), Clare Winnicott (1970) and James and Joyce Robertson (1967; 1968). Their works were, and probably still are, essential reading for all child care students, and the films made by the Robertsons ('Young Children in Brief Separation') must have been seen by the majority of those working in child care. Evidence from fieldwork practice, and the poor prognosis for children in care, lent support to the belief that continuity of care should be a fundamental principle for child placement. Hence the increasing stress on preventive work and keeping the family together, which was officially recognised in Section 1 of the 1963 Children and Young Persons Act quoted above.

Almost from the date of Bowlby's World Health Organisation report, however, there has been a debate about the interpretation and importance of his work (see Rutter, 1972). It was quickly accepted that the father or a mother substitute could take the place of the mother, and that the crucial factors were stability, commitment and continuity of care. In other words, 'psychological' parenthood could replace 'natural' or 'biological' parenthood, without damaging the child. This view is central to Goldstein's thesis, and from it he argues that full adoption rather than fostering is desirable for children in care, in order to ensure the 'psychological parent-wanted child relationship essential to healthy development' (Goldstein et al., 1973, pp.17-21). Whilst many social workers would argue with his conclusions, they would accept his view that a child's concept of time differs with age, and that, especially for the very young child, delays in placement must be avoided if at all possible.

Rutter (1972), J. and B. Tizard (1971) and Wolkind (1974) have extended the debate by examining more closely in a series of research studies the nature of maternal care and of deprivation. They show that a child living in his own home can also suffer from maternal deprivation. The nature of the mother-child relationship, or the lack of any such relationship, may be the damaging factor, and not the separation itself. Mia Kellmer-Pringle (1974, p.84), following a similar line of argument, sees a misinterpretation of Bowlby's work leading to 'the dictum "better a bad family than a good institution". While there is no evidence to support this assertion, it has led to some official reluctance to remove children, even from appallingly bad homes. This view ignores the msot crucial factor in mothering, namely its quality, stability and intensity. Instead, it postulates a powerful bond, commonly referred to as the "blood tie".' Kellmer-Pringle, Howells (1974), and Tizard (1977) accuse social workers of putting too much weight on the 'blood tie', and thus endangering the future emotional health, and possibly the lives, of the children about whom they make decisions. (3)

This argument is extended by a series of research studies on children who have been adopted. A study of children in the 1958 cohort who were adopted (Crellin et al., 1971) showed that in all respects at the age of 7 they were ahead of those illegitimate children who had remained with their natural parents. Others, notably Tizard's (1977) and Kadushin's (1970) studies of children who were adopted suggest that children even from deprived backgrounds can successfully relate to substitute parents. It is now generally accepted that early deprivation of maternal care need not necessarily cause permanent damage, and that much depends on a child's ability to cope with the stresses to which he is exposed, his age, and the degree of deprivation. Most writers also stress the need for the child to become attached to an adult who can meet his needs as early as possible.

Bowlby's work has been more fundamentally challenged in the last few years especially by contributors to A.M. and A.D. Clarke (1976) and by Morgan (1975). Morgan questions the value to a child of a close relationship with one adult, and would support a pattern of child care where less close relationships are formed with a number of adults. This philosophy has been adopted by some communes, and by some feminist groups who call for a massive expansion of day and residential nursery provision. It has not, however, had much if any influence on placement policies for children in care. Group residential care is seen as necessary and valuable for some children, but for long term care family placements are usually preferred. Indeed, there is a move towards the placement of young children needing day care with subsidised daily minders rather than in day nurseries, on the grounds that this is not only cheaper but better for the child's emotional development.

THE 'CYCLE OF DEPRIVATION' (Joseph, 1972)

Alongside this essentially psychological debate, and equally important to the social worker making decisions about placement, is the debate about what Sir Keith Joseph, speaking to the Pre-school Playgroups Association in 1972, referred to as the 'cycle of deprivation' (see Rutter and Madge, 1976, for an assessment of this concept). Parents who were themselves brought up in depriving circumstances are likely, it was suggested, to bring up their own children in similarly depriving circumstances. Whether this is the case, and if so, the reasons for it and the possible solutions, are subjects for debate by sociologists, psychologists, social administrators, and politicians. Does the problem lie in some psychological inadequacy on the part of the parents, as Keith Joseph seemed to be suggesting, to be remedied by family planning, more caseworkers, and perhaps by rescuing children from 'bad' homes? Or does it result from the debilitating lives which poor families lead, and the inadequacies of our social services which place families under intolerable stress, as Holman (1973a; 1976), Wilson (1974) and the publications of the Child Poverty Action Group, Shelter, and the Mind campaign would suggest? Holman (1973a; 1976), Jordan (1974; 1976), Wilson (1974; 1976) and Wilson and Herbert (1978), in looking at the relationship between material deprivation and the failure to function adequately as a family, apply this debate to the role of the social worker. Jordan (1974) states that the 'poverty lobby' has done poor families a disservice in accepting the view that poverty is a social rather than an economic problem. Social workers should concentrate on helping those who have problems of adjustment, and throw the problem of poverty back to the politicians to sort out. Harriett Wilson (1976) comes to a similar conclusion as a result of her study of families receiving social work help in an inner city area.

> Poverty is not generated by 'inadequate' people; it is the consequence of too much inequality. In the final analysis we must all work for a better distribution of the nation's resources.

Families whose children appear before the courts and come into statutory care are central to this debate. Has this happened because they are 'inadequate' (H. and E. Schaffer, 1968), or because the circumstances of their lives have put them under undue stress? Wilson counters the arguments of the Schaffers by pointing to the 'incidence of emotional instability, neurosis, or psychosis among families who are well to do' and yet whose children rarely come into care. She suggests that families lacking resources for decent living may, under stress

> reach a stage of functioning which is adapted to their resources but which has adverse effects on child development, so that the social services or the educational authorities feel compelled to intervene. And this includes the tragic circumstances in which 'total failure to act in a protective capacity' results in physical damage to children (Wilson, 1976).

Holman (1976) argues that a local authority should be required to show that it has fulfilled its duties under Section 1 of the 1963 Act to provide practical help to keep children out of care, before being able to assume parental rights over a child. He sees the lack of day care and other support services and the low level of financial support, especially to single-parent families, as being one of the reasons why parents fail to fulfil their duty to their children. (4) Jean Packman (1968), Rosamund Thorpe (1974b) and Jane Aldgate (1978a), in their studies of children in care, found that the poor, the homeless, and children from single-parent families were particularly at risk of coming into care. The British Association of Social Workers (1974) in its evidence on the Children Bill, makes a similar point; and Stuart Wier, writing on behalf of the Child Poverty Action Group (1975) points to the 2,700 children received into care because of homelessness in 1973, and stresses that this was an under-estimate, in that it did not include those where the 'lack of a secure home is the root cause of the separation'.

The Bill has been presented to Parliament as politically neutral. In fact it represents a deliberate political choice - to 'rescue' children from poor and deprived homes rather than to provide the resources and services which would enable the majority of families with children 'at risk' or in care to provide secure and caring homes for them.

The pressure groups continue to ask the politicians to improve the impoverished and stigmatising environment in which thousands of children are being brought up. To some, however, they cannot succeed within the capitalist system. Wilding and George (1975, p.385) write:

> Stigmatising procedures may be a latent rather than a manifest
> function of welfare policies, but such procedures are necessary,
> inevitable, and functional in a capitalist economic system.
> They are necessary to reinforce the value system on which
> capitalism depends.

Looking at the relationship between social work and poverty from a Marxist point of view, Peter Leonard (1975, p.6) sees social work as having a 'legitimating function' essential to the maintenance of the capitalist system:

> We have seen that the ruling class cannot maintain its exploitive
> domination simply by the direct repressive state apparatus of
> the army, police, courts and prisons. Its legitimation has to
> be engineered through a range of ideological mechanisms. Social
> work operates primarily as part of these mechanisms.

How has social work practice, particularly in respect of families whose children are at risk, responded to this debate about the 'cycle of deprivation'? In the 1950s, as a reading of social work journals will show, social workers tended to concentrate on the personalities of parents whose children needed help. The 'problem family', and how to improve its functioning, was a central concern. This is not to accept the view that no attention was paid to social conditions as Barbara Wootton would suggest in her caricature of the social worker of the time, 'Daddy Knows Best' (1959b). It was, after all, the social workers who pressed most strongly to be given powers to help families in practical ways in the 1963 Children and Young Persons Act. Since that time more weight has been placed on environmental factors, and practice has changed accordingly. As early as 1959 in 'Social Science and Social Pathology' Barbara Wootton was asking social workers to give up social casework and instead to concentrate on helping clients to improve their environment. Her message was perhaps too early and too extreme, but when Adrian Sinfield (1969) in a post-Seebohm Report analysis of social work practice took a similar line, the social work profession took more notice. Social workers, he said, should be social investigators, mediators, and interpreters.

The teaching of sociology and of community work and welfare rights are now given greater prominence in the training of social workers. In 1972 the British Association of Social Workers published 'Social Action and Social Work', which stated that 'social action is an integral part of social work and a commitment to it has always been implicit in social work values'. The BASW Code of Ethics approved in 1975 implies an acceptance of the importance of environment in contributing to social distress:

> The social worker's responsibility for the relief and prevention
> of hardship and suffering is not always fully discharged by
> direct service to individuals, families and groups. He has the
> right and duty to bring to the attention of those in power, and
> of the general public, ways in which the activities of government,
> society, or agencies, create or contribute to hardship and
> suffering, or militate against their relief.

On the whole, however, social workers in accepting the importance of poor environment as a cause of family problems, have not rejected the view that in some cases the personality of the parents is of great importance. Peter Leonard, in trying to define an 'oppositional function for social workers' states:

Perhaps I should say at this point that a structural analysis of
social work is not intended to suggest that people do not have
psychological problems which need responding to individually as
well as collectively (Leonard, 1975, p.6).

In this study I set these attempts to explain why families fail
to meet their children's needs against the views of the parents and
the social workers. To what extent are social workers influenced by
these theories in deciding whether to remove a child from home, where
to place him, how to balance the child's rights against those of the
parents, and how to help parents and children?

STUDIES OF CHILD PLACEMENT

Child care social workers, as has been noted above, have traditionally
stressed the desirability of keeping the child with his natural or
adoptive family, or, if care is necessary, returning him to his home
as soon as possible. However, a series of research studies, both in
Britain and in North America, has shown that there is a gap between
theory and practice. George (1970), Adamson (1973), Rowe and Lambert
(1973), Holman (1973b), Thorpe (1974a, b), Shaw and Lebens (1976), and
Aldgate (1978a), analysing how social workers actually work with
children in care, found that little time is in fact spent visiting
parents, and helping them to resume care of the children. In America
a five-year study (Fanshel and Shinn, 1978) of 640 children who came
into care in the same year found that the best indicators of whether
children would return home were the frequency of parental visiting,
the level of social work activity, and the personality of the mother.
As part of this study Jenkins and Norman (1972) interviewed 390
parents of these children, and suggest that most parents suffer from
what they describe as 'filial deprivation'. With greater understanding of how the parents feel, and time spent helping them with
these feelings, they suggest that more children could be reunited
with their parents. Thorpe (1974a, b) and Aldgate (1978a) in
similar studies in Britain came to similar conclusions. As part of
a study of 121 foster children Thorpe interviewed 40 parents in an
attempt to discover why their children were still in care. She
found that instead of being helped with their feelings when the
children went away:

> Often their sense of failure was reinforced by their contact with
> social workers. Many felt that from the time their children
> entered care they were tacitly, if not directly, excluded from
> their lives (Thorpe, 1974a, p.694).

Aldgate studied 222 families of children who remained in care for
at least three months, and compared the 65 families where the
children returned home with those whose children remained in care.
She also interviewed 62 parents, and her conclusions are similar to
those of Thorpe and Jenkins. In all these studies the question of
parental visits to children in care is seen to be of great importance,
not only because it facilitates the return home, but also because it
helps the children to retain a sense of identity which is considered
by many to be related to emotional well-being (Weinstein, 1960).
Although some of these studies have included children who came into
care through the courts, none has looked at them as a group, and in

this study I follow similar lines of enquiry to see if this
particularly vulnerable group of children and parents differed in
any marked way, or received different treatment.

A further question I have posed centres around child placement.
It was noted above that the likelihood of a child recovering from
the stresses of early maternal deprivation, whether resulting from
separation or care in his own home which was not good enough to
meet his needs, was related amongst other things to the stresses
subsequently placed upon him. Jones (1978, p.101), in discussing
follow-up studies of children who have been abused by parents or
others, noted that 'hospitalisation, separation from parents,
frequent home changes, and poor quality foster homes or institutional placements may be more damaging to the child in the long term
than the physical trauma itself'. Having removed a child from home,
it is incumbent upon the local authority to provide good enough
care, yet it frequently fails to do so. Space precludes a detailed
review of the literature on children in different caring environments, but of particular interest are Juliet Berry's (1975)
detailed study of residential care; Holman's (1973b) and George's
(1970) books on foster care; and Olive Stevenson's (1977) book
written for foster parents; the readings edited by Tod (1968; 1973);
and the National Children's Bureau reviews of research (Dinnage and
Pringle, 1967a; 1967b; Prosser, 1978a; 1978b).

In this study I was particularly concerned to examine the
placement of those children for whom return home seemed likely to
offer the least detrimental alternative. What factors in a placement
facilitated this end, or made it more difficult to achieve? The
above-mentioned research shows that a crucial factor in determining
whether a child goes home is parental contact, but that, particularly
in respect of foster care, there are important differences between
theory and practice so far as parental visits are concerned. In
particular, the image of the foster parent as a colleague of the
social worker, welcoming the parent's visits and working towards
rehabilitation or links with home being maintained, is not shared
by the majority of foster parents, who tend to see themselves as
long-term substitute parents. Holman (1975) refers to these two
types of foster care as 'inclusive' and 'exclusive'. Thorpe (1974b),
Holman (1975) and Aldgate (1978a) suggest that more use should be
made of 'inclusive' foster homes - those where the natural family
is welcomed in the foster home, and seen to have a continuing role
to play in a child's life - if more children are to be enabled to
return home from care. Shaw and Lebens (1976, p.27), on the other
hand, referring to the possible implications of the 1975 Children
Act for foster parents, express a different point of view:

> Do we seek out potentially professional, 'inclusive' foster
> parents to be socialised into a caring role, (as perceived by
> social workers), or do we settle for ordinary families who will
> bring up foster children as they would a child of their own?
> If, as seems more feasible, the latter course is resorted to,
> preferably with an ideology which fits, the logical policy will
> be to tailor the law to the real situation.

Cooper (1978), Parker (1978) and Rowe (1977), in three important
papers on fostering, comment on new developments and clarify the
issues with respect to 'professional' fostering. Jane Rowe believes

that 'professional' fostering and substitute parenting both have a
part to play, and stresses the importance of 'proper diagnosis and
good planning'.

A foster parent's role must always depend on which aspects of the
parental role are still being exercised by the natural parents,
and which are being undertaken by the agency. The foster parent's
difficult task is to fill in the gaps so that the child's needs
are met without unnecessary overlapping of function (Rowe, 1977,
p.15).

That a hasty decision about placement can effectively close options
for the future and increase the stresses on the child is illustrated
by Olive Stevenson in her report on the early life of Maria Colwell.
She examines placement options open to the social workers when Maria
came into care as an infant, and suggests that the decision to place
her with relatives against the wishes of her mother made future
decisions considerably more difficult.

Viewed in retrospect, it is possible to argue that in this humane
and seemingly obvious choice lay the seeds of the tragic 'tug-
of-love' which was to follow (Stevenson, 1974, p.91).

STUDIES OF SOCIAL WORK INTERVENTION

In recent years several research studies have explored the relationship between disadvantaged groups and the social services designed
to help them. Recent British 'consumer' studies of families in
difficulties have included those of Marsden (1969) and Marsden and
Duff (1975) on single mothers and the unemployed, Kenyon and Gould
(1972) and Stevenson (1976) also on the unemployed, and George and
Wilding (1972) on motherless families. Others, notably Goldberg
(1970), Goldberg and her colleagues (1976; 1977; 1978), Stevenson
and Parsloe (1978) and the members of the Home Office research team
(Davies, 1974; Shaw, 1974; and Folkard et al., 1974; 1976) have
examined the nature and effectiveness of social work in the statutory settings of the probation, prison, and local authority
services. Of particular relevance to this study, also, are the
studies of Sainsbury (1975), Mayer and Timms (1970), and Baher
and her colleagues in the NSPCC research team (1976), which have
analysed the social work service to children and families offered
by specialist voluntary agencies. These studies have highlighted
the problems of assessing the effectiveness of social work.

Folkard found no difference in reconviction rates between clients
who had received a 'more intensive, situationally oriented' form
of probation supervision and those who had received less attention
as a normal part of a probation officer's caseload. Shaw, on the
other hand, reported that increased casework help by prison welfare
officers was associated with lower reconviction rates. She also
attempted to evaluate effectiveness by introducing other criteria
of measurement.

While reconviction is one of the main criteria for measuring
the effectiveness of a type of treatment, it is a crude measure
and does not provide much information about how the treatment
has worked.... A second method is for the caseworker or some
other expert to make assessments about the nature and extent of

changes in the client's behaviour or social functioning (M. Shaw, 1974, p.6).

Goldberg (1970), Goldberg and Fruin (1976), Mayer and Timms (1970) and R. and N. Timms (1977) also call for evaluative studies to assess client satisfaction as well as changes in social functioning. R. and N. Timms (p.75) comment that

> Social workers are deeply involved in the area of planning with people so that they can better meet their needs, attain their goals, serve their interests. In this kind of enterprise seeking consumer opinion is not a frill, not a public relations exercise; it is the heart of the matter.

Goldberg and Fruin (1976, p.8), discussing accountability in social work suggests that

> Thought and research need to be devoted to the professional accountability to individual clients and to the community.
> Studies of client attitudes and satisfactions could help to make social work more relevant and useful to clients.

Three-quarters of the experimental group in Shaw's study, including some who were reconvicted, felt that they had been helped by the social workers.

Goldberg and Fruin (1976), I. Shaw (1975) and R. and N. Timms (1977) have summarised the now fairly considerable body of 'consumer' research in the broad field of social welfare and commented on methodological problems, as well as its limitations as a basis for changes in social policy. Shaw points out that despite its importance for informed debate, it provides only a partial picture, and concludes:

> The research is at its best when it comes to terms with its research method and does not purport to give rigorous measures of the incidence of opinions in the population, and when client opinion is utilised in conjunction with other kinds of research evidence (I. Shaw, 1975, p.32).

Apart from these methodological points, these studies, especially Goldberg et al. (1978) and Stevenson and Parsloe's (1978) recent reports, are important to this study in that they give a detailed picture of the present state of social work practice and morale in local authority social services departments. The interviews on which this book is based were carried out shortly after two major reorganisations which set up multi-purpose social service agencies in enlarged local authorities, to replace the smaller specialist children's, mental health, and welfare departments. In analysing the service offered to the families in the study, the relevance of these changes to the nature and quality of service, the degree of specialist skill, and the morale of the workers has to be considered. Although not available in the early stages of the research, these two major research reports have provided important information about current social services practice against which to view the attitudes of clients and workers outlined in the following chapters.

Goldberg examines in detail the way in which referrals to one area team are dealt with, and particularly focuses on the reasons why some are offered a short-term service by the intake team, and others go on to long-term caseloads. Stevenson and her colleagues cover similar ground in a detailed study of social workers and their caseloads in area teams throughout Britain, and use an 'in depth' interview approach rather than a statistical one. In this case the social workers themselves are the ones interviewed as 'consumers' of organisational systems in which they work. Both found that child care cases, especially where children were identified as being at risk, were given high priority, were more likely to be allocated to the long-term caseload of a qualified social worker, and took up a very high proportion of qualified social worker time as compared with other client groups.

> The chronically disorganised and disturbed families presented the greatest challenge to social work skills. We saw that they took up an inordinate amount of social work resources, sometimes over many years, with few visible results (Goldberg et al., 1978).

Goldberg and her colleagues note, however, that less severe family cases tended to be closed at intake after the presenting problem had been alleviated, and questions the wisdom

> of closing within the intake phase as 'low priority' those family cases whose problems are not as yet very severe. It may prove more effective in the long run to reverse this policy and to limit the resources which are at present poured into the chronically disorganised families and to spend more casework resources on work with families who have not as yet become severely disrupted.

Stevenson and Goldberg both comment on the anxiety which such cases raise in the social workers, and Stevenson discusses in some detail the relationship between management structure, supervision, and support arrangements for social workers, and this anxiety.

> More elaborate procedures, although arguably of value in child protection, have served also to increase the fear of the social workers, lest failure to follow the letter of the procedures will adversely affect their reputations, regardless of their general professional competence.... Some social workers also felt that departmental anxiety to 'play safe' might lead to pressure to remove a child against their better professional judgment, leading to the infringement of parental rights (Stevenson and Parsloe, 1978, p.323).

A further body of work which I have drawn on has been work on the nature of social work intervention with families whose care of the children has been deemed unsatisfactory. This has ranged from earlier but still influential work such as that of Reiner and Kaufmann (1959), through reports of the work of the Family Service Units (Sainsbury, 1975) and the NSPCC (1974 and Baher et al., 1977) to more recent theories of social work practice which are usefully summarised by Browne in her chapter on social work activities in the recent report to the DHSS (Browne, 1978). Recent work on services to children at risk of physical abuse and their families, summarised in the Open University Text and Reader (Carver, 1978; Lee, 1978), especially the contributions of Roberts and Lynch on their work at the Park Hospital, have emphasised the need for preventive and supportive services to families where the children are at risk. The social worker's role in offering material and practical help to families is discussed by Hill (1978) in the report to the DHSS on local authority social services departments, Goldberg et al. (1977; 1978), Mayer and Timms (1970), Jordan (1974;

1976) and Newman (1975). All this work on the nature of social work help to families will be referred to in more detail in Chapter 6.

Chapter 2

OUTLINE OF THE STUDY AND METHODS USED

This study had its origins in the debate about the least detrimental alternative for children in care outlined in Chapter 1. How, in practice, are decisions reached about when a child in care should return to his parents, or whether he should remain in long-term care? It is generally recognised, and confirmed most recently by the work of Thorpe (1974b) and Aldgate (1978a), that a high proportion of children coming into care do so for practical reasons such as homelessness, lack of day care, or illness of a parent, rather than because of the inability of the parents to meet the child's emotional needs. In this study I set out to look at those children who came into care for reasons which were not purely practical, and where there could be some room for argument as to whether the least detrimental alternative for them could best be achieved by return home or by placement with long-term substitute caretakers. The thirty-four children who are the subject of this study had all been assessed by a court or Social Services Committee as being in need of care, and therefore it seemed reasonable to assume that the twenty-five families had been assessed objectively as being unable to meet their children's needs without the statutory intervention of social workers. At the same time, the fact that all returned home on trial at some stage could be taken as indicating that there was no clear-cut case for their being placed with long-term substitute families.

The study aimed to examine the nature of the social work help offered to such families and the decisions made about placement by looking in some detail at children who went home, to see how these decisions were reached, and whether any factors or patterns of circumstances could be identified with successful return home. The numbers in the study were small, and the families were not selected on a random basis, so that no statistical significance can be claimed for the findings. (1) However, a small study allowed me to go into areas which would not have fitted easily into a large-scale survey. Marsden and Duff (1975), in discussing their 'small-scale' research study on the unemployed, make a plea 'for the possibility of arriving at an understanding of social processes and more subjective and sensitive social phenomena by methods other than statistical techniques'.

> For the kinds of questions we raise in our study and the
> exploration of people's feelings, any gains in statistical
> 'validity' from conducting research on a larger scale are to
> some extent bought at the expense of a loss of subtlety in the
> collection of the data, which may lead to superficiality and
> to a possibly misleading fragmentation of the experience of
> individuals (p.20).

In an area as sensitive as child neglect statistical techniques and a standardised questionnaire would have led to a loss of individual subtleties which are essential for a proper understanding of such a complex and highly individual subject.

The detailed study of the families and the social work service offered to them is followed by a discussion of some of the issues raised. What does it mean to parents to have their children taken into care? Are they satisfied with the resources and services offered to them, and are social workers satisfied with what they offer? How do parents and social workers manage the delicate task of sharing the care and control of the children? How does the experience of court action affect parents, children, and their relationship with the social workers?

The problems of this type of research are numerous, the principal difficulties encountered being:

1 to obtain a balance between identifying a reasonably representative sample of families, and yet covering important areas for debate;
2 to obtain a complete set of data for each family;
3 to get a picture which, even if not unbiased, was as little distorted by the interview as possible;
4 to define 'success' and 'failure'. This was possible in only a very rudimentary way. In Chapter 4 the well-being of the families and children is assessed but not in proportional terms, given that the sample was deliberately selected to include a proportion of the least successful placements (judged in terms of breakdown of placement). Breakdown figures are given for the fifty-six children from whom the study children were selected, however, in order to give a general idea of the breakdown position for children home 'on trial'. As mentioned above in the discussion of studies of effectiveness, re-conviction rates or rates of placement breakdown are not the most adequate measures of success;
5 to report the findings without betraying the trust of the families, who were assured that they would not be identifiable;
6 to make sure that the interviews were in no way detrimental to the families and the children, in that many were still at the time of interview extremely vulnerable;
7 to convince management and social workers that the study would not be detrimental to the families and the children.

These difficulties will be expanded on in this chapter.

FINDING THE FAMILIES

The only possible way of meeting the families I wished to interview was through the social services department, as the Juvenile Courts do not publish names of children, and, for obvious reasons, confidentiality is extremely important. All 'consumer' research involves some invasion of privacy, but in this study I was asking about experiences which were not only personal, but inevitably painful, and about difficulties which were often still unresolved. In that few of the care orders had been revoked, it was reasonable to assume that these children were still considered to be 'at risk'. It was decided, therefore, that families should be contacted only if the team leader and social worker agreed;' that the letter asking parents if they were willing to take part should come from the Director of Social Services; and that there should be some definite indication from the parents that they were willing to take part before any visit was made.

The idea of a random sample was therefore ruled out for reasons of confidentiality, but also because, with such small numbers, it seemed more important to select from a list of families which fell within defined terms of reference, those which would give a representative picture of the issues I wished to cover. It seemed important to include children who had been in different placements in care, and also a number where the placement at home had not been satisfactory and the child had been removed. Children over school-leaving age at the time of interview were also excluded, as I was studying children in relation to their parents (older children might be expected to have a strong influence on the decision about where they should live, even if not actually old enough to fend for themselves). I also included some children who were in care under Section 2 of the 1948 Children Act, (2) and some who, although their circumstances were similar, were the subject of supervision orders. These were included as I was interested in the distinction, if any, made by social workers and parents between children at home on trial and those on supervision orders.

The study took place in a county authority in the southern half of England, which resulted from the amalgamation in 1974 of a rural county (containing some country towns and new town developments) with former county boroughs whose population was more urban in character. When compared with other similar county authorities the county studied had a lower than average percentage of children in care. (3) However, when one looks at the proportion of children in care who were there under care orders at a given date (31 March 1975) the difference is less marked (46 per cent for the county studied, 49 per cent for England as a whole). Nationally, and in the county studied, there has been a tendency towards a higher proportion of children in care being there under care orders.

The sample for the study was drawn from seven of the twelve social work teams, which included rural areas, urban areas, and new towns in roughly the same proportions as in the county as a whole. Fifty-one families from these areas were identified, being, as far as could be ascertained, all those who had gone home on trial since 1967, (4) and those on supervision orders where there was concern about the standard of care in the home. (5) Thirteen of the families were not contacted, either because the parents had moved out of the area, or because the social workers thought that this could be harmful to the families. It was decided to include five of these in the study without interviewing the parents, because

a brief look at the files showed that they included some of the
most difficult cases, and raised questions which should not be
left out in a descriptive study of work with such families. In
four of these cases the children were back in care, and had they not
been included, it seemed likely that cases where home placement had
failed would be under-represented.

Letters were then sent to thirty-seven families, including in
roughly equal proportions children who had gone directly home on
trial from court or were on supervision orders, those placed
initially in residential care, and those placed in foster care.
The letter (Appendix II) was signed by the Director of Social
Services, as it was felt that it would be preferable for the families
to see the research as separate from their normal contact with the
department, so that they would neither feel compelled to take part
out of loyalty to their social worker or a desire to 'do the right
thing', nor, on the other hand, decide not to take part because of
antagonism towards the social worker. As a result of the letter,
thirteen families sent back the form agreeing to take part, or saying
that they would like me to call to give them more information. (All
of this latter group agreed to take part when I called.) Two wrote
back saying that they did not wish to take part, and seven agreed to
take part via their social worker. Thus, twenty-two of the thirty-
seven families contacted replied, twenty agreeing to take part;
together with the five cases mentioned above, which were included
without interview, these made up the twenty-five families studied.
All those interviewed had been willing to take part, and this could
have led to some bias. However, by no means all of them had positive
views about the service, and one of those who replied saying he did
not wish to take part added 'but we have no complaints'.

In the original letter it was stated that a small fee would be
paid. It is not clear to what extent the fee affected the response
rate, and whether it distorted the interviews. My conclusion after
the study was that it did not seem to be significant, and I doubt
if anyone was persuaded to take part against his better judgment.
Some social workers told me that clients indicated to them that the
money would be useful, and it may therefore have increased the
response rate. One of the reasons for payment was to give concrete
proof to the parents that their comments were valued, and the time
taken up not wasted. The interviews took at least an hour, and
often longer, and many were emotionally demanding. One mother who
wrote agreeing to take part said she did so because the offer of
payment indicated to her that her views were of value.

Despite the problems of identifying a sample, the families studied
were very similar to those of children on care orders in the county
as a whole, both in terms of geographical area and sex. The main
systematic bias is that a higher proportion of the children was
younger on coming into care, they were more likely to be placed in
foster care, and there were fewer offenders. The children on
supervision orders were not typical of those on supervision orders
in the county as a whole, in that only those children were included
where there was most likely to be a breakdown, and the majority of
fairly straightforward supervision order cases was excluded.

Chapter 2

THE INTERVIEWS WITH THE PARENTS

All the interviews were conducted by myself, by appointment, and in all except one case in the family home. In common with others doing similar research, I rather left it to chance as to which family members would be interviewed. As the original letter asked for convenient times, it was possible for some element of choice to be exercised by the parents, in that they could select a time when some members of the family would be present, and others not. Of the thirteen two-parent families, five of the interviews were with mother and father, and six were with the mother, with the father joining in towards the end in two cases, and the children either present or putting in an appearance in two cases. Two interviews were with the step-mother on her own, two with single fathers, and five with single mothers. Apart from one 15-year-old who was present for part of the time, and a mentally handicapped toddler, none of the children who were the subjects of the interviews were present. However, five children from two families were interviewed separately at a later date, and others were seen briefly before or after interviews.

The shortest interview lasted half an hour, the longest about three hours. A guided interview schedule was used, and parents agreed to the use of a cassette recorder in all cases except one. Almost all had deliberately chosen a time when interruptions would be minimal, and gave me their full attention. Most had given some thought before I arrived to what they wanted to tell me. At the start of every interview I outlined the study, and said that I wanted their views about the services offered to families in difficulties. One of the problems mentioned above was to get a reasonably balanced picture. Clearly I would be given a personal and one-sided view, but I hoped it would not be distorted by any hopes or fears of any results from the interview. It was explained that although the social services department had contacted them for me, and would be interested in my findings in general, I was quite independent of the local authority and in my report they would not be identifiable as individuals. Many, including some with positive and some with negative comments, said they did not mind if they were identifiable; and one woman said that she had been so grateful for the help she had received, and felt so guilty about the harm she had done her child, that she would like the interview to be used in any way it could help. Several expressed the hope that their own experiences might help others in similar positions in the future, particularly in so far as they felt that agency policy had added to their difficulties, and wanted to suggest changes in the way cases like theirs were handled.

The fact that the children were mostly still in care, and that for some the long-term future of the children was still in the balance, made it more necessary to guard against distortion by making it clear that I was not connected with the department. (This was another reason for paying a fee - social workers do not pay for interviews!) It is my impression that in most cases the parents did feel free to talk openly. In two cases where I was uncertain whether the parents fully accepted my powerlessness to change anything, I did not use the Rutter Behaviour Questionnaire (see

Chapter 5) to assess the child's well-being, as I felt that it might be seen that I was testing the child for some official purpose. In Chapter 5 the question of assessment is discussed at more length, but it is possible that the parents were not prepared to be completely honest with me about their children's adjustment.

One further possible reason for distortion could arise out of the fact that, as a former child care officer, I was acutely conscious of the pain they had experienced, and my sympathy for their position must have been clear to them. Indeed, I would argue that had I attempted to be an impassive observer, I might not have been trusted with their confidence. I did not probe about the reasons for court action, but most wanted to tell me what happened so that I could the better understand how they came to the conclusions they did about the help offered. Several sought assurance that I could understand how it could have happened that they harmed their own children. In sifting through the material and writing up the report I have tried to guard against bias, but I would suggest that it is probably impossible to write a completely objective report on such an emotive issue as child neglect. On the positive side, my experience as a social worker was invaluable during the interview, as without it I should have had difficulty in understanding the complexity of the legal position, and the significance of certain procedures. It may well be, also, that social workers were more prepared to allow me to interview in some of the more delicately poised situations, knowing that I was sympathetic to their difficulties and to those of the families.

THE INTERVIEWS WITH THE SOCIAL WORKERS

For the interviews with the social workers a questionnaire was used, and the interviews were also recorded so that opinions and attitudes could be examined in more detail. Some of the questions were about work with specific families, but others were about general attitudes and the decision-making process. Most interviews took between one and two hours. Twenty social workers were interviewed, as five had two cases each. At times it seemed almost as painful a process for the workers as for the parents, as, with the benefit of hindsight, they looked at what might have been if they had made different decisions, or if other resources had been available. In only nine cases had the same social worker been involved since the original reception into care or court appearance. In all cases the current social worker was interviewed, and details of previous events were filled in from the files. However, some of the files, especially those going back several years, were very brief, and others were long on description but short on facts and analysis.

I was particularly anxious to get a picture of the nature of social work help at the various stages, and the reasons for the placements, but in both these areas it was not possible to get a complete picture in some cases. If anything, the amount of help in the early stages may, in a few cases, have been underestimated. It should be noted that time, and the complexity of the material already obtained, prevented me from getting the perspectives of children, social services managers, foster parents, and residential workers, though the findings were discussed with some in each group. This should be borne in mind, especially when issues of social policy and placement are discussed.

THE REPORT

In this sort of study there must always be some dilemma about confidentiality and the right to privacy. The need for confidentiality precluded the straightforward narrative approach, even if details were changed, as, with so small a sample, families would be easily identified by the social workers involved. As much of the interview was about the nature of the social work help offered it was not possible to attribute individual comments to individual families. I have therefore 'scrambled' the families, sometimes changing the sexes of those I have quoted, and leaving out certain details, without altering the significance and context of what was said. Some of the social workers will recognise their own words, and those of their clients in so far as clients have said to them what they said to me. If any of the families read it, and some might, they too will recognise bits of themselves. Inevitably the need to protect the identities of those involved has meant that the story loses something in the telling.

Chapter 3

SOME ILLUSTRATIVE CASE STUDIES

The brief histories which follow are included in order to give a sense of continuity to the analysis of cases, and to illustrate the legal and administrative processes for those readers who are less familiar with the child care procedures outlined in Appendix I. To preserve anonymity details have been changed, and events from more than one case have been included. Some important points are hurried over for the sake of brevity but are returned to in the following chapters.

INFANTS: OFTEN ACTUAL OR SUSPECTED CASES OF NON-ACCIDENTAL INJURY

Jim Peters

Mr and Mrs Peters married when he was 18 and she was 16, against their parents' advice. Mrs Peters was pregnant, and the marriage was never a happy one.
    Mrs Peters: '...We never did get on. We should never have got married. I didn't love my husband. He was there. That was it. All I was was the skivvy - washing and ironing, and when he wanted sex I did it. He used to knock me about, and when I was pregnant he broke my nose. When you get married at sixteen, you don't know. I was headstrong. I still am. I do what I want to do, and even if I got hurt, I wouldn't admit it....'
Mr Peters was often working away from home, and frequently went out with his unmarried friends. His wife, a lively, attractive person, kept in touch with her friends and family, and took philosophically the inadequacies of her marriage. On the surface she was a capable and contented mother to her first child, if anything a little over-anxious about her housekeeping.
    The Peters had two children, a girl and a boy, within eighteen months. When pregnant for the second time Mrs Peters was excessively tired, and after the birth of the baby she felt unable to cope.
    '....I was always tired. I was on my own with two babies. I put my housework before his feeds. The more he cried, the more I panicked, because I had got to get the living-room clean.

Don't ask me why, but I am still like it. You will never change
me. But I just couldn't cope. I couldn't admit it to my
parents, when I started hitting him, because my pride would have
been hurt. I told nobody at first. I daren't tell anybody. I
knew I was doing it. One day my mother came. I shouted and
screamed and chucked him in the cot. She sent me to the doctor.
I said he was getting on my nerves. The doctor wasn't bothered.
He said, "Take these pills and come back next week." I don't
know if I actually said I was hitting him. I mean, you don't
admit that, you are too frightened, aren't you? Because you are
ashamed....'

Shortly afterwards Jim was taken to hospital by his grandmother and found to have a fractured skull, and healing fractures of his arms and legs.

'.... She took him to hospital. I wouldn't have anything to
do with it. I went to hospital the next day, and the doctors
questioned me and I told them. There is no point in denying
it....'

A Place of Safety Order was obtained, to ensure that Jim was not taken out of hospital before a decision was made about the action to be taken. The Peters were interviewed by a social worker and by the police, and at a case conference it was recommended that care proceedings should be taken by the local authority social services department, and that Mrs Peters should be formally cautioned by the police, but not prosecuted for her assault on Jim. Psychiatric and social work help was to be offered to Mr and Mrs Peters. The social worker was also to offer help with marital problems, and keep an eye on Jenny's progress. Jim's name was to be placed on the register of children at risk (the forerunner of the present central child abuse register). The Peters were told of the case conference, but not asked if they would like to attend, and were not aware of the existence of the register. The social worker started to visit Mr and Mrs Peters twice weekly, although Mr Peters was rarely present, and hostile when he was there. Mrs Peters and her mother visited Jim almost daily in hospital. He made good progress, and there seemed to be no lasting physical damage as a result of his injuries. Mrs Peters was prescribed tranquillisers and also went fortnightly to see a psychiatrist at the out-patient department of the local hospital. Her comments about this period were:

'...The police were in on it, but I wasn't prosecuted. I had
to go and be cautioned. I suppose now it was necessary, but
at the time I resented it. You don't know what that's like till
it happens to you. Now I have to live with it. I know I've
done wrong. I thought the social worker was a bloody nuisance.
She wasn't, but then I saw her as nosey, interfering - what
right had she got? - who did she think she was? - all those
personal questions! But it was necessary for him to go away,
because I couldn't love him as a mother should.'

At the Juvenile Court a care order was made, but the chairman of the bench indicated that it might be possible for Jim to return home in the future. Mr Peters did not go to court.

'The court was all above my head, I didn't really care at the
time, I was taking so many drugs. When you are taking drugs,
they change your mood. They just said they would take him into

care. I was asked had I anything to say and I said no. What could I say? That was for the best. I just asked if I could have him back as soon as I could. Not that I really wanted him back at the time, because I didn't. I was glad he had gone, you know, the pressure was off.'

The social worker continued to visit at least twice weekly, but outpatient psychiatric visits ended after about two months, at Mrs Peters's suggestion. After six weeks in hospital, Jim was gradually introduced to foster parents, and remained in the same foster home for about eighteen months. Mrs Peters was involved in the decision about where he should be placed, and was most insistent that he should be near enough for her to visit regularly. Despite her acceptance of the need for care, she was always adamant that she wanted to have him back as soon as possible.

Because of the uncertainty about Mr and Mrs Peters's feelings towards him, he was placed in a foster home where he would be able to stay for an indeterminate period, but where the foster parents accepted that his family would visit, and that if possible he would return home. His mother and grandmother visited before placement and then twice weekly, taking Jenny with them. His father never went, despite the attempts of the social worker to persuade him to do so. The social worker continued to visit at least weekly, offering the sort of dependable relationship and opportunity to talk about feelings and long-term plans which is described by Baher and her colleagues (1976). Mr Peters became slightly less hostile, but was rarely at home, and remained a shadowy figure in the background, uncertainty about whose reactions made decisions about Jim's future even more difficult.

Jim settled well in the foster home, where the atmosphere was warm and loving.

'She gave him the love he needed, which I couldn't have given. I love them in my own way, but I will never be a lovey-dovey mother. I think he used to know I was his mummy, but he used to call her mummy. She was ever so good about that, though I didn't appreciate it at the time. I hated visiting. I used to think she was watching me all the time.'

After about nine months the numbness diminished, and Mrs Peters was no longer on medication. She began to take Jim out, and then to have him home for weekends. Her feelings of returning to normality were accompanied by increasing impatience with the visits to the foster home. She began to be critical of the foster home, and to press the social worker to allow Jim to return home permanently. Jim was then about eighteen months old. A departmental case conference came to the conclusion that there were still too many uncertainties to allow him to return home on trial. On the one hand, Mrs Peters was physically much stronger, coping well with Jenny, and anxious to have him back. She had continued to have a great deal of support from her mother and a close friend. Jim was a fairly placid child, clearly attached to his foster parents, but apparently at ease also with his mother, his granny, and his sister. He saw his father on his weekends at home, and was getting used to him again. His development seemed to be normal for his age, despite the severity of his injuries, and his two moves. If he was going home, a prolonged stay would make parting

from his foster parents even more difficult for him, and for them.
Mrs Peters had a good relationship with the social worker, and it
seemed likely that she would ask for help if she needed it. The
social worker had visited Jim regularly in the foster home, and
when he was at home at weekends, and felt confident that she would
be able to recognise any signs of distress. His granny also would
keep a watchful eye on him, and help out when needed.

On the other hand, Mrs Peters was still rather distant from Jim,
and still not able to talk with warmth about him; the marriage was
still far from ideal, and Mr Peters was still resisting any attempt
to get close enough to him to gauge his feelings about either his
wife or Jim. Mrs Peters was still extremely houseproud, and would
clearly find the presence of a toddler, who had not yet been toilet
trained, difficult to cope with.

On being told that Jim would not be allowed to return home for a
few months Mrs Peters reacted angrily, and stopped visiting for a
while. When interviewed about this decision, the social worker
said that the conference had to balance the advantages of leaving
Jim where he was until he became less dependent on physical
mothering against the fact that the longer he stayed, the more
difficult would the parting become; and also the anxiety that
Mrs Peters's emotional state and readiness to resume Jim's care
would deteriorate if she were too frustrated by delay. She commented
that her observation of Jim and his mother together led her to
believe that there was enough basic commitment on the mother's part
towards making the relationship work. At the case conference she
had been in favour of Jim's returning sooner rather than later, but
had not felt sufficiently confident to stand out against the
majority view. She managed to persuade Mrs Peters to resume
visiting, and at the next review of the case strongly pressed for
him to go home. By this time, Mr Peters had left his wife and
gone to live with another woman.

Jim returned hom on trial when he was almost 2 years old.
'At first he was whiney, because I couldn't pick him up like
she did. It took him about three months to settle. He was still
at risk till I had got him in my way. I never told my social
worker, or she would have taken him straight back. The "home
on trial" meant that if I couldn't cope he would go back. But
then, I wouldn't have admitted I couldn't cope. You still
won't ask for it, because you want to prove to yourself and them
that it is all right, even it it isn't.'

Jim was still at home four years later. He was still technically
in care, but the department was about to apply to the Juvenile Court
for the order to be revoked. Jim was not interviewed, but school
reports showed that his performance was average, and there were no
obvious signs of difficulties. (School reports are provided for
all children in care, even those living at home.) His score on the
Rutter scale (see Chapters 2 and 5) was eleven (thirteen being the
score indicating slight disturbance), and the areas where there
were problems indicated that he had a tendency towards being anti-
social rather than neurotic. His mother described him as an
independent child, if anything with a tendency to be quarrelsome.

'He's all right now. I said to him the other day, "I don't
shout at you as much now, do I?" And he said, "That's because

I'm not so naughty." And I think, is it them or is it me?
They are only children. I think it's me. Little things irritate
me. Stupid little things.'

Philip Jones

Mr and Mrs Peters accepted the need for court action, but as this
is frequently not the case a brief outline follows of the case of
Philip Jones, who was admitted to hospital also aged 6 weeks with
similar injuries, where the parents insisted that the injuries were
caused accidentally. In such cases the legal process is more
complex, with the possibility of appeals. Mr and Mrs Jones were a
young couple whose only child, Philip, was born after they had been
married for three years. Mr Jones worked long hours at a local
engineering factory, and Mrs Jones gave up her job in the canteen
there just before Philip was born. The Joneses were very close to
each other, had little contact with their parents, and seemed not
to have any friends. Their marriage was under stress, principally
because of financial worries due to their high standards and
reduced income. They had both wanted a child, had high hopes for
his future, and both took a hand in the practical aspects of care.
They both showed affection for him, but were at the same time, as
the social worker put it, 'a bit nervous of him', especially as he
was a slow feeder and cried a lot. At 6 weeks, both parents took
him to hospital after he had had what they described as a fit.
A full skeletal survey revealed that he had a subdural haematoma
(head injury), and grip marks on his arms.
  Mrs Jones: 'They kept him in for tests. Then the social
  worker came and said she had taken him into care on a Place
  of Safety Order. Her first remarks were, "We are taking him
  away because you are not capable".'
At a case conference called under the procedures laid down by
the area review committee it was decided that a care order should
be sought. The parents had no explanation for the injuries, except
that they resulted from the fit he had, the bruising being the
accidental result of picking him up at the time. They were both
distressed because he was so ill, and visited him daily in
hospital. It was decided at the case conference that there was
insufficient evidence on which to base a prosecution of the
parents, and that in any case this was not desirable. The GP also
said that Mr Jones had been consulting him about anxiety symptoms,
and that he was prescribing medication for this. It was agreed
that the social worker should visit to offer help with marital
and financial problems which seemed to be causing Mr Jones's
anxiety symptoms, and also to get some idea of how the injuries
had occurred, the degree of risk to Philip if he were to return
home, and thus the recommendation to be made to the court.
  In this case the social worker failed to establish herself with
the parents as capable of helping them.
  Mr Jones: 'We were just a case to her. She kept coming back
  to it - did you do it? Then she didn't come at all, and I had
  to chase her up. She said she would help with our financial
  problems. She said I will get this done for you, and that done
  dor you, but nothing ever happened.'

When the case came to Juvenile Court the parents, who had consulted a solicitor to act on behalf of Philip, denied having caused his injuries. The magistrates found that he was in need of care, 'which he is unlikely to receive unless the court makes an order' (1969 Children and Young Persons Act), but made a supervision order rather than the care order which the social services department had recommended. A clause inserted in the order required the parents to give the social worker access to the child when requested to do so.

Philip was still in hospital with the parents visiting regularly. He returned home to them after two more weeks. The relationship between the parents and the social worker improved slightly, but they never saw her as being able to help them. When she left several months later the new social worker was more able to combine his roles as supervisor and helper, and began to help with financial and marital problems.

Mrs Jones: 'It wasn't just that the first one took him away and this one didn't. She didn't know her job. It was as simple as that. This one doesn't make you feel as if he is watching you all the time.'

The Joneses were interviewed when Philip was two and a half, and after they had had another child. They still insisted that they had not caused the injury. Philip still seemed to be making normal progress, and his mother still took him fortnightly to the clinic, as requested when the supervision order was made. The parents were still rather anxious and isolated people, but were affectionate with Philip, and the social worker no longer felt that he was at risk.

Mr Jones: 'You are hurt, because it makes you feel you are incapable. If there had been a proper social worker to start with, that would not have been so bad.'

Mrs Jones: 'I don't know. It still comes down to it. If you are accused of something you didn't do. If you do a thing, fair enough. Nobody proved it, but the doubt is still there. I am still on nerve tablets, and I never had one in my life till then.'

YOUNGER CHILDREN WHOSE HOME CONDITIONS WERE UNSATISFACTORY

Jean, Paul, and Eva Smith

Mr Smith's father left home when he was 2 years old, and he was brought up by his mother and grandmother. At the age of 10 he was received into care at his mother's request, and placed in a small children's home because of his aggressive behaviour, and staying out all night. He remained in care, but at the age of 17 was sentenced to Borstal training after wounding another boy at the hostel. At 19 he married Pat, aged 17. She had been adopted as an infant by a professional family, but had been committed to care at the age of 13 because of promiscuous behaviour and frequently running away from home. Both still had contact with their families, but felt a mixture of affection and antagonism towards them, so that they would not, or could not, trust them to help when they set up home together.

They had a similar relationship with the social services department, at times demanding help, at other times refusing any help which was offered.

They had many difficulties, in their relationships with each other, their families and neighbours, and in the practical aspects of living. They moved house five times in three years before being offered a council house. Mr Smith was a good worker, but was unreliable, largely because he often had to stay at home to look after the children. Thus their income fluctuated, making budgeting difficult, and there were many debts. Mrs Smith left home on two occasions for several days, and often stayed out overnight. From time to time the family asked for practical help from the social services department, as, for instance, when Mr Smith was without food at the weekend because his wife had left home taking all the money with her. The children were never received into care, however. Both parents were affectionate if rather inconsistent with them, and they seemed to be developing normally.

When Jean was 5, Paul 3, and Eva 8 months, Mrs Smith left home again, and her whereabouts were unknown for over two weeks. Mr Smith, who had always expressed a great deal of affection for her, became very depressed and collapsed, physically and mentally. His GP telephoned the social services department duty officer saying that he had come to the surgery, leaving the children unattended at home, and that he was not fit to care for them. The GP and the social worker tried to persuade Mr Smith to enter psychiatric hospital as a voluntary patient, and allow the children to be placed temporarily in care. He turned down both suggestions and threatened to harm himself and them if any attempt was made to take them away. A Place of Safety Order was obtained and the children placed together in a foster home.

On hearing that the children were in care, Mrs Smith came home, and together the Smiths asked for the children to be returned to them. A case conference was held, and it was agreed that court action should continue as the children were at risk of being hurt emotionally by their parents' impulsive behaviour. It was agreed that both parents were fond of the children and would not intentionally harm them, and therefore that the court should be recommended to return the children home under a supervision order. In order to show that the children were in need of care 'which they would be unlikely to receive unless the court made an order' the social workers had to give evidence going back over several years about the times when Mrs Smith had left home, and financial help had been sought. The Smiths were very angry about this.

Mr Smith: 'We were angry at court. They twisted things. Things came out that weren't accurate, and we couldn't fight back. They more or less ganged up on us. When you have a child taken away, you say things you don't mean. The social worker wrote it all down. I don't think that was right to bring up what I said when I was upset.'

A supervision order was made, and the children returned home. They had settled well in the foster home, and were described as pleasant, outgoing children who were very much attached to each other. Before reception into care, the Smiths had not been on a particular worker's caseload, and different duty workers had responded to their requests for help. Once the supervision order had been made, the social worker visited at least weekly, focusing her attention on the tensions within the marriage and financial problems, and trying to see as much as possible of the children. Six months later, the Smiths had a violent argument, and Mrs Smith telephoned the department asking for the children to be taken into care, since she was going to leave her husband, and he was threatening to harm the children. The social worker who had been visiting was on leave, so the duty officer visited. He persuaded Mr Smith to agree to the children going into care under Section 1 of the 1948 Children Act to give the parents time to sort out their future plans. There were no vacancies at the previous foster home and it was not possible to place all three children together, so Eva was fostered separately.

Mrs Smith left her husband and went to live with her parents. A case conference was held, and it was decided that despite their affection for the children both parents were too unstable to care for them. The social services committee therefore assumed the parental rights of both parents under Section 2 of the 1948 Children Act on the grounds that they 'had so persistently failed without reasonable cause to discharge the obligations of parents as to be unfit to have the care of the children'. Mrs Smith consented to the resolution, but Mr Smith was extremely angry and threatened to take the children and hide them.

Mr Smith: 'They conned me. They said if you need help, just ask. So my wife phoned when we had that trouble. We asked for help, and the next we knew they brought the piece of paper to sign away my rights. I couldn't appeal, only by going to court. I had enough of that the first time. Anyway my solicitor said it was no use, if the welfare were against me.'

The social worker felt that had she not been on leave at the time, she might have been able to calm the situation so that care would not have been necessary. However, she accepted the need for the Section 2 resolution as she saw a danger of the children's being caught up in the battle between the parents.

Both parents visited both foster homes separately once a week. At first Mr Smith was only allowed to go when taken by the social worker, as he continued to threaten to take the children away. In this case the decision to be made was not only whether the children should go home, but which parent they should go home to if they did. Mrs Smith had been the less reliable in the past, but seemed more stable when the children were in care, and talked about making a home for them. Mr Smith's aggressive threats and previous record of violence were not encouraging. He admitted, 'To the welfare, I am a bad case, let's put it that way'.

Jean and Paul were pleased to see both parents, but if anything Mr Smith was more at ease with them. Mrs Smith was offered help with housing, but seemed uncertain about having the children back, and after about three months had a row with her mother and left the area without leaving an address. Mr Smith continued to visit the children regularly, went back to work, and started paying off his debts. His relationship with Jean and Paul continued to be a warm one, and they began to ask to go home. They went first for weekends, and then went home on trial after they had been away for

a year. Eva, however, had been younger when she came into care, and
it was more difficult for Mr Smith to maintain a close relationship
with her, though she continued to know him, and was relaxed when she
was with him. She rather lost contact with her brother and sister,
though occasional visits were arranged. Her foster parents became
increasingly attached to her. Although initially they had been
short-stay foster parents, they were a childless couple who would
really have liked to adopt a child. For a while after Eva started
to call her foster parents mummy and daddy, Mr Smith was so upset
that he stopped visiting.

When Eva was three and a half, Mr Smith, who had stopped work
when Jean and Paul came home, decided to go back to work and found
a housekeeper, a former nurse with a 6-month-old baby. Contrary to
expectations, Mr Smith, who had shown himself to be a concerned and
fairly competent mother and father to Jean and Paul, seemed to
mature even more under the influence of his housekeeper, Rita, who
soon became his common law wife. Rita encouraged him to resume
visiting Eva, with the possibility of asking for her to return home.
When Jean and Paul had gone home, the social worker had decided not
to allow Eva to do so because of the strong bonds existing between
her and her foster parents, and because at the time Mr Smith was
refusing to visit, and would not accept the need for a gradual
reintroduction for her. As it became clear that Mr Smith was able
to offer a stable home to the children, and that Rita was attached
to the whole family, and likely to be a positive and stabilising
influence in the home, visits to Eva in the foster home were
encouraged, and she began to spend weekends at home.

This was a difficult time for Eva, who became increasingly torn
between her foster parents and her father, brother and sister. She
began to wet herself during the day, and the foster parents asked
for the visits home to stop. The social worker, who had by this
time established herself in Mr Smith's eyes as a reasonably
benevolent representative of authority who could be useful at
times, spent many hours with the foster parents, Mr Smith, Rita,
Paul, Jean, and especially Eva.

Rita: 'The social worker met us several times, separately.
She was interested in Eva. The main thing she had to think
about me was whether I loved her, and short of having had her,
could be her mother, and whether she was going to be happy. I
think at first she would have liked her to be adopted by the
foster parents. She was the only one, really, the link between
the foster parents and us. Eva really trusts her.'

Social worker: 'Mr Smith was building up his confidence and
maturing. I thought Rita had a fair bit of insight, but I
didn't know if she had the strength to cope with the problems
Eva would have if she went home. The move would have been
difficult for her anyway, but the foster parents couldn't help
her. I had to do the preparation. They were tugging from the
other end.'

Eva went home on trial when she was 4 years old. The period of
re-introduction had to be cut short because she began to show signs
of distress which were thought to be a reflection of the distress of
the foster parents, on top of her own anxiety about leaving them.

After apparently settling well, she began to wet herself several times a day, and became quarrelsome at school and aggressive towards Rita's child. As her father was at work all day, Rita had the major role in caring for her, and helping her through these difficulties. The social worker made a point of visiting frequently, taking Eva out on her own and letting her express her confused feelings.

At the time of the interview with Mr and Mrs Smith, the children were still at home on trial, and were now aged six, eight, and ten. The divorce court had awarded custody of the children to Mr Smith, but care and control to the local authority. Paul and Jean were doing well at school. Eva had relaxed considerably, and was no longer showing overt signs of distress, but was still an anxious, controlled child.

> Rita: 'That has affected her. She has got a lot of love in her, but she is hard. She often acts unkind. But I know she is not wanting to. She is wanting right at that minute to say, I'm sorry, but she won't give in.'

Both the social worker and the parents described her as 'slightly disturbed'.

Carol Dunn

Other cases in this group involved different legal processes and had different outcomes. Mr and Mrs Dunn had themselves both been in care as children. They were offered supportive social work help from before the time that their first child was born, but the marital situation continued to deteriorate to the detriment of their baby daughter, Carol, who was twice received into voluntary care in her first two years. Care proceedings were taken in very similar circumstances to those in the case of the Smiths, except that there was a clear plan to return Carol to her parents after a few weeks. It was hoped that the care order would allow the social worker to intervene more positively in ensuring higher standards of care for Carol. Although extremely anxious to keep her with them, and apparently fond of her, the parents were too caught up in their own problems to be able to meet her needs adequately. After a violent marital row, when Mrs Dunn sent Carol to the social services department with a neighbour, she was placed in a long-term foster home, where she is likely to remain. Both parents visit occasionally, but accept that her best interest lies in remaining with her foster parents. The social worker is working towards the parents' consenting to Carol being adopted by the foster parents, and it seems likely that they will give their consent, provided that they can see her from time to time. The foster parents, who get on well with both parents, now separated, are in favour of this plan.

OLDER CHILDREN WITH BEHAVIOUR, DELINQUENCY, OR SCHOOL PROBLEMS

Patrick and Peter Jackson

Almost all the children in the first two groups went away from home initially, whereas older children were more likely to be placed at home. (1)

Mr and Mrs Jackson had five children. They lived on a council estate which was part of a London overspill scheme. They had had seven different homes since they were married, and had twice been evicted because of rent arrears. Mr Jackson was in receipt of supplementary benefit, but was thought to have other sources of income, and had served a prison sentence for theft, in which his oldest son had also been involved. The family had been visited by a succession of social workers because of the evictions, poor school attendance of all the children, and the delinquency of the oldest boy. The second two children, Patrick, aged 14, and Peter, aged 13, had been cautioned for minor offences on two occasions, and were then prosecuted in the Juvenile Court for stealing milk from a doorstep. A care order was recommended for Patrick, and a supervision order for Peter, and these orders were made by the court.

The social worker argued for a care order for Patrick, even though the offence was a minor one, because he had been truanting from school, and because he seemed rather withdrawn and listless at home. Peter, on the other hand, enjoyed school and was much more outgoing and apparently relaxed. Even though he recommended a care order the intention, which was approved by the magistrates, was to allow Patrick to return home on trial, in the hope that the power given by the care order to allow him to intervene more forcefully, would allow him to help Patrick without the need for him to leave home.

Social worker: 'The care order gave me the legal right to come into the house. It allowed me to push my way into this massive family. You walk in - nothing stops - the TV blares - . There is some damage to the parents because of taking away parental rights. But thinking of the child, if it is necessary to be more involved with a family, the care order gives more scope, and you can use all the resources of the department.'

The social worker visited the family twice weekly, and spent considerable time with the boys on their own. The parents were angry that what they saw as a 'sentence' until Patrick was eighteen was imposed for such a minor offence. However, they appreciated the amount of time the social worker spent with the boys, his straightforward approach, and his obvious concern for them, and for the other children in the family. At the time of interview, although still expressing hostility towards 'the welfare', they expressed goodwill and some affection towards the social worker.

This situation went on for twelve months, during which time Patrick attended school regularly, and began to modify some of his anti-authority attitudes. A camping holiday was also arranged, which was attended by the social worker and both boys. Patrick did not commit any further offences and his self-confidence was increasing, and showing itself in his smarter appearance and improved relationships with his peer group. However, his head teacher had opposed his return home after court, and was reluctant to work with the social worker on ways of making his behaviour at school more acceptable. Lateness, cheek to the teachers, and smoking, were constant sources of friction, and after a year at home he was excluded from school.

The Education Department felt unable to transfer him to another school in view of the transport problems, and a case conference

decided that he should go to an observation and assessment centre.
Despite his reluctance to leave his mother in particular, Patrick
settled well and continued to gain in self-confidence in the caring
atmosphere at the centre. His social worker continued to see him
weekly, and group work helped his relationships with his own age
group. His parents visited weekly, and he then started to go home
at weekends. When interviewed, the parents praised the home, and
said that Patrick had been happy there. After three months' stay,
it was decided by a case conference that he should stay in care, as
this seemed to offer the best chance of his not following the
delinquent careers of his father and older brother. Although Patrick
said he wanted to go home, he and his parents had been so satisfied
with the assessment centre that they agreed reluctantly to his
staying away from home. Unfortunately, this necessitated a move,
and no long-term community home could be found which would continue
the sort of care which had been offered at the centre. With some
misgivings from Patrick and the social worker he was introduced to
a family group home, and then moved there. However, he did not get
on with the child care staff, and staffing ratios did not allow them
to spend the time with him which might have helped him to get over
his difficulties. The social worker continued to visit weekly,
seeing him on his own, and jointly with the house parents, to try
to improve the relationship problems in the home. Patrick kept
threatening to run away, and finally did so after three months. He
was missing for a month, occasionally telephoning the social worker
and the assessment centre staff to say he would not go back to the
family group home.

He finally agreed over the phone to go back to the assessment
centre pending a decision about his future. He was now over
school-leaving age, and it was agreed that he should go back home
and be allowed to stay there provided he got a job. This he did,
and he was still at home at the time of the interview a month later.
Peter's supervision order had by this time been successfully
completed.

Social worker: 'The children were not neglected in the parents'
terms, or in my terms. They are actually sturdy children. But
in society's terms, there was no guidance. No going to bed at
a reasonable time. No respect for law or authority. Anything
left lying around at home is taken. As soon as the children
walk they are individuals in that family, and have to fend for
themselves. But they are a close family who do show affection
for the children They thought the only problem was that
neighbours and the school were picking on them.'

Chapter 4

PARENTS AND CHILDREN

It is important to say at the outset that although these parents had in common that they had been unable to meet their children's needs without state intervention, they were not a homogeneous group. Some seemed to be 'ordinary people' who had just married the wrong person or been overwhelmed by a combination of circumstances; others, as one social worker put it, 'had the scales weighted against them from the start'. The point must also be made that the study covers a considerable period of time in some cases, and important factors, such as family composition, housing and income, changed.

Perhaps more significant to the study, a single adult during this time sometimes had several 'careers', and might have been a failure in one role, but reasonably successful in another. Thus, Mr Smith, whose story was outlined in Chapter 3, was at the start of the study seen as a failure as a husband and breadwinner but became a reasonably successful mother and father to his children. Information was collected about the emotional and material circumstances of parents and children before the court orders were made, whilst the children were in care, and when the children were home on trial. Even with the use of files a full record was not always available except for the time of the interview, and at times parents and social workers gave conflicting information or opinions. In places, therefore, I have given my own professional assessment of the position based on the material available from all sources.

MATERIAL CIRCUMSTANCES OF THE FAMILIES

The material circumstances of the families, and the parents' and social workers' comments about the relationship between practical problems and the need for care for the children, are reported in some detail in the report of the study (Thoburn, 1977). For the sake of brevity, and because they tend to confirm and add little to the findings from larger studies of families of children at risk, they are merely summarised here. (1) In a survey of the research on the circumstances of parents of children in care Holman (1976, p.9) comments:

The children of the poor are more likely than other sections of
the population to be taken away from their parents. The reasons
cannot simply and wholly be attributed to personality or family
interaction as though these occurred quite separately from the
environment. The inequality which is revealed in their lack of
access to income, housing, health, education and so on, is also
shown in a greater probability that they will lose their
families.

Family composition

In this study, at the time leading up to the children being taken
into care, twenty-one of the families consisted of mother, father
and children. (In three of these the children in question were
adopted, but the rest were with both natural parents.) There was
one single father, a widower, and three single mothers (two
unmarried, one divorced). However, in several cases a traumatic
end to the marriage led to care, so that at the time of interview
the number of single-parent households had doubled, and in four
other cases the children were living with a step-parent. Thus,
in more than half of the families one of the natural parents had
left the home. One family had completely disintegrated, with the
parents in different parts of the country and the children in
long-term care. Aldgate (1978a) found that 31.1 per cent of the
222 families in her study were single-parent families at the time
when the children came into care, as compared with 10 per cent
of all families.

Housing

For about half of the families housing presented a problem
immediately before care, and for even more it had done so in the
early stages of the marriage when the children were young.
    Social worker: 'Accommodation has been a big problem all the
    way through. If we had been in a position to offer them a
    decent house from the start, that might have helped.'
Thirteen of the families changed their address in the period between
care and the interview, three of them moving three times or more.
At the end of the study a high proportion of the families was in
council accommodation, and there was a tendency for improved
housing to precede the return home of the children. In fourteen
cases help with housing was one of the services mentioned by the
social worker. It is interesting to compare this group, where the
children went home, with the parents in Thorpe's (1974a) study
whose children remained in care: 'The majority of natural parents
interviewed lived in private rented accommodation or in ancient
property.' Even allowing for possible differences in the availability of council housing in the two areas studied, one may ask
just how significant in determining whether children go home are
the efforts of social workers in helping parents with their housing
problems.
    Related to the question of housing is that of the state of upkeep

TABLE 4.1 Summary of Circumstances of Parents

	Before care	When home on trial		Before care	When home on trial
Family composition			**Social class**		
Both parents	18	10	Higher professional (1)	0	0
Adoptive parents	3	3	Other professional (2)	1	2
Father alone	1	2	Skilled manual (3.2)	1	1
Mother alone	3	6	Semi-skilled (4)	9	8
Natural parent and step-parent	0	4	Unskilled manual (5)	14	14
Housing			**Family size** (number of school-age children at home)		
Council	11	16	1-2 children	16	17
Temporary accommodation	6	4	3 children	2	4
Owner-occupier	0	1	4 children	5	2
Private rented	6	2	5 children	1	2
With relatives	1	0	6 children	1	0
Tied housing	1	1			
Mobile home	0	1			
Source of income			**Health*** (before care, 46 adults; after care, 42 adults)		
One parent in work	12	9	Physical health problems	11	11
Both parents in work (including part-time)	1	5	Mental illness	11	2
Parent in irregular work	6	2	Personality problems	15	20
Single parent on benefit	4	7	In care or adopted as child	12	9
Sickness or unemployment benefit	2	2	Mental handicap	7	7

* These are minimum numbers as records were incomplete and not all adults were interviewed.

of the house. In a few cases homes were described as overcrowded, dingy, or muddled, but in no case did social workers describe standards of cleanliness as unacceptably low.

Income and employment

Twenty-three of the heads of households were in social classes four or five, (unskilled or semi-skilled manual workers), but two of the fathers held professional or technical posts. However, neither of these was free from financial worries, either because of high housing costs, or because there were several children and 'appearances had to be kept up'. No parent in the study was earning the average industrial wage, except occasionally by working overtime, or by doing two jobs, and at the time when care became necessary eighteen families had incomes at or below supplementary benefit level. Typical of the social workers' comments was:
> 'I'm always very pleased, as I am with many of my families, when the school term starts and they get school dinners.'

There were indications that financial problems were less for some of the families than they had been at an earlier stage in the marriage, and that these had led to stress over a period of years. One mother said: 'The odd thing is, these things have happened when we have had more financial security than we have ever had', and went on to describe the effect on their early married life of acute financial difficulties. Another factor which social workers and parents mentioned as important was whether the income was regular. Interruptions because of sickness, unemployment, or the frequent family crises added to the problems of budgeting on a low income.

As with housing, there was a tendency for income to be less of a problem at the end of the study. In some cases this was because the children were older and both parents working, and in others because although income was still low, it was less likely to be interrupted by family crises. In the majority of families at least one parent was usually in paid employment, although six were in receipt of social security benefits at the beginning of the study and nine at the end. This increase was totally accounted for by marriage breakdown.

Most of the parents were uncomplaining about or resigned to their low income, but some of the separated mothers who had known better times found it particularly depressing. Court appearances leading to loss of income, and costs associated with the children being placed away from home added to the financial problems in several cases, and this point will be returned to in Chapter 6. Typical comments of parents showing the range of views were:
> 'We haven't been well off, but we've never bothered much. We don't go out much. I've got a house, a roof over my head. My husband pays the rent. They could have gone on holiday with the school but it was £10 and pocket money. They would have liked it but we couldn't afford it.'

> Single mother: 'Rows with Mary always start with money. She is not extravagant. Just over shoes and things. You don't have it to give them pocket money like other children. You have got to make them understand your bills have got to come first.'

> Single mother: 'Feel badly off? Yes, I do. Social Security don't realise you have got to live. They are now taking £2 out of my money for clothing, and I could do with that for food. The oven doesn't get hot enough to heat a meal. If I washed the curtains they would fall to pieces. I've tried to save for a TV licence. I've got debts up to my eyeballs what he left me, and I don't know which way to turn.'

To conclude this section, it seems that although almost as many families were existing on low incomes at the time of interview there was some improvement, in that low income was creating fewer problems, largely because it fluctuated less. Social workers and parents were asked if practical help, including extra money, could have prevented the children from going into care. For all those on low incomes or who were inadequately housed, this was just one problem, and not the major one. But perhaps, as Harriett Wilson (1974; 1976) and Holman (1976) suggest, the connection between material deprivation and the inability of parents to care adequately for their children is that deprivation can lead to inappropriate child care practices or marital difficulties, which in turn lead to relationship problems, delinquency, abuse or neglect. What, for these families, has been the effect of low or irregular income and poor housing at an earlier stage on physical and mental health, on their marriages, and on the way they brought up their children? Their generally disadvantaged circumstances and the comments of some about their early married life suggest that this question is worth asking.

PHYSICAL HEALTH OF PARENTS AND CHILDREN

Of the fifty-one adults involved in caring for the children (including step-parents but excluding the natural parents of the adopted children about whom little was known) eleven were known to have a physical illness or handicap either of a debilitating or acute nature. This figure is almost certainly an under-estimate, as information was not available about parents who were not interviewed, and social workers and files were unreliable sources as far as illness was concerned. Health problems ranged from anaemia, migraine, persistent boils, to having lost a leg, hysterectomy, severe diabetes, and loss of one kidney. One mother was, for a period of months, going into hospital for several days each week. Where such illness did occur it was associated by those parents who were interviewed with problems in coping with the emotional and sexual demands of marriage, or with the children. Although in some cases the significance of the illness or disability as a factor influencing child care was mentioned by the social workers, this was not always the case. Mrs Peters linked her anaemia during pregnancy and consequent tiredness after the baby's birth with her ill-treatment of him:

> 'I was always tired. I used to sleep during the day when I was pregnant. But when he was born, there was extra pressure, extra work, and I couldn't sleep, could I?'

Another mother talked of the effect of a serious operation on her marriage as in part leading to ill-treatment of her son:

'I think, in all fairness, the smacking he got which he was taken away for was because I was ill. I was terrible after the operation. It affected my marriage. It was a bad time for my husband with a wife who couldn't do anything and was going round sobbing all the time.'

Eight of the children who went into care also had physical health problems, as did five of their siblings. These included 'mild malnutrition', 'more than their fair share of infections', eczema, severe and frequent stomach aches, as well as more serious complaints including epilepsy, mild spasticity (not diagnosed until the child came into care), fractures and brain damage. Several of these symptoms were related to emotional problems, or to parental abuse or lack of competence, and also increased the parent/child difficulties. One older child missed a lot of schooling because of an accident, and then found it hard to go back again. A baby was found to be undernourished because the milk formula was being mixed at half strength. His parents' frustration at being unable to stop the crying of their hungry child had led to his being admitted to hospital with a fractured skull and broken ribs. In another case a mother illtreated her child over a period of months, but was unaware of the resulting fractures which increased his crying, and her ill-treatment of him. In another case, which is on record as a case of child abuse, there is still considerable doubt as to whether the child was injured at birth or congenitally handicapped:

Mother: 'She was taken in at 5 weeks with screaming problems. I knew there was something wrong since she was born.'

Certainly these parents had spoken to their GP on several occasions about their anxieties in those first five weeks. This was the only case where a serious handicap prevented the child from leading a normal life.

MENTAL HEALTH AND EMOTIONAL PROBLEMS OF PARENTS

The link between physical and emotional problems is clearly established, and was made by parents and social workers in this study.

Mother: 'Jim had pleurisy, depression, an ulcer, irregular employment because of illness. But when he is in work, he works very long hours. He is a glutton for work. He was taking five different lots of pills.'

In two cases social workers put down a series of debilitating complaints to physical reactions to stress, these being more acceptable to the parents than the emotional symptoms shown by others. In other cases stress symptoms were linked with loss, in the one case of a mother, in other cases of the marriage partners through death or separation. As George and Wilding (1972) found, the depression was sometimes very slow to abate.

'If I didn't have Jenny to look after I think I would go and jump in the river,' said one mother, speaking of her sense of loss two years after her husband had left her. A father whose depression was still in evidence five years after his wife's death said in a flat monotone:

'I suppose I shall have to pack up my job. I don't know, I shall
have to pack it up, or pack myself up. Last week I couldn't
remember where I had left the car, and I even forgot when my
wife's funeral memorial was. After five years, I think I
deserve a holiday or something.'

Sometimes also problems with the children, and reactions to their
going away, exacerbated the emotional or physical problems.

In other cases the mental illness or serious personality difficulties had their origins long before child care or marital problems
became apparent, although they contributed to those problems and
were, in turn, aggravated by them. One young mother whose obsessional need for cleanliness led her to wash the walls of her modern
coundil flat every other day did not see this as a problem until
the demands made by two small children made it impossible to live
up to her own standards:

'I always have been a bit neurotic, if you like to put it in
those words. I had to do my housework. That had to come first.
I think the problem was me. Now. But at the time I didn't.'

The degree of emotional disturbance varied between diagnosed mental
illness, often involving in-patient treatment and in some cases
under an order of the Mental Health Act, to incidences of
depression or personality problems for which no medical treatment
had been sought. Of the fifty-one adults, eleven were known to
have had serious episodes of diagnosed mental illness, and ten of
those had had in-patient treatment. After care, only two of the
parents were described as having episodes of mental illness requiring
in-patient treatment. This was in part because some of the more
seriously ill parents were no longer actively involved with their
children and information about them was not known.

With seven parents low intelligence was mentioned as a problem,
but in only four of these cases was the parent known to have had
special schooling. As well as those who had been diagnosed as
suffering from a mental disorder, fifteen more parents were known
before care became necessary to have had some form of serious
emotional problem involving depression, alcohilism, suicide
attempts, or personality difficulties seriously affecting their
functioning. Most of these were prescribed drugs by their GPs
but had no other treatment. At the time of the interview twenty
of the parents came into this category, including several who had
previously been described as mentally ill.

Social workers' comments about the mental health of the parents
varied from: 'Not diagnosed mental ill-health. He's a hyperactive
chap, very money conscious, wound up, tense', to 'Persistently
drunk, suicide attempts, then a complete breakdown and into
psychiatric hospital. A highly unstable chap with convictions for
violence.' This man, although sometimes still needing treatment,
had improved to such an extent that the social worker said at the
time of interview: 'I find it very hard to recognise him as he is
now.'

Thus, twenty-nine of the adults were known to have some mental
or serious emotional problem, and only with one family was this not
mentioned by either social worker or parent. Detailed information
is not available in most cases about diagnosis, but even when in-patient treatment was involved descriptions lead to the conclusion

that we are usually talking about either behaviour difficulties or depression, both of which are likely to be associated with other problems, to exacerbate or cause problems, and in turn to be alleviated by an improvement in relationships and diminishing of environmental stress. This seems to have happened in most cases, so that when the child was home on trial serious emotional problems were no longer present in five families, and the scale of the problem had diminished in all other cases.

CHILDHOOD EXPERIENCES OF PARENTS, AND CONTACT WITH THE EXTENDED FAMILY

In view of the controversies mentioned in Chapter 1 about the significance of maternal deprivation and about 'transmitted deprivation', social workers and parents were asked about the parents' own family background. At least eleven of the parents had experienced serious discontinuity of parental care, and another was adopted as an infant. Seven of these spent most of their childhood in care (mostly residential care but including spells in foster homes); three others spent fairly long periods in care, usually as teenagers, and two were brought up by a succession of relatives, due to desertion by the mother or prolonged illness. In the cases of two of the families, both parents were in care for long periods.

One of the parents brought up by relatives described herself as having had a disrupted but fairly happy childhood, but for the rest experiences of separation were linked with unhappiness, and increased the sadness when their own children went into care. A young mother whose own first child was born when she was still in care herself, and placed for adoption, said:

'My mother walked off and left me. By gran' died and they put me in a children's home. I had no life. They ran my life. I was in a foster home but that didn't work out. They unsettled my life. They moved me around.'

Both of the parents who came into care as teenagers because of their own difficult behaviour were described as 'runners'. 'I started running away at eleven', said one mother. However, it is clear with both these that there was a long history of unhappiness at home, and in one case of physical abuse. Of the twelve parents who were in care or adopted, six had been in a psychiatric hospital, three were described as having severe personality problems, and two were described as being grossly deprived and immature in their relationships. Four had dropped out of the lives of their children by the end of the study.

The parents were not directly asked about their early lives and information from files and social workers was sketchy; but there was some indication that several of the other parents had experienced some unhappiness in their childhood.

'The mother had an unhappy childhood. Her parents were disappointed in her. They had very high expectations', said one social worker.

There are indications that unhappiness at home figured in the lives of many of the parents, and few received support from their own parents over their difficulties with their children. In only eight of the families was help from the children's grandparents mentioned. To put the other side of the story, some of the parents clearly did come from supportive backgrounds and were given a great deal of help by the children's grandparents, aunts and uncles. In seven cases there was evidence of a warm extended family network. One interview was constantly interrupted by relatives popping in, and the mother said: 'We are a very close family. If anything upsets one member of the family, the whole lot are upset.'

FRIENDS AND NEIGHBOURS

In the majority of cases there was no indication that relationships with neighbours were any better or worse than average, and in two cases neighbours were mentioned as offering positive help.
    Mother: 'Two of my friends have been really good. A lot has
    happened they can remember. One of my friends says: "Social
    workers - I ought to be your social worker. They can pay me."
    She carried me along more than my parents. She has five
    children and does everything for them. She is ever such a good
    mother.'
With eleven families social isolation was mentioned as a problem by either the parents or the social workers. Sometimes problems of isolation were linked with disapproval of whatever led to care:
    Mother: 'I felt people were looking at me. That they thought
    I couldn't look after kids. I thought people were two-faced.
    When you turn your back to them they talk about you.'
But usually problems related to isolation existed before care became necessary.
    Social worker: 'They felt threatened. Everybody knew what
    happened. But social isolation was probably a problem before
    this happened. You try to talk about their friends, their
    contacts, and there is a funny look between them as if to say,
    "We don't have any friends!"'
Others related their social isolation to living in an 'undesirable area'. Several of the families lived on known 'problem estates', though one social worker commented that this reduced his anxiety about whether the children would be neglected, as he visited so many other families in the street that someone would be bound to tell him if things were going wrong. Another talked about a 'hierarchy of families' in a deprived area, and of the others looking down on the family in question. The problem of social isolation was even greater for families living in rural communities and not conforming.
    Social worker: 'The community was a problem: the great feeling
    in the village - why were they saddled with this family. That
    house is now kept up to a reasonable standard, but we still get
    complaints from the community about grubbiness. But the housing
    manager admits that the house is quite clean.'

DELINQUENCY OF PARENTS

Information about parents' delinquency is incomplete, but it is known that eleven of the fifty-one adults had a criminal record, in two cases as juveniles. In one other case, and with three of the above eleven, 'social' delinquency was mentioned, involving frauds concerning social security or hire purchase, detected or otherwise. Three of the women and three of the men had been in prison, two for soliciting, two for violence and two for theft. Interestingly, these did not include any of the parents whose children came into care because of physical abuse, and none of this latter group was in fact prosecuted for violence towards the children.

ATTITUDES TO MARRIAGE, AND MARITAL PROBLEMS

As indicated above, several of the parents separated, and some formed other relationships in the course of the period studied. In seventeen cases the social workers commented about serious problems in the marriage before care; and this was mentioned as a problem, though usually less severe, with thirteen of the families when the child was at home on trial. Six of the families where there had been marital problems no longer had them, either because they had separated and were now alone, or were happily remarried. Two families who were not described as having marital problems before care were having difficulties after the children went home. (In one case a single mother formed a stormy relationship after the child had returned to her, and in the other it seems likely that difficulties below the surface were increased by the stresses of court action.)
 Mother: 'Our relationship has deteriorated since they went away. We will always be worried and insecure as a result.'
Only in six cases was there no mention of marital difficulties. Problems varied from 'florid, with frequent separations and violence', to difficulties which were hardly obvious on the surface but which were felt to have had an adverse effect on the children. In five cases the mother was physically injured by the father, but in only two of these five did the father injure the children (and in one of these it was rather that the children got in the way, than that the violence was deliberately aimed at them). In only one of these five cases were the parents still together at the time of interview, and with the others the violence was a fairly minor symptom of a generally unhappy marriage.
 In some cases, however, even when the marriage eventually broke up there had been considerable affection. One mother who had twice been injured by her husband said:
 'This is the odd thing about it, which I've had great difficulty convincing the social services, that apart from when he was ill normally we have had a pretty happy marriage. We don't go round chucking things at each other. We have differences of opinion, but these things are isolated incidents which came out of a period of extreme stress which would drive anyone up the wall.'
At least one of the separated partners seemed to regret the loss of the other. One father said, 'Whatever she was, and whatever she wasn't, when she left that broke my heart.' A mother who had gone to a great deal of effort to get her husband back when he left to live with another woman said: 'I've been married over twenty years. I've got used to him. I can't imagine my life without him.'

Sometimes marital problems were related to financial difficulties, different attitudes to priorities, or whether the wife should work; sometimes jealousy played a big part, and sometimes alcohol. In many cases the problems were clearly linked with the personality difficulties or mental illness referred to above, which in some cases led to unrealistic hopes about the other partner, and frustration at these hopes being disappointed.

Social worker: '*She* thought it was because he couldn't be kind to her. And *he* thought it was because she was completely hopeless.'

In all cases where marital problems were mentioned, these were linked directly or indirectly with the children coming into care.

Social worker: 'If they could have just managed the relationship between them, they could have coped with the children.'

Separated mother: 'You see, I didn't seem to have control over them. I relied on my husband, and when he wasn't there, I went to pieces.'

For some of the children a happier remarriage was playing its part in healing their wounds.

Mother: 'I didn't love my first husband and I never used to consider his feelings. But now I consider my husband. With my first husband, I never thought I didn't ought to do that because he wouldn't like it. Now I ask my husband. I say, "Do you mind if I do this or that?"'

SINGLE-PARENT FAMILIES

It might be thought, in view of the severe marital difficulties in so many of the families, that the lot of single-parent families would be better. However, being a lone parent brings its own problems, as documented by Marsden (1973) and George and Wilding (1972). Only one single-parent family in the study did not attribute difficulties with the children to being a lone parent. Often the problems described were financial, and for some women the drop in standard of living added to the bitterness of being left to cope alone.

'I had a good home, but it's completely falling to bits, and I can't get nothing to replace it. Why should I have to pay? My husband is getting away with nothing. He doesn't seem to realise he has got children.'

In this and similar cases the children had the worst of both worlds. They experienced the disadvantages of being brought up by only one parent, but were still constantly reminded of previous marital strife. The other main problems were loneliness and feelings of guilt at depriving the children of a father or a mother.

Mother: 'There was a man at the welfare. My boy says, "Is this where you come to get daddies?" That hurt.'

Father: 'Perhaps if I had a woman in the house I would be different from the way I am. Someone about the house to talk to. I'd like to go somewhere to meet people in the same position as I am.'

Getting a housekeeper is often suggested for men on their own with children, and three of the four men in the study had considered or tried this. One had had two housekeepers with on the whole unhappy results.

> Father: 'I had one for a year and she got married. I suppose I could have married her but I didn't. They don't take the place of your wife, but I suppose you think they are your wife. Or you live as man and wife. I think to employ a housekeeper and to keep her as a housekeeper is nearly impossible.'

Despite the fact that increasingly men are taking on the role of caring for the children, this is still a step which many feel unable to take. Two of the men in the study who were given custody of the children did not feel able to take over their care until they had remarried.

> Stepmother: 'I think he would have given up if I hadn't been around as the sign of a real family for the future. Yes. I do think he would have given up and stopped visiting.'

ATTITUDES TO CHILDREN

It has been suggested that all the above factors affected the way the children were brought up. During the interviews parents were asked for their views about how children should be brought up, as it seemed important to consider whether their views about children differed noticeably from the average (which, as we know from the studies of the Newsons (1963; 1968) covers a very wide range of child-rearing practices). In Chapter 1 reference was made to Wilson and Herbert's (1978) research, in which they suggest that many parents whose care of their children is considered inadequate, are forced by their environment to adopt child care practices of which they themselves do not approve.

Social workers were asked whether they thought this applied to parents in the study. In eleven cases it was thought that families were satisfied with the way they brought up their children, and in eleven cases it was thought they were not. In two cases the husband seemed to be satisfied, but the wife not. Five of those who were thought to be satisfied were amongst those whose care of the children was thought to be adequate until some crisis led to the need for statutory action, but with six of these families the care offered the children was a matter for concern. This apparent discrepancy between other people's views about the adequacy of child care and those of the parents may in part explain why court action had been necessary, and the figures might have been different with a sample of parents whose children were receiving voluntary help. Amongst the answers given by social workers were:

> 'I don't think he is happy about his relationship with his children. I think he thinks, as father he has to have a relationship with them. But he is not satisfied with that relationship.'

> 'They were two grossly deprived people who were desperate to try to do for their children what they just couldn't manage to do.'

What, then did the parents say about the way they treated their children? The predominant impression from those interviewed was of basically concerned people whose views about children's needs, with perhaps one or two exceptions, were not at all out of the ordinary. Some were bewildered by their children's disturbed behaviour:

'I just don't think people understand these children yet. I think they are just working it out, like you see it on the telly. What's the cause of the children doing all these things?'

Some were so caught up with their own problems that they could not even see their children's needs. One separated father, when asked whether the children missed their mother said: 'The children? It ain't nothing to do with them. They haven't got the worries I've got.'

The majority, however, talked with considerable feeling about their children's emotional needs.

Lone father: 'I wouldn't put those children against their mother. I think, when a person grows up, their mother is very handy.'

Stepmother: 'I took to Jenny straight away because I could see she was a bit of a handful but I could see just how her mind worked.'

Many spoke of their love for their children, but sometimes this was mixed with their own great need for love.

Mother: 'I said to the judge, "I don't care what the case is, I love these children and I always will".'

Mother: 'Although the kids have been away a lot, I don't know what I would have done without them. They kept me going. I'd have been back in mental hospital without them.'

Love was sometimes linked with inappropriate behaviour towards the children:

Mother: 'I never go out at night. These kids don't know what it is for me to leave them. I talk to them about his (husband's) woman. Mike (aged 12) was very angry. He called his dad a dirty old man. He is very protective.'

Love for the children also caused considerable anguish on separation, as will be discussed in the next chapter; and this was often turned on the social workers as anger:

Father: 'I wanted to speak to the children, and the social worker said you cannot speak to the children. So I hit him.'

Mother: 'The social worker wouldn't tell me where the children were because she said I was too upset. I said, "Stop being so officious," and I got really angry, so I walked out because I didn't want to get upset in front of Ann. She told my mother if I had been reasonable she would have taken me to see the place. I asked her nicely. It is not very nice when they say they are taking your children away and you can't have them back.'

Sometimes, as has been found in other research (Baher et al., 1976), parents had unreasonable expectations of their children, as these comments by social workers show:

'The new baby cries and is called all sorts of things. It is the baby's fault.'

'It's the old problem. As soon as they walk, they have to fend for themselves.'

'They lavished beautiful standards of care on her (adopted child) but she was expected to show gratitude. They couldn't face it when she began to grow up.'

On the whole, the parents were either inconsistent in the way they disciplined the children, or over-indulgent. For some there was a fear that if they used physical punishment they might go too far:

>Social worker: 'She can be firm with enough backing that by being firm she is being a good mother. But she is afraid of hitting them. She confesses with shame when she has hit them in temper.'
>
>Father: 'I don't want to knock them about. Because if I start, I could do some damage.'

Consequently several parents used the threat of going into care as a means of discipline. This was particularly the case with those who had themselves been in care.

>Mother: 'I felt bad about having him put away, but I felt it had to be done if I was to have any peace of mind. I didn't mean permanently. It was a lesson for him really.'

PARENTAL BEHAVIOUR LEADING TO STATUTORY ACTION

Given, then, the apparent concern which most of the parents had for their children's well-being, why was statutory action necessary? The situation is complicated by the fact that in some families some of the children were well cared for, and showing no obvious problems, whilst others were not. On the basis of the interviews with social workers and parents, and using my own judgment, I estimated that eighteen of the families were seriously incapable of meeting the child's needs, or were physically harming him, though in three of these the problem was with one child only and other children of the family were adequately cared for. In the remaining seven families, exceptional family problems or the child's own difficulties made care necessary, though whether statutory action was necessary is debatable and will be discussed later.

When the children went home on trial there had been considerable improvement in the parents' ability to care adequately for the children. Although thirteen of the families were still offering a level of care which gave cause for anxiety (usually for emotional rather than physical reasons), twelve of the families now could be regarded as providing a standard of care which was at least average, and sometimes above average. Of the thirteen who still gave cause for concern, two did so for only brief periods at times of stress, and with six there was a great deal of love for the children but the ability to care was hampered by low intelligence or personality problems. (In one case the social worker spoke of 'an all-pervading atmosphere of chaotic love'.)

Tables 4.2 and 4.3 summarise the answers to the two questions which attempted to relate the families' problems to the reasons why the children came into statutory care or appeared before the court. It will be noted that the choices offered vary between straight descriptions and more or less judgmental comments. Social workers

TABLE 4.2 Patterns of behaviour leading to care according to social workers

	Number of families
Physical neglect	3
Emotional neglect	9
Physical abuse	4
Emotional abuse	3
Persecuting	1
Lacking moral standards	2
Anti-social	1
Sexual assault on child	1
Lack of parental control	3
Child delinquent	2
Inadequate	9
Disorganised	8
Marital breakdown	3
Trying but unable to cope	8

were asked to give the main reason, but rarely were they able to give only one answer, particularly as answers sometimes differed for each parent.

This was particularly the case for Table 4.2, which was asking about underlying problems. In so far as patterns were discernible, it was interesting that the four families who were described as physically abusing did not physically neglect the children, though two of them were described as inadequate, and one as disorganised. Four physically neglectful or abusive parents were also mentioned as being emotionally neglectful or abusive, but three were not thought to be emotionally neglectful. The largest groups consisted of combinations of 'inadequate', and 'trying but unable to cope'; and 'disorganised' and 'emotional neglect'. 'Trying but unable to cope' could be related to difficulty with a particular child, or could just be another more positive way of saying 'inadequate'. Several social workers objected to the term 'inadequate' as being vague and pejorative, but it was included as it is frequently used in case records.

> 'They definitely wanted to look after their children. They just couldn't manage it.'

> 'They were trying but just unable to cope with a new baby rather than physically cruel.'

Relating the long list in Table 4.3 to theories about the 'cycle of deprivation' referred to in Chapter 1 and earlier in this chapter, it seems clear that poor environment as such cannot be seen as a major reason for these children coming into care, although as suggested above it did contribute to more deep-seated problems. These figures lend support to the conclusions of Rutter (1972; 1975) and others that 'maternal deprivation' can occur even when a child is not physically separated from his parents.

Social worker: 'The deep-seated reason for the failure of the home on trial placement was the mother's emotional neglect. There were practical things, but they were less important. She just "went off the boil", and he responded to it and acted out, and did everything he could to get attention.'

TABLE 4.3 Parents' inability to meet child's needs related to: (Social workers' assessments)

Emotional problems	20	
Immaturity	2	
Low moral standards	2	
Low social standards	1	
Financial mismanagement	1	Personal or inter-
Marital problems	17	personal difficulties
Inability to mother young baby	3	mentioned 52 times
Problem with adopted child	3	
Guilt at ill-treatment and problems of bonding resulting from separation	3	
Deprived background	11	
Poor mental health	8	Physical or mental health problems
Poor physical health	3	mentioned 29 times
Low intelligence		
Poor material conditions	4	
Low income	1	Environmental problems
Poor social environment	4	mentioned 14 times
Homelessness	2	
Lack of day care	3	

EMOTIONAL AND BEHAVIOUR DIFFICULTIES OF CHILDREN

Having examined the problems of the parents, one must now consider to what extent the children's own behaviour contributed to the need for care. 'Parent/child difficulties' were mentioned with nineteen of the thirty-four children. This term was used to describe problems which had their origins mainly in parental handling, and where it seemed likely that with a different parental approach the problem would not exist, whereas 'behaviour difficulties of children' was used to imply that, for whatever reason, the child's behaviour was objectively difficult. Under 'parent/child difficulties' the most frequent comments of social workers were 'lack of control', 'inconsistent handling', and 'lack of guidance'. With children as with parents, mental, emotional and physical health problems were often inextricably combined. Six of the children were described as having emotional or mental health problems, the most frequent symptom being enuresis. Four of the children in the study, and five siblings were attending special schools for the educationally handicapped. Seven of the study children had attended child guidance clinics, but it is perhaps more useful to describe the children's symptoms, as information about diagnoses was rather vague.

Social worker about a 2-year-old: 'He had disturbed relation-

TABLE 4.4 Summary of circumstances of children

Numbers of children	At time of care/court	At time of interview
Age		
Under 2	12	0
2-4 years	5	6
5-11 years	8	16
12-16 years	9	12
Reason for care/court action		
Infants 'at risk'	10	
Unsatisfactory home conditions	14	
Delinquent/beyond control/ school problems	10	
Problems of children		
Parent/child difficulties	19	23
Mental health problems of child (including mental handicap)	6	8
School problems	11	8
Behaviour difficulties	6	13
Delinquency	11	5
Initial placement		
Home on trial or supervision order	11	
Hospital	3	
Foster care	14	
Residential care	6	
Main placement		
Home on trial	7	
Foster care	16	
Residential care	11	
Number of different placements in care (other than home)		
None	2	
1 only	7	
2-3	17	
4 or more	8	
Length of time placed away from home		
None	2	
Under 1 year	15	
1-3 years	10	
4 or 5 years	7	

ships with both his parents. He was withdrawn, and not passing his milestones. Generally he was unstimulated. He was frightened at night and difficult to put down. Generally a jumpy alarmed boy.'

Social worker about a 5-year-old: 'He was like a little robot. He used to curl himself up like a dormouse. He was depressed and desperately disturbed. And so much at risk because his behaviour was so frustrating.'

Mother of a 15-year-old: "He is a funny boy. It's his nerves. He always has stomach upsets and every night he still has nightmares all night.'

Included in this group of children with serious emotional problems were the three adopted children. Six other children also had behaviour problems which were sufficiently marked as to be seen as more than just the result of inappropriate parental handling.

Mother: 'You never know what he is going to do when he is in a temper. He is giving me a nervous breakdown.'

Mother: 'He is a problem child. He doesn't like standing out in anything new. He has enormous holes in all his clothes.'

Sometimes difficult behaviour started at an early age.

Mother: 'It used to break my heart that I would go to cuddle him when he was about two and he would push me away.'

In other cases it was a reaction to stressful circumstances.

Mother: 'He just gives me hell instead of his father. I suffer from migraines. He's got no sympathy. He calls me a fat pig, an old pro', etcetera. He misses his father, you see.'

One adolescent boy's behaviour deteriorated whilst he was committing a series of offences and before they came to light.

Father: 'While this was happening he was bouncing up and down, and couldn't sleep. I took him to the doctor and he put him on tranquillisers. So what he was doing, he was worrying about. When it was all out in the open, it was all right. He was relieved.'

School problems were mentioned in respect of eleven of the children. For two children this meant under-achievement, but for the others the problem was a reluctance to go to school at all, coupled with unhappiness when there. Sometimes the teachers and education welfare officers offered a great deal of help, taking children to school, and arranging transfers to more suitable schools, but all too often school difficulties were not tackled positively until after the court appearance.

Mother: 'I don't think there was hardly a night when I wasn't up at that school on my bike. I used to take him to school. He used to be terrible, he just couldn't stand it. I don't think he would have been in trouble if he hadn't had to go to that school.'

In nine of the eleven cases where delinquency was a problem, there were also school problems, and in all of these the social workers and parents thought the main problem was not delinquency but difficulties with school.

Delinquency figured as a reason for care in eleven cases, but was the main reason in only two cases. Usually a fairly minor offence, such as stealing two bottles of milk or a roll of chicken wire, was used as a hook on which to hang care proceedings, and this caused some parents to feel that their children were being 'picked on'. In all the cases where delinquency was the reason for the care order the case was taken under criminal proceedings rather than under the 1969 Act (see Appendix I), and it was therefore not necessary to prove that 'he is in need of care or control which he is unlikely to receive unless the court makes an order'. Several of the children had been in court on previous occasions and five were already the subjects of supervision orders, but it was still difficult for parents to understand the 'treatment' principle behind the care order if the offence was a minor one, especially given the atmosphere in court, which was seen in all cases except one as punitive. In two cases there was a long list of offences committed jointly by several boys; all the charges related to theft or burglary. However, none of the children in the study fitted the stereotyped image of a persistent offender.

These comments about the children all refer to the period before statutory action was taken. In the following chapter the behaviour and problems of the children when at home on trial or on supervision orders are discussed, and Table 4.4 compares the behaviour of the children before and after statutory action.

Chapter 5

THE PROCESS OF CARE: ITS IMPACT ON PARENTS AND CHILDREN

THE CHILDREN IN THE STUDY

There were thirty-four children in the study, but another nine children of these families were statutorily involved with the social services department in some way (either in care and away from home, or on supervision orders). In addition there were a further twenty children living at home with whom the social workers were often involved in a voluntary capacity. Five children from two families in the 4 to 11 age bracket were interviewed, and I met another nine of the sample children and briefly chatted with them. During six interviews older or younger siblings who had been in care or were on supervision orders were present and gave me their views. Some parents suggested I talk to the children, but for most it was clear that they did not wish the interview to continue if the children were in the room. Most deliberately gave a time when the child we would be discussing would not be present.

The children could be roughly divided into three groups, with their different characteristics requiring broadly different approaches from the social workers. Group A were young children, often actual or suspected cases of non-accidental injury. Group B were children under ten loosely covered by the heading 'unsatisfactory home conditions', though in some cases there was also physical ill-treatment. Group C were mostly over ten, and were themselves the presenting problem, either because of delinquency, school problems, or being beyond parental control. There were ten children in group A (nine families), fourteen in group B (seven families), and ten in group C (nine families). There were twenty-one boys and thirteen girls. At the time of care or court action twelve were under 2 years of age, five were between 2 and 4, eight were aged between 5 and 11, and nine between 12 and 15. Seven came from rural areas, nineteen from older urban areas, and eight from 'overspill' developments.

Although this is not a statistical study, it is important to assess to what extent the children are representative of children home on trial in the county. Twenty-three of the children were home on trial at the time of the interview, the rest being back in care away from home, or on supervision orders. This figure

52 Chapter 5

represents over 30 per cent of the sixty-six children who were home on trial in the areas from which the sample was selected. Thus, although the numbers are small, they can be expected to be reasonably representative. They were in fact found to be similar to the total population of children home on trial in the county in terms of sex and the geographical area from which they came. The main systematic bias was that more of the children came into care at a younger age, and as a result of this they were more likely to stay in care longer than average, and to be placed initially in foster care. There were also fewer offenders, and more children 'at risk' than was the case for children in care on care orders in the county as a whole. Also the sample was deliberately chosen to include a fair proportion of cases where the placement at home broke down, and 'unsuccessful' home placements were in fact over-represented. The children on supervision orders are not representative of all children on supervision orders in that they are younger and were deliberately selected because there was anxiety about the home circumstances.

THE CHILDREN IN CARE

One of the difficulties of studying children who are found to be in need of care or supervision is that their legal status tends to change. The cases of all except one of the children were at some stage considered by a Juvenile Court or a Magistrate's Court (matrimonial proceedings), and that one, together with eight other children who later appeared in court, was the subject of a parental rights resolution by the social services committee. (See Appendix I for an explanation of this procedure.)

TABLE 5.1 The legal position of the children

	Children	Families
Care order only	17	15
Supervision order only	2	2
Voluntary care → Matrimonial care order	3	2
Voluntary care → Section 2, 1948 Act → Matrimonial care order	4	1
Voluntary care → Section 2, 1948 Act → Supervision order	1	1
Care order → Supervision order	1	1
Interim care order → Supervision order → Voluntary care → Section 2, 1948 Act	3	1
Voluntary care → Section 2, 1948 Act	1	1
Interim care order → Supervision order	2	2
	34	26*

* In one family the legal position was different for the two children

Statutory action was taken in twenty-four cases because the children were considered to be at risk of emotional or physical ill-treatment, and in ten cases the action was taken because the child had committed an offence, although, as mentioned previously, there were other factors in all cases.

Eleven of the children were initially placed at home, either under a care order or a supervision order, six were placed in residential care, and seventeen in foster care. The average length of time in care for those on care orders was three years, but some had been in care for over seven years. However, on average 40 per cent of the time technically 'in care' was spent living at home on trial. Two children never left home, but seven spent over four years away before returning home. The thirty-four children spent a total of a hundred years in care, but forty of those years were spent at home.

TABLE 5.2 Age at admission to care/supervision order, compared with length of time in care/on supervision order

Age at admission	Less than 2 years	3-4 years	5-6 years	7-8 years	Total
Under 2	3	3	3	3	12
2-4	1	3	1	0	5
5-11	2	3	0	3	8
12-15	6	3	0	0	9
Total	12	12	4	6	34

Table 5.2 compares the age at the time of admission to care or court action with the length of time in care (including time spent home on trial), and suggests that children admitted to statutory care at an early age are likely to be in care for a period of years. Thirteen of the seventeen children admitted when under five were in care for three or more years, and eight of these were actually away from home for three or more years. This is in line with the findings of other studies of children in care. Aldgate (1978a) found that 40 per cent of the children who remained in care were under two years of age on admission, as compared with only 15.3 per cent of the children who returned home.

THE CHILDREN WHEN AWAY FROM HOME

Thirty-two of the children, then, were in care away from home at some stage, including one child in hospital on an interim care order who returned home on a supervision order. Ten of the children had also been in care at their parents' request before the occasion when statutory powers were sought, and the three adopted children had had a change of home, two as small babies, one as a toddler. Of all the children, only one had not experienced separation from at least one parent, for a period of months, or indefinitely. Having been separated from parents, the children were more likely than not to experience further separations whilst in care, and here again the study supports findings of other writers (Rowe and Lambert, 1973; Aldgate, 1978a; George, 1970). If one includes earlier periods in care, only seven, mostly older children, had only one placement, whilst eight of the children lived in four or more different substitute homes. One of the regrettable facts about these moves was that only six children went back to a placement they had known before if they came back into care.

The social work help offered will be considered in more detail in Chapters 6 and 7, but it seems appropriate here to look briefly at the children's move from home, their experience in placement, and the parents' reactions to placement. Altogether twenty-nine different foster placements were used, and one child was fostered with his grandmother. The other placements used were three local authority community homes, two local authority observation and assessment centres, two community schools, one residential school for the educationally handicapped, one voluntary children's home, and one private boarding school. Eight of the sixteen children who were in residential care had more than one residential placement. Thirteen of the twenty-two children who were fostered had more than one foster home, and eight children had both foster and residential placements.

It is generally agreed that children are more likely to settle well on leaving home if they and their parents have been able to make a preliminary visit, and there is research evidence to support the view that the child's well-being is increased if the parents visit regularly. (1) The question of visiting will be discussed in more detail in Chapter 7, but at this stage when considering the children in care, the way the placement was made and the frequency of visits will be briefly discussed. Despite the generally accepted view, repeated in the DHSS publication, 'Foster Care: A Guide to Practice' (1976), that pre-placement visits by children and parents are desirable, only in four cases were parents known to have visited the placements before the children went there. Sometimes social workers said this was not practicable; in other cases they said they had not thought about it; and in a few cases they had discussed the possibility with the parents but either they or the parents did not think it was a good idea. Even when children changed placements parents rarely had the opportunity of visiting, and were usually told after the event.

Mother: 'I should have thought at least they would have taken me to see her, to see if she was really suitable for him.'

Mother: 'I went to see them one day, and she said, oh, they have been moved.'

Only nine children were known to have made a pre-placement visit, a very small number when one considers that a total number of seventy-three placements were made. In addition, four sets of foster parents visited children in hospital before placement. It may be that other visits were made and not recorded; but my impression was that this particular piece of child care theory was seen as a good idea (though a few social workers had obviously not even thought about it), but that in practice it was a bit of a luxury. Similarly with parents going with children when they were placed, only in six cases was this known to have happened. For most the day of placement was a very distressing one, and several said they would have welcomed the opportunity to talk to the caretakers about their children's habits, likes and dislikes.

Mother: 'I wrote them a long letter telling them their personal habits. Nobody asked me, but I told them anyway.'

In other cases the parents themselves were too numb to think about it until after the event, and it was clear that, given the state of shock and depression of some of the parents, more guidance on the part of the social workers about how the placement should be achieved, and how the parents could be involved, was necessary.

Mother: 'I don't know really whether I would have wanted to have gone with her or not. Because you are numb. It's just as if something is happening and you are standing outside watching it.'

It may well be that the notes of guidance on reception into care which were issued by the DHSS after the implementation of parts of the 1975 Children Act will have a beneficial effect on this aspect of practice, in that the requirement to ask parents for detailed information about their children will serve to remind social workers of the role which parents can play in helping their children to settle. In seventeen cases parents knew how to contact their children, but in twelve cases they had no address or telephone number other than that of the department. One mother phoned several children's homes in the area to ask if they had her children, and was eventually successful. One wonders whether this lack of involvement of the parents in the placement was because, being a group of parents of children coming into statutory care, they were thought to have little constructive to offer, or whether the situation would have been the same for children coming into voluntary care. Aldgate's (1978a) finding that only 9 per cent of the parents in her sample of children in voluntary care made a pre-placement visit suggests that it would.

On the question of visiting, Rowe and Lambert (1973), George (1970), Holman (1973b) and Thorpe (1974b) all found that, contrary to the theory of good child care practice, children in long-term care were not visited frequently by their parents. Aldgate (1978a) and Jenkins and Norman (1972) found that children who returned home were visited significantly more often than those who remained in care. In my study I found that parents did visit their children regularly. Only one child was not visited at least once a month, if one includes the times when the children went home to see their parents. However, for some there was a considerable time before the first visit, this fact probably being linked with the above findings about lack of involvement of parents in the placement. Twenty children saw their parents within a week of placement, but ten did not see them within the first month. Once visiting was established, eighteen of the children saw their parents at least once a week, and all except one at least once a month.

Although, as we shall see in Chapter 7, the majority of parents did not enjoy visiting, twenty-two of the children were thought to enjoy visits, five were thought to find them confusing, and three to be too young for the question to be answered with any certainty. The children I interviewed said they enjoyed their parents' visits and thought they did not visit often enough (visits in the case of both families being once a fortnight). They also liked to speak to their parents on the telephone, and one child said that one of the things he disliked most about his present placement as opposed to a previous foster placement was that he was not allowed to phone his parents.

Apart from parental visiting, being with siblings was also a link with home which parents and children saw as important. Nine children were placed separately from brothers or sisters also in care, and in several cases other siblings remained at home. 'I wouldn't want to go anywhere by myself,' was the first comment of a 5-year-old girl when I asked what she would like to tell me about being away from home, and her 10-year-old brother chimed in, 'I'm glad we were all together'. 'We were glad we were together,' said another boy of 9. 'We used to talk to each other at night about whether we would be able to go home.' Although attempts were sometimes made to keep children in touch with siblings in different placements and still at home, it was clear from one child's comments that this was not easy: 'We don't really like visiting them. They don't know us any more, really, and we feel shy.'

Since few children were interviewed it was not possible to know how most had felt on leaving home, but the ones I spoke to were predominantly scared and anxious.

'I was scared. I had butterflies in my tummy. I wasn't mad. I was just worried about mum and dad, and worried about where we were going.'

'I kept on thinking I was never going home.'

'We weren't afraid, because we knew Mr Brown (social worker), but I was afraid it would be for ever.'

'I knew it was necessary for me to go away, but I didn't want to go.'

Social workers were asked to describe the children in care. Eleven were said to be happy or fairly happy, six were described as fairly happy but anxious, eleven as anxious, apathetic, or confused, and one as violent and unhappy. It was noted above that several of the children experienced changes in placement, in eleven cases as a result of a breakdown in relationships with the consequent anxieties. In nine cases the children's anxiety was increased by uncertainty on the part of the parents about whether or when they wanted them home; in three cases anxiety, confusion and apathy were the results of conflict between the natural parents and the foster parents who did not want them to return home.

The general picture emerging from the interviews with parents and social workers was of general satisfaction with the care given to the children whilst away from home. However, in only eleven cases was this the placement which the social worker would have opted for if something more suitable had been available. In fifteen cases they would have preferred a 'professional' foster home, as discussed in Chapter 1, with foster parents more able to work with them at the task of rehabilitation; and in three other cases they would have preferred respectively a family group home, a boarding school, and a small adolescent unit. Several of the social workers said that if 'professional' foster parents were not available they would prefer community home placements, even for children under five. This is in line with the views of Thorpe (1974b), Aldgate (1978a, 1978b) and others that more use should be made of community home care for children who are likely to return home, especially as visiting, which is closely linked with the likelihood of return home, seems to be more successful if children are placed in residential care. There was some evidence to support this view in my study. Eight of the ten community home or school placements positively encouraged visiting, and the other two adopted a neutral stance, whereas parental visiting was actively encouraged in only six foster homes. Most foster parents adopted a neutral stance, whilst some were actively discouraging. In four cases the original neutral position changed to discouragement as the likelihood of return home increased. Of the twenty-two sets of parents whose children were placed away from home, only eight said they enjoyed visiting their children, and seven of these were visiting residential establishments.

Despite the fact that there were clear advantages in residential care for natural parents and children in terms of more relaxed visiting, it is interesting to note that when asked which type of placement they preferred for their children, ten of the eighteen parents interviewed whose children were away from home at some stage said they preferred foster care. (Most of those who preferred residential care had older children.) However, when they went on to talk about the sort of care they had in mind, it was clear that they were thinking in terms of the sort of foster care which would allow them to retain a meaningful relationship with their children. Several had had experience of this sort of care in that, although only six sets of foster parents were described by social workers as 'professional' (in attitudes if not always in levels of pay), several of the children had passed through their care, even if only briefly. In contrast, it was thought that the foster parents of six of the children would have liked to adopt them. This very important question of placement is returned to in Chapter 7, when its implications for policy and social work practice are discussed.

Another issue of possible relevance to the child's return home is that of the material standards in the substitute home. Chapter 4 showed that the families were not well off, but neither were they, at least when the children came into care, exceptionally deprived. Material standards were thought to be better for sixteen of the children when in care, but about the same in ten cases, and worse in four cases. Some of the children had a very different experience of life, including outings to the seaside, and more experience of being played with than when at home. Some parents were afraid that higher standards would affect their children's attitude to themselves when they went home, and there were minor problems; but only in six cases were differences in material standards or patterns of care felt to have made return home more difficult for the child. In four of these, problems resulted from the standards of the foster home or children's home being, in the eyes of the parents, lower than their own, or at least to different values and priorities.

'Mother: 'I think matching of values is important if there is to be a reunion. All our problems are about values. When they got Christmas presents, they didn't send thank you letters. None of our family got thank you letters.'

Mother: 'When they come home, they get bored, they want to be entertained. They are used to having everything done for them. And Jenny is worried all the time she will get her shoes dirty.'

Sometimes the placement did make children more aware and critical of deficiencies in their own homes.

Social worker: 'She is beginning to say, "I love my mum but I hate living in this horrible house".'

However, in such cases the problem would probably have been there if the child had not left home, as was clear in another case where a boy remained at home on a supervision order.

Social worker: 'It does worry him that he is coming out of a dirty home.'

The most frequent response to a drop in standard of living on return home was one of acceptance of one drawback which was more than compensated for by being back in familiar surroundings.

Mother: 'You put a plate of dinner in front of him, and he turns round and says, "Is this all I get?" He says to me, "I got better treated in the home." I say, "I know you did." He was used to having three good meals a day, and a snack at night. He came back and he wanted more to eat. He's glad to be back, though.'

In one case where the father had expressed reservations about having his children home because they were so much better off when in care, the 10-year-old son said:

'We have more things at home than we had there. We can go out of the house when we want, here. We had no friends there, but here we have millions of friends.'

On the whole, parents were satisfied with the care given to their children, and apart from the cases discussed below where there were divided loyalties which led to considerable unhappiness on all sides, most either thought their children had gained from the experience or come to no harm. Several, however, were unhappy at the way their children were moved around whilst in care.

In some cases the foster parents or residential workers had helped very disturbed children through the emotional difficulties resulting from the traumatic circumstances which led to care; in others they had helped children to think through their problems, and to look at themselves and where they were going; and in some cases they had provided for young babies the 'good-enough' care which their parents had been unable to provide.

Mother: 'I never worried about him. I knew he was in the best place. She was untidy because she cared about her children, and to her that didn't matter. I was really nasty to her in the end. I never even said thank you. Now, when she sees me, she always asks me how he is. I say, all right, thinking to myself, she would have done a better job than I could.'

When they returned home, seven children told their parents they would like to go back to visit, though none actually said they would like to go back to stay. It was felt that ten children had divided loyalties at first, but that this situation did not last longer than a few weeks for all except one of the children. It was thought that nineteen of the children, including one child who had been in the same foster home for five years, did not experience divided loyalties. Five of those who said they would like to go back to visit did so, and two babies also went back for brief periods to give the parents a break.

REACTIONS OF PARENTS WHEN CHILDREN WENT AWAY

In Chapter 1 mention was made of the work of Jenkins and Norman (1972) in the USA and Thorpe (1974b) and Aldgate (1978a) in this country, on the attitudes and feelings of parents when the children went into care. Jenkins postulated that 'filial deprivation', characterised by distress and anger followed by despair, was as relevant a concept as 'maternal deprivation'. She concluded that the feelings of parents, and the help they received in overcoming their sense of loss and depression, were related to the likelihood of their visiting their children, and of the children returning home. Aldgate noted that parents of children who returned home were more likely at the time of reception into care to experience feelings of anger, sadness, and loss, whilst parents whose children remained in care were more likely to feel relief or guilt.

As one of the aims of my study was to clarify why these particular children went home, questions were asked about parents' feelings when children went away. The answers were more difficult to interpret than in other studies because reactions changed according to the actions taken by courts or committees. Some parents were relieved when children went into voluntary care at a time of crisis, or worried about the children, but angry when court action or parental rights were subsequently taken.

Father: 'He said, "She needs help, would you mind if she went away somewhere?" and we said no. We were relieved that they thought they could do something. Then he brought the form asking us to sign over responsibility. We were disgusted. You see, we had *asked* for help. We were blazing mad.'

Mother: "I did need a rest. I was tired with all that screaming. But then when she said they were taking her into care and we couldn't have her back, well, you just don't believe it. We were that stunned. Then we were angry.'

Table 5.3 gives the answers of parents and social workers when asked about the parents' reactions. Although there were some differences, the social workers' answers should not be discounted, as many of them had talked to the parents at the time, whereas parents were more likely to remember one predominant feeling. Social workers tended to list several reactions, whereas parents tended to give one or two answers (most often anger combined with some indication of their own distress or worry about the child). Sometimes the two parents reacted differently.

The parents were more likely to remember feelings of anger, whilst social workers were more likely to mention feelings of distress. These findings will be discussed in more detail in Chapter 7, but are of interest in that they differ from those of Thorpe with her sample of parents of children who were still in care (distressed,

TABLE 5.3 Parents' reactions when children went away

		According to parents (20 families)	According to social workers (25 families)
Worry 8-21	Worried about self	0	2
	Worried about child	8	16
	Worried about what others would say	0	3
Distress 8-41	Sad or upset	2	10
	Guilty	1	7
	Depressed or empty	1	9
	Hopeless	1	6
	Apathetic	0	5
	Stunned/numb	3	4
Relief 4-10	Relieved/thankful	4	10
Anger 15-29	Angry towards social worker	8	14
	Angry towards magistrates	2	3
	Angry towards self	0	2
	Angry towards spouse	4	6
	Angry towards child	0	3
	Angry towards school	1	1

44; relieved/thankful, 4; angry, 5) and tend to confirm the findings of Jenkins and Norman (1972) and Aldgate (1978a) about the correlation between anger and the return home of the children.

Although the parents tended not to emphasise their own distress, perhaps because their anger was so strongly felt that it had blotted out other feelings, their descriptions of the time their children went away did support the concept of filial deprivation.

Mother: 'I took an overdose. Life just wasn't worth living if I couldn't get them back.'

Father: 'I had to hide all their things away, because when I came home, that really upset me.'

Mother: 'I used to ring him every night. I never slept for nights.'

However, where these parents did seem to differ from those in Thorpe's study was in their determination to fight to get their children back. The extent to which parental determination resulted from anger, from fear of losing control, from feelings of 'possession' or the 'blood tie', or from the existence of strong bonds with the children differed in each case, but all four played a part. Whatever the reason, it led them to overcome the pain of visiting, and in some cases fight long legal battles or make strenuous efforts to improve their circumstances or behaviour to get the children back home.

Mother: 'I thought I'm going to fight them, and fight till the end until I get them back.'

Mother: 'I thought, what they could give him, I could give him the same, so I was determined to get him back.'

Sixteen of the parents interviewed said that when the child was away from home they used to worry about him. The sorts of anxiety mentioned were: that he would not be allowed to return home; that he would turn against them and not want to come home; that he would be unhappy; that he would run away and get into trouble; that he would be hit or ill-treated in the substitute home; that he would be brought up in a way they did not approve of; that he would not recover mentally or physically; and that he would be emotionally damaged by being in care, especially by being moved about.

Parents and social workers were asked if they thought the parents would consent to adoption if the child could not return home. None of the parents said they would, although two had threatened that they would give the child up for adoption, but said they did not mean it, and had done so to put pressure on the social workers to let the child come home. In two cases the social workers thought the parents might consent to adoption, but thought definitely not in the rest.

THE RETURN HOME OF THE CHILDREN

Social workers were asked if the return home was planned, or if, in the case of children remaining at home, this was the placement of choice or because no suitable alternative was available. Of the twenty-three children who were initially placed away from home, return home was planned for nineteen. For two children from one family a holiday with a father whose chances of caring for his children had seemed remote was so successful that it was decided they should remain with him; for one, a breakdown in the placement led to what proved to be a rather short-lived return home; and for another the Juvenile Court returned a child quite unexpectedly against the advice of the department. Of the eleven children placed directly at home, the placement was part of the treatment plan in six cases; in three cases it was described as unsatisfactory but the best alternative available, with in one case the clear understanding that the child was awaiting an assessment placement; and in two cases the court made supervision orders returning the children home against the advice of the department. It is of interest here, in view of the criticism levelled at courts when such action is not successful, to note that in the three cases where courts returned children against the advice of the social services department (all children under two in the 'at risk' category), the children were still at home at the time of interview. The social workers were no longer worried about the care given in two cases, and only worried about the rather haphazard way of life of the third mother, rather than about deliberate neglect or ill-treatment.

Social workers were also asked whether they had always worked for return home, or whether the original plan had changed. For the total group of thirty-two children who were away from home at some stage, return home was eventually planned in twenty-five cases, but in nineteen cases the original plan had been for the child to remain in long-term care. Why these plans changed will be discussed in Chapter 7, when I consider how decisions were made about placement, but at this stage it can be said that sometimes it added to the confusion of the children and the parents, though sometimes it was as a result of pressure from them.

    Social worker: 'Bill was so desperate to go home, we just had to see if this was possible after all.'

For the older children there was a pattern of being in care for a few months; returning home as part of a plan, usually on the recommendation of a departmental case conference; and settling back home usually with some relief, but often with fairly positive feelings about care, and almost always showing some improvement in behaviour. For those older children who were in care for longer periods, return home was much more difficult, and in all four cases ended in the child going away from home again. With the younger children, who were more likely to be hurt by the change of environment (partly because of their age and partly because they tended to remain away from home for longer periods), return home was usually carefully prepared. However, in some cases the foster parents' own feelings of distress at parting with the child were such that they were unable to help him with his anxiety. Most younger children showed anxiety symptoms for a while but most parents seemed to cope with this and the symptoms gradually disappeared.

    Mother: 'One weekend he didn't go back to the foster parents. It was strange for him, because weekends, that's nothing. It took time for him to get used to us again. He was upset the first few weeks, but then he got used to it.'

Hearing the parents talking about their children's behaviour when they came home, one might have been discussing children's reactions to foster care, which is not surprising in view of their length of time in care. 'Testing out' behaviour sometimes started fairly quickly, but in other cases it followed a 'honeymoon period', both types of behaviour which Olive Stevenson (1977) describes vividly in her book written to help foster parents to understand the behaviour of children placed with them.

    Mother: 'They were all right at first, but after three months it was terrible. I took him down to the welfare.'

    Social worker: 'He tested out like mad. They had a tough time. He went into the toilet when they were on holiday, and smeared himself all over.'

In cases where there was serious conflict between foster parents and natural parents (fortunately few), the children experienced very severe difficulties, as shown in this description of a 4-year-old:

    Mother: 'I didn't really understand her until the summer holidays, six months after she came home. She would be trailing round me every day, and making bits and pieces, and she would be wet three or four times a day. I was getting to the point where I was not going to give in. The next day she gave me five pairs of wet pants. I rounded on her. She burst into tears. I gave her a hug and a kiss. The next day she nipped Billy. I said, don't do that. She did it again. I slapped her fingers. She went white in the face and screamed and could not stop herself. I hugged her but she couldn't stop. When the screaming had died down and she was only sobbing, she said: "You don't love me. I knew you wouldn't love me," and it went on for an hour. I couldn't stop her. She was so "up tight" after all these months of bottling it up. She really believed I didn't love her. We still got wet pants, but not so often. I made a point of doing everything with her for a while. I knew if I let her go then, I would never get her back.'

In another case a 5-year-old who had been in the same foster home for four years abruptly rejected her foster parents, so that the reintroductory period had to be curtailed.

Stepmother: 'She used to come for weekends. It got more difficult to take her back. I used to have to practically drag her. She would sit and cry, and the foster mother would get upset. It was like one big nightmare in the end. She was supposed to come back gradually, but in the end the social worker said she couldn't divide herself up to them. She was so attached to her dad, she just wanted to be here.'

In contrast, the following account of another stepmother of a 5-year-old in placement for three years tells a different story.

'As Jill grew older, I'm sure she felt the tension. When she came home for days she and her sister used to have fearful rows. Her sister used to say, "When daddy marries auntie we can live in a house together." "I'm not," she would say. "I don't have to if I don't want to. My mummy says" (foster mother). Right up to the week before the wedding, it went the same. I went to buy her a coat for the wedding. "Who is this coat for? - Daddy's and auntie's wedding. - Which daddy? - Your proper daddy. - Which one is that? - The one we have just been talking to. - Is he my proper daddy? Are you sure? I want a blue coat. But my mummy hasn't said anything. Can I come to the wedding? Can I wear a rose?" After the wedding she said, "Am I going home now?" We had one or two ups and downs but she seemed to settle all right. It was all new, and it was coming up to Christmas. It was several months before the real problems started. She used to sit and say nothing. She never actually said she wanted to go back. It was partly my fault, I suppose. I would go up to her and cuddle her and ask her what she did at school. "Nothing. What did you used to do at auntie's? - Nothing. - Let's do something exciting." I used to make out we were better. It's terrible to say it. I bought her a complete new wardrobe.'

The pain of these situations for children, parents, siblings, and foster parents and their children, came through these interviews so clearly. In five cases there was the extra dimension of step-parents, which further confused the children.

Stepmother: 'In the end she said to me, "Will you be my mum?" She never sees her own mum. She will sometimes say to me, "Who put me in my cot?" I say, "Another lady".'

None of the children who went home to step-parents had regular contact with the parent who had left home, though social workers sometimes arranged rather spasmodic contacts.

The above quotations show very clearly that placing a child back home who has been in long-term care presents many problems for child, parents, caretakers, and social workers who have to recognise the anxiety and sometimes pain of all those involved. Some parents took the move in their stride and accepted the problems as not unexpected. Others, notably, in this study, the two step-parents interviewed, were more aware of the risks in what they were doing.

Stepmother: 'What I really did think about in the beginning when she first came back, her foster mother said she would not have her back. I thought if she is really unhappy and pining, it's going to affect her and she couldn't go back.'

Despite these problems, most of the children did get over at least their most obvious symptoms, and none of those who experienced difficulties in adjusting to the return home went back into care primarily because of those difficulties.

Mother: 'I wondered whether things were going to be all right. If it was going to be one big mad battle, it wasn't going to be any kind of life for anybody, but that soon settled down.'

THE CHILDREN WHEN AT HOME

Placement at the time of the study

Although this was essentially a descriptive study, some attempt was made to assess whether return home had offered 'the least detrimental alternative'. The crudest measure of success was whether the children were still at home at the time of interview, at least two years after placement at home. Children from eighteen of the families were at home, though some had had brief spells, mostly planned, back in care. As the children were not selected on a random basis, Tables 5.4 and 5.5 also show the outcome of the placements of the fifty-six children who were placed at home in the areas of the county from which the sample was selected. Seventy-one per cent of these children were at home at the time of the study, a figure which compares favourably with the approximately 50 per cent of long-term foster home placements which break down within two years.

TABLE 5.4 Placement of children at time of study compared with reason for care (Study children and total group)

	Still at home		Not at home	
	Study Group	Total Group	Study Group	Total Group
Infants 'at risk'	7	8	3	3
Unsatisfactory home conditions	9	19	5	7
Older children with behaviour or school problems, or delinquency	7	13	3	6
Total	23(68%)	40(71%)	11(32%)	16(29%)

TABLE 5.5 Placement of children at time of study compared with initial placement (Study children and total group)

	Still at home		Not at home	
	Study group	Total group	Study group	Total group
Initially placed at home	6	10	5	8
Initially placed away	17	30	6	8
Total	23	40	11	16

Of the children away from home at the time of the study it was thought that three (the three infants 'at risk'), were likely to remain in long-term care, and these had substitute family placements. It was thought that the remaining eight were likely to return home at some stage, and all except one of these had close contact with the parents. Four children went back into care because of serious marital difficulties which placed them at risk; two children were physically ill-treated though neither was seriously hurt; one child came into care because his mother was quite unable to relate to him; and four went back into care because of difficult behaviour. Where home placement did break down, this was likely to occur within the first three months, and none of the children returned to care after two years at home. At the time of interview care orders had been discharged on only three children, two after five years, one after eighteen months.

Ill-treatment or neglect

Of the ten children who were in care or on supervision orders because of actual or suspected ill-treatment, two were back in care because of further incidences of ill-treatment, and in one other case there was some anxiety about non-deliberate neglect. In the remaining seven cases the social workers were confident that the children were no longer physically at risk.
   Social worker: 'There obviously was ill-treatment at one stage, but she is now happy and cheerful and not afraid.'
In three cases, though, there was still some anxiety about relationships.
   Social worker: 'I'm still not entirely happy about the relationship between him and his parents, but I don't think he is physically at risk.'
Sometimes the focus of the family problems had shifted from the ill-treated child.
   Social worker: 'He is as safe as houses now, but there are still marital problems.'
Of the eleven children in care or on supervision orders principally because of physical or emotional neglect, three were back in care because it was felt they had continued to be neglected when back at

home, and the two younger ones were likely to remain with their long-term foster parents. The older child who was in residential care was described as 'desperately deprived and increasingly looking towards home again as he gets older'. With the remaining eight, there was felt to be no risk of deliberate neglect, but the social workers, although considering that the children and parents had warm relationships, were still concerned about the general well-being of seven of the children, usually because of the problems of the parents.

Delinquency and school problems

For several of the children who had been experiencing problems at school, the making of a care order or supervision order did seem to improve the situation, although in two cases this may have been because remedial or special units opened in the home area about the same time.
   Mother: ' She used to have problems with school. Not now in the new unit. She really likes it there. Why couldn't they have done this without putting her away?'

   Father: 'The headmaster came here to see him and took him the first day. His mother had to sit with him a week before he would stay. He was lucky because they had just finished building this school, so they didn't have to take him away.'
For the remaining eight children school remained a problem when they went home, though usually more under control, and with the social workers trying to ease the difficulties as they arose. Only in one case did school problems lead to a child returning to care. Of the fifteen younger children now at school, only two were noted as having difficulties, and three were said to be doing surprisingly well.
   Although five of the older children had been involved in further delinquent episodes, only two had returned to care or custody for this reason, and two of the five had not re-offended within the previous year. The remaining six had not re-offended since the care order or supervision order was made. None of the children who were younger at the time of statutory action, but old enough to be committing offences at the time of the study, had been involved in delinquency.

General behaviour and well-being

For most of these children the problems of their early lives, the continuing problems of some of the parents, and the upheavals and pains of their removal to care and return home, mean that not until they themselves become parents will one be able to see what damage has been done, and to what extent the return home allowed for recovery and normal growth. A description of the position at the end of the study may, however, give some pointers which can be set alongside other studies of children in residential and foster care, and placed for adoption (Thorpe, 1974b; Wolkind, 1974; Berry, 1975; George, 1970; Weinstein, 1960; Holman, 1973b; Parker, 1966; Aldgate, 1978a; Kadushin, 1970; Tizard, 1977). To compare these

children with the average child would be to pretend that the
circumstances which led to care had never happened, a point which
several of the parents made:
   Mother: 'Comparing these children with a friend's children of
   the same age, hers have far more trust than either of my two
   have. I don't think we will ever have quite the same sort of
   relationship.'
   It was noted in Chapter 2 that the children were not interviewed
and no systematic testing of their functioning was attempted.
Parents and social workers were asked to say whether they thought
the children were emotionally disturbed, and whether their emotional
and material well-being was better or worse than at the time when
care became necessary. No comparison was attempted between the
group of children who were still at home at the time of the study,
and those who had returned to care. There were in fact disturbed
children, and apparently well-adjusted children in both groups.
   In recent years researchers and professionals in this field
have been turning their attention to ways of assessing the degree
and nature of the damage suffered by children who are subjected to
neglect or ill-treatment, and to ways of helping such children. (2)
In assessing whether the children were disturbed the views of the
parents and the social workers, and information on file (including,
in some cases school reports) were taken into account. Also for
twelve children in the appropriate age-range Rutter's Behaviour
Questionnaire A2 for parents (Rutter and Graham, 1968) was used.
The questionnaire lent itself well to this sort of study in that
it was quick and simply understood, but I doubt whether parents
were completely honest with me, and not tempted to underestimate
their children's problems. Of the twelve children with whose
parents the scale was used, three had scores which would indicate
some disorder, two of an 'anti-social' type, one of a 'neurotic'
type. Social workers said they considered twelve of the children
to be slightly disturbed, one to be very disturbed, and twenty not
to be disturbed, though two of these were described as immature.
One child was too severely mentally handicapped for the question
to be relevant. The parents interviewed tended to agree with the
social workers' assessments of their children. Twelve of the
twenty-nine children whose parents were interviewed were thought
by their parents to be slightly disturbed. These figures give a
proportion of disturbed children similar to that found by Thorpe
in her study (1974b) of foster children, 39 per cent of whom were
considered to be disturbed. Wolkind (1974) and Wolkind and Rutter
(1973), using the Rutter questionnaire, found 46 per cent of a
group of children in residential care to be disturbed. (When used
with general populations of children in the Isle of Wight and
Camberwell these scales identified 7 per cent and 23 per cent
respectively as being disturbed.)
   Table 4.4 compared the behaviour of the children when at home
with their behaviour and problems before care. As can be seen,
more children were described as having behaviour difficulties, and
more parents had difficulty in relating appropriately to them when
they were home on trial. This was mainly for two related reasons.
First, parent/child difficulties and behaviour problems were not yet
apparent with several of the children who went into care as young

babies, but on return home they were in the age-range when such difficulties were more obvious; and second, some of these difficulties could be related to problems resulting from separation, from divided loyalties, and from moves when in care.

> Social worker: 'The father says that the separation from the baby has made him feel that he is not his child.'

> Social worker: 'For this particular mother, the separation of the child at three months, on top of separation at birth because he was premature, with her own deprived background, was disastrous.'

Sometimes it was clear that a child was returned home just at the wrong time and the parent/child difficulties were aggravated. Because his foster parents were going on holiday, one 3-year-old went home on the day his mother moved house.

> Mother: 'They just gave me a new house, and they gave me Peter the day I moved in. I said I wanted him home, but he kept following me everywhere I went. I just couldn't stand it.'

In another case a child was returned to his obsessionally clean mother before he was toilet-trained, and both mother and social worker commented in retrospect on the extra risk under which this placed him.

> Mother: 'I got him dry, day and night, in a few weeks. I was determined. Oh yes, I used to get angry. I would smack him, but I knew how far I could go. Perhaps I shouldn't have had him home just then, honestly speaking.'

In several cases parents noted that children were more aggressive when they came home, and other parents found their children to be clinging or less able to amuse themselves. In some cases parents could understand why foster parents had found their children difficult.

> Mother: 'She felt she couldn't cope with him. I've felt the same myself sometimes.'

Some children did not show obviously disturbed behaviour but had 'put up their defences', and there were worries about the future. One social worker, talking about a 6-year-old who was back in long-term care, said:

> 'She is not exactly difficult, but I find her threatening. She is very aloof and seems arrogant in her manner. She has a barrage of defences.'

Another child who was back in residential care was described as: 'not cheeky or difficult, but attention-seeking. With very much the symptoms of a child deprived over a period of years.'

Two other factors are seen by many writers as being important to a child's future well-being. It is felt to be important that a child has a sense of his own identity (Weinstein, 1960), and also feels secure enough that he is not going to be suddenly uprooted to allow himself to make close relationships with those caring for him (Rowe and Lambert, 1973). In terms of identity, this group of children had a clear advantage over other samples of children in care referred to above. All except one saw at least one parent at least once a month (although only one of the adopted children was in touch with the family of origin). Rowe in particular has pointed to the dangers of children remaining 'in limbo' with no long-term plans being made, and without the opportunity of making lasting relationships. Social workers were asked if they envisaged any further change of placement for the children. Apart from short-term care which might be necessary, especially for the single-parent families who had no one to fall back on for help at times of illness or other difficulties, twenty-eight children were likely to stay where they were, with some of the older ones probably returning home by choice at a later stage. The positions of one 5-year-old and two adolescents at home were causing some concern, and return to care was a possibility. Three children from one family who were in residential care were likely to go home shortly.

Table 5.6 shows the answers to a question the social workers were asked about the children when at home. (The numbers add up to more than thirty-four as the position changed over time for some.) All the children who were described as either ambivalent or frightened were away from home at the time of the study. Five of the ten children who were described as happy were also away from home (largely because of their parents' continuing problems), as were two of those described as 'not very happy but not wanting to leave'.

TABLE 5.6 The children when at home as described by the social workers

Happy	10
Fairly happy	12
Not very happy but not wanting to leave	8
Apathetic	1
Ambivalent	5
Frightened	1

As stated above, the evidence presented cannot be clearly interpreted to allow an assessment of success or failure in each case. At best one can ask whether the placement at home seemed to be the least detrimental alternative for each child. In the light of all the evidence available, and using my own professional judgment, I assessed that nineteen of the thirty-four had a reasonable chance of having no further serious problems (these included six who were back in care). For the other fifteen (seven from group A, two from group B, and six from group C - five away from home and ten at home) the situation at the time was fairly stable, but there were serious question marks in my mind about their future. For these it can be said that their chances were probably no better nor worse than those of a random sample of children in care, except that only one was described as 'institutionalised', all still had a sense of their identity, and all except perhaps two knew that, in their own way, at least one of their parents (whether by birth or adoption) still loved them and cared about them.

Chapter 6

THE SOCIAL WORKERS AND THE HELP THEY OFFERED

The previous two chapters have examined the problems which led to care, and described the families and the children whilst they were in contact with the social services department. In this chapter the nature of the social work help offered will be examined, as will some of the attitudes of the parents towards this help, and of the social workers towards working with families of children in statutory care. It must be stated here that the social workers' task in such cases is complex, in that they are on the one hand given the statutory role of acting either as parents or as supervisors of the children, and on the other hand required to use their expertise as professional social workers to help the children, the parents, and the substitute caretakers with their difficulties. There has been some discussion, especially in 'At Risk' (Baher et al., 1976), as to whether these two roles can successfully be combined in all cases. The social workers interviewed had obviously given some thought to this question, and on the whole thought that the roles could be combined, with their helping role having a strong influence on the way they exercised their supervisory or parental functions.

For the parents, there was more confusion, as illustrated by these comments:

'But she is only supposed to be concerned with Mary. She isn't supposed to be bothering about our marriage, is she?'

'Help me? No. He wasn't *my* social worker. He was in charge of Jim.'

At the same time, parents complained when they were not helped with their own difficulties, implying that they did understand that the social workers might be expected to help them as well as the children. To the parents, the major action of the social worker was the statutory one of either placing or not placing their child away from home in the first place, deciding where to place him, and whether and when he should come home, and then deciding whether he should remain at home. This applied even to the children on supervision orders, as all were conscious that the social workers might initiate action which could lead to the children leaving home, and this did in fact happen.

The way decisions were made about placement, and attitudes towards the different placements, will be discussed in the following chapter. However, it is important to note here that there was a strong element of authority always present, and that, for the parents at least, the social workers' parental or supervisory roles were almost always paramount. The most obvious implication of this, which makes this group of clients different from most recipients of social services, is that they had little choice in the matter. As stated in the Preface, they were 'captive clients'. They might refuse to accept certain aspects of what was offered, but they could not, without going back to court, terminate their connection with the department. The result, as one might expect, was that this lack of freedom of choice, to say nothing of the anger often felt about statutory action, sometimes led to resentment which distorted the relationship, and the view of the help offered. Indeed, it is surprising that this did not happen more often. That it did not was probably due to the fact that several parents differentiated between the social worker and the 'system', and this reaction will be discussed in more detail below.

THE SOCIAL WORKERS

All the recent inquiries after the deaths of children in their own homes or in care have looked at the role of social workers. Some of the writers, notably in the cases of John Auckland and Steven Meurs, and certainly many media commentators, have commented on whether they were thought to be too young, or inexperienced, or unsuitable because they had not had children of their own. The parents in this study had their views about the sort of social workers they preferred, although their views were less simplistic than those of the media. Because of this, a few basic details were collected about each worker.

In all, twenty workers were interviewed, as some were involved in more than one case. One social worker had at some stage been the worker for four of the families studied, and another for three, which seems to indicate a degree of specialisation in working with 'at risk' families. (Indeed, two of the areas covered had specialist family care teams.) Ten of the social workers were men, and ten were women. Fourteen were professionally qualified, and these were the workers for eighteen of the families. Thus, 76 per cent of the families had a qualified worker. The proportion of qualified social workers in the county as a whole was approximately 40 per cent; and thus it is clear that there was a policy of allocating these statutory child care cases to the qualified workers whenever possible. It is not the purpose of this study to look in any detail at the differences between the work of qualified and unqualified workers, but a few general comments may be appropriate, as the quality of work may well be related to outcome. Although only seven of the families had unqualified workers at the time of the interview, in at least eight other cases previous workers had been unqualified.

On the whole, qualified workers were more familiar with the child care theories referred to in the introduction, and were more likely to base their work and their decisions on these theories, whereas the unqualified workers relied more on 'common sense'. However, some of the unqualified workers had clearly thought very carefully about the decisions they made, and whether through supervision, reading or in-service training, were familiar with child care literature. Conversely, the comments of some of the qualified workers seemed to indicate that they were basing decisions more on 'common sense' than on good child care practice. This was particularly the case with issues such as parental contact with children in care when the child was upset after visits. There were examples of clients preferring qualified workers, and also examples of them preferring workers who were unqualified, and there were examples of sensitive, skilled, and time-consuming work, often out of office hours, by both qualified and unqualified workers. Some of the unqualified workers did say that they felt ill-equipped to handle cases of such complexity, and sometimes this came through to their clients. They were also more likely to be overawed by the non-accidental injury procedures, so that their anxiety and inexperience led them to antagonise clients in a way which more experienced workers might have avoided.

Unqualified worker: 'I probably mishandled the investigation at the beginning. I was new to the department. It was my first N.A.I. case. I was terribly anxious about it. I didn't know how to handle it. I upset them in trying to get them to say how the injuries occurred. They never did. I think it was the case conference that made me feel I had to find out. I was a bit heavy handed. I never really got over that initial bad patch. My senior came in later. They could respond to her. She was much more relaxed about it.'

Mother: 'I think they should be trained before they are let on cases. He was practising on us. He didn't know his job. He once said, "I don't care how you feel, I've taken her away and that is that", which didn't go down well. We were just a case. With this new social worker I feel like a person. I don't feel like a convict any more.'

Mother: 'That social worker was hopeless: I think I could do it better. All she could ever say was, "I'll have to ask my superiors".'

On the other hand, this comment was also made about an unqualified worker:

Mother: 'I don't know if he had any experience but he was good at his job. I didn't know then that he wasn't trained. He never put me under pressure. If he said something, he did it. You could rely on him.'

Closely linked with the question of training is that of experience in social work practice, and more specifically in child care social work. The British Association of Social Workers' code of practice for working with cases of non-accidental injury to children (BASW, 1975b) states that workers in this field should be not only qualified social workers but should also have particular skills in communicating with children. At the time of the study five of the workers had over eight years' experience, five had been in social work for four to seven years, and the remaining ten for one to four years.

These figures refer to the time of the study, and some of the workers had far less experience when they first started working with these cases. However, the fact that ten social workers serving twelve of the twenty-five families had four or more years experience in social work does not support the stereotype of the inexperienced social worker. Again, as with training, it may be that the more experienced workers are working with statutory child care cases.

The question of experience in child care social work was mentioned above, and it is often brought up as a criticism of local authority social services departments that social workers no longer have expertise with particular client groups, especially children at risk (Howells, 1975). Nine of the social workers were working from 'family care' teams, and several of the others were clearly specialising to some extent in child care cases. Although I did not discuss individual cases with senior social workers or managers, it was clear from the interviews that most of the social workers, whether qualified or unqualified, were influenced by the senior social workers, and that having a senior with child care experience was of considerable help, especially where the workers had little experience in such cases. There were some cases where neither senior nor social worker had much experience in child care, but these were a small minority.

Another comment often made about social workers is that they are too young (linked with inexperience). None of the social workers was under 25, eighteen were aged between 25 and 40, and two were over 40. Like the media commentators, the clients had their own views about whether they preferred older or younger social workers, men or women, those with children of their own or without. They did, however, by no means agree with each other, and my general conclusion was that they rationalised around the social worker they preferred, and that personality and the quality of the social work help offered were the relevant factors. The following comments illustrate the range of views expressed:

Mother: 'We had a few words, because she said, "I understand how you feel", and I said, "How can you; you haven't got kids?" Our second social worker had no kids, though, and she understood. She didn't have children but she was very good and helpful.'

Mother: 'She had no children of her own. She tended to see things in black and white. She couldn't understand the pull of a child.'

Father: 'She was a nice person. The boy liked her, and he could talk to her. She would come in here and sit down. She was a young person, hadn't any children. The next one was older. She had children of her own, and just told us what to do. She didn't seem to understand our problems.'

Father: 'I had a young woman on the case and she was about nineteen or twenty. I think most people look for somebody older.'

Mother: 'The last three I remember very well. Because they were younger. More my age-group for a start. You could have a laugh with them.'

Another problem which is often mentioned is the frequency with which social workers move. One family had had six different social workers over an eight-year period, but fifteen families had had only one or two different workers. Thus, whilst not allowing for complacency, the picture is of fewer changes of worker than in some other studies. Most of the families who mentioned it found the prospect of a change of social worker difficult.

Mother: 'I dreaded it. I didn't really get on with her but I thought the next one might be worse.'

The change of worker reminded parents of the precarious nature of their child's stay with them, though on balance those who got on well with their social worker could accept change more easily, if with regret at losing someone whose visits they valued.

Mother: 'I don't resent her going. She had to get trained, That's what she wanted. But I did miss her.'

At least three of the families were left for long periods without a social worker, which led to problems for the new worker when he came on the scene, usually at a point of crisis. For example, a child was returned home after court because there was no assessment place available, and was then not visited for several months. During this time parents and child were left anxiously wondering whether the 'reprieve' was temporary or permanent, and were not surprisingly angry when a new social worker, with no relationship with the child, arrived to say that their son would be going away in two days' time.

For some, though, it was the fresh look given by a new social worker which had led to a change of emphasis towards the children returning home.

THE SOCIAL WORK HELP OFFERED

Help offered by other agencies

This study is principally concerned with the help offered by social workers from the social services department, and there was no systematic attempt to ascertain what help was offered by other agencies. Parents were asked if any other agencies had been helpful, but the nature of the help offered by other agencies was not explored in detail. Sixteen of the twenty families interviewed mentioned either going for help with their problems, or receiving help from other social workers (mainly NSPCC workers, probation officers, education welfare officers, and child guidance social workers), from teachers, health visitors, general practitioners, psychiatrists, and personnel officers.

The tendency was for other social workers to be less involved after statutory action, but three probation officers and the other professionals continued to have a role, and there were cases where the major helping role was shared between local authority social workers and teachers, general practitioners, psychiatrists or health visitors. Only in two cases (one where the mother was in psychiatric hospital for a period of years) were psychiatrists involved in therapy after the children were in care, although a psychiatric assessment was obtained in several cases for parents or children, and two of the children had been going regularly to child guidance clinics before care.

On the whole, comments about social workers from other agencies tended to be favourable, if rather vague.

Mother: 'The probation officer was a good man. I can't say nothing against him. He put in a good report. She never missed going up to see him.'

Mother: 'The NSPCC helped. He gave me clothes for the children, and one week he helped me out with groceries.'

Parents who mentioned the police did not feel that they had been helpful, although one mother was, in retrospect, grateful that she had not been prosecuted for assault on her child.

Mother: 'The police won't leave him alone. They took him one day when he was walking in the street, and kept him in the cell with no boots on.'

One family was receiving considerable help from a health visitor, but others tended to feel that they would have liked more help.

Mother: 'Having never had a mother, although I've been a nurse, there are problems, and the health visitor didn't visit.'

Mother (about the period when she was ill-treating her child): 'I had a health visitor then, and then she changed. That's where it goes wrong. She had got me on the pill, and everything. I was just getting round to telling her and then she left to get married. You get another, it takes you a month to get used to her - and it was too late.'

Parents had far more to say about their general practitioners, either for good or ill. Generally they were supportive and prescribed pills, occasionally they were unhelpful, but in some cases they took on a major therapy and supervisory role.

Father: 'I didn't get any help after my wife died. The GP gave me some sleeping tablets though.'

Mother: 'The day before I took her to the hospital, she kept being sick, so I took her to the surgery. The doctor said to me, "Take her home and feed her and stop fussing".'

Mother: 'Our GP said the other day, "If he does get you down, don't touch him, come and see me, because I can see what he's like." He is very understanding.'

Mother: 'I went to the doctor and he told me I was completely run down and gave me some tablets. You can sit and talk to him.'

The parents also had a fair amount to say about the psychiatric services, either of the health service or the education department. On the whole, they were disappointed with what was offered, having hoped for more, or positively hostile. There was confusion in the minds of parents about the assessment role and the therapeutic role. Some who had clearly been referred for assessment were disappointed that they were not offered therapy. Others were disappointed because, having overcome their inhibitions about them or their child going to see a psychiatrist, no magic cure could be offered.

Mother: 'He'd been to a psychiatrist while I was away, but he said that it was a marital problem, he wasn't mental or insane.'

Mother: 'The psychiatrist came round to my house first. I thought they were going to take me away. Then I used to go to see her twice a week at first. I never used to tell her how I felt. I couldn't express myself. I did go, but I hated it.'

It may be that some of the children were receiving some psychiatric help, either at special schools or in residential care; but on the whole the role of the psychiatric services, other than their assessment role, was minimal in these cases. In view of the amount of mental illness or personality difficulties referred to in Chapter 3, this is perhaps surprising. It may indicate that the problems the parents had, even though in several cases severe enough to require admission to psychiatric hospital, were more likely to be alleviated by improvement of the environment and support with relationships within the home, than by a more traditionally medical model of treatment; or it may be that the psychiatric services at that time within the area were not offering a service relevant to the needs of this particular group of families, except on an emergency basis.

An overview of help offered by the local authority social workers

In order to examine in more detail the nature of the help offered, social workers were asked to indicate on a check list the way in which they had tried to help. Families were asked what sort of help they had received at the various stages, and whether this had been appropriate. They were also asked more generally about what in their opinion were the attributes of a good social worker.

Eleven of the families were known to the department long before the events which led to statutory action. Indeed, eight of these parents had themselves been in the care of the county. Only six families were offered long-term help on a planned basis, the other five being helped out of crises from time to time, usually by a different social worker each time. The children from nine of these families had been in short-term care, and in two cases children had been placed for adoption. All these eleven families were known to be 'high risk' families, and it is perhaps surprising that all were not on a social worker's caseload under the provisions of the 1963 Act (Section 1), although one was receiving support from the probation service. Three of the five families not being consistently helped were at this time going to the department for help and advice, and three of the parents interviewed felt that if they had been helped more consistently and positively at this stage, statutory action might not have been necessary. In another case, the current social worker felt that the mishandling of the adoption of a previous child had been one of the factors leading to a mother's inability to cope subsequently:

Social worker: 'It worries me that a girl who has spent her whole life in care wasn't picked up earlier at the time of the adoption, as needing casework help. She regretted having him placed. She felt pushed. And that had an effect on what happened later.'

Mother: 'I went up there about the way he behaved. That really worried me. The social worker just didn't want to know. After they took him away, they did everything for him.'

The lack of a comprehensive preventive service for these families will be discussed at the end of this chapter, and the question of practical resources as aids to prevention is discussed in Chapter 7.

Although care proceedings did become necessary in the six cases where regular help was being offered, when the children came into care the thorough knowledge of the family made for more realistic planning of placement, and the children were at least placed and visited by a familiar figure. Also the actual occasion of the taking of statutory action was less traumatic for parents and social workers as in all six cases this had been discussed as a possibility which might become necessary, and parents, social workers and older children all acknowledged that a great deal of effort had been put into trying to avoid such action.

Although almost half of the families were known to the department, three became known only when help was sought about the problem which subsequently led to care, and eleven were not known to the department at all. These eleven included five of the suspected abuse cases, and six of the older delinquent group.

In most cases there was an increased amount of contact with the parents when the children came into care, at least initially, and some social workers who had been unable to establish any helpful contact with a family before court found that the statutory powers allowed them to 'get to grips' with a situation, even if the child remained at home. However, three parents complained that, when the children went away, they were rather left to their own devices, although it must be added that in two cases their extreme anger and threatening behaviour must have been something of a deterrent! The three who complained about not being visited when the child went away, had all complained of a low level of service before care.

Mother: 'When the children went, they just cut me off completely. They never bothered. I was in most of the time too.'

Table 6.1 gives a detailed analysis of the forms of help offered by the social worker interviewed, and therefore in most cases refers to the time when the children were at home. In all cases more than one form of help was offered, and also the nature of the service changed over time. As mentioned above, the principal form of intervention in most cases was the placement of the child away from home, but this will be discussed in more detail in Chapter 7.

The list was roughly divided into verbal help and practical help, but there was some overlap in that, for example, much of the negotiating was in fact in order to get financial or other practical help. The various forms of intervention will be commented on below, but at the outset it will be clear that in these cases a great deal of help was being offered when the children were home, and in a variety of ways. Certainly the image of the non-directive social worker offering 'casework' help and little else does not seem applicable. The average number of forms of help offered was ten,

TABLE 6.1 Help offered by social services department when children home on trial or on supervision orders

Verbal/supportive help		Number of families	
Supportive visits		22	
Supervisory visits		22	
Casework/therapy with	a) mother	11	
	b) father	6	19 families
	c) whole family	13	in all
	d) children	11	
Groupwork with	a) mother	5	
	b) father	0	
	c) children	2	
Negotiating		18	
Advocacy		5	
Legal advice		12	
Controlling		15	
Advice giving		20	

Practical help	
Help with housing/rehousing/repairs	13
Help with employment	4
Home help	1
Budgeting	11
Financial help	14
Clothing and other material aid	11
Holidays for parents	6
Holidays for children	10
Volunteer visits	3
Playgroup/day care	8
'Voluntary' care	10

with the lowest number being two, and the highest, nineteen. Usually a combination of practical and verbal help was offered, but in five cases no practical help was offered.

Mother: 'How did she help: only by talking. I needed somebody to talk to. She never took me anywhere or did anything like that, because there was no need. We just used to talk. I never had any financial help, except when he did come home, she clothed him.'

Social worker: 'There is a consistent them of supporting him through his mental health problems, using various means. It is often financial, helping him out in muddles, reassuring him about the children. We are keeping the family going as much as possible to the advantage of the children - to give them the best environment we can, using whatever skills are available. If casework is a planned commitment, that is what it is. There are key times when I work with the family as a group.'

The nature of the service offered varied throughout the period studied, with the usual pattern being that the level of help was stepped up at the time when the child returned home, or at other points of stress, with spells of less frequent supportive visiting in between.

Social workers were asked about the frequency of visits when the children were at home, and Table 6.2 shows the answers.

TABLE 6.2 Frequency of visits by social worker when children were home on trial or under supervision

	More than once a week	Weekly	Every 2 weeks	Every month	6-weekly
To parents	2	14	2	6	1
To children	2	9	5	8	1

The nature of the help offered to the children will be discussed below, but it is interesting to note here that although supervisory visits were mentioned in twenty-one cases, there was a pattern of the children being seen less regularly than the parents, and in fourteen cases children were not seen more often than fortnightly. However, for some cases of children at risk, arrangements were made for a child to be seen at the clinic or by the family doctor in between social work visits, or the child was at school.

Social workers were asked to say which of the services they offered was most important, and which the family thought was most important. Again, this tended to be different at different points in time, but wherever possible they were asked to give only one answer. The answers are summarised in Table 6.3. This table will

TABLE 6.3 Most important service offered according to social workers and families (as assessed by social workers and families)

	According to social worker	According to family (assessed by social worker)	According to family (20 families)
Supportive visits	9	7	2
Supervisory visits	3	4	9
Casework/therapy	10	6	7
Negotiating	0	1	0
Controlling	0	2	0
Advice giving	0	3	0
Practical help	1	3	1
Care for children and getting them home	2	2	1

be commented on in more detail as I consider the different forms of intervention. The third column is in fact my own assessment of what the parent interviewed thought was most important, as answers to the question about the help offered were usually lengthy, and it was a matter for interpretation as to whether we were talking, in particular, about casework or supportive visits.

Where clients stressed the importance of a relationship with the worker combined with the value of talking about their problems this was put under the heading of casework. The social workers often referred to changes in the clients' view of the main help offered, usually from supervisory or supportive visits to advice giving and casework. In one case it took well over twelve months for this change to occur.

Social worker: 'They just saw me as the policeman. They had to let me in because of the supervision order. The hard work in this was the sheer dread of visiting. Now, there is nothing I would call casework, but he loves talking about himself, and I plan to go more often in the evening.'

Relationships

As mentioned above, one of the ways in which I assessed whether casework was an appropriate description of the help offered as perceived by the parents, was to assess whether the relationship with the social worker was seen as being helpful. Much has been written about the nature of the casework relationship, and certainly this study confirms the view that to the client this aspect of the help offered is of crucial importance. (1) In these cases the nature of the relationship was complicated by the statutory role of the social worker, which, as we have seen, often provoked aggression or resentment. Only nine of the social workers interviewed had been responsible for removing the children from home, but families often commented about previous social workers who had taken their children into care and the effect this had on the relationship. Sometimes also there were very mixed feelings about social workers of the past from those who had been in care themselves. The question of the authoritarian aspects of the social work will be discussed under the heading of supervisory visits, but it can be said here that either removing the child, or representing the agency which did so, proved a serious handicap to the establishing of a helpful relationship in some cases but not in others.

Mother: 'Well, he'd got a job to do, hadn't he? How I felt didn't alter the fact that he had to take her there. He talked to me. I think maybe he did understand. He's a nice person.'

Mother: 'It turned me against the social worker for putting them in care. I was nasty with them after that. I would have been against anybody who took them away.'

Father: 'I seem to get on with this social worker better, but that could be time. If he had been the one that took them, I would probably have punched him.'

Mother: 'I hate that social worker for what happened, and I always will. Underneath, in fifty years time, I will still hate her.'

When discussing the qualities which they most valued in a social worker the parents tended to come to roughly the same conclusions: they needed to know that they were valued as people, and were not just cases; they wanted their social workers to be honest with them about what they were planning for the children and if they said they would do something to do it or say why they could not; they wanted them to empathise – to listen, and to try to understand how they felt; (2) and they wanted them to be caring, helpful, and sometimes controlling, towards their children. Like Sainsbury (1975), I found that social workers were approved of, not because of the material aid they gave, but rather for the values they seemed to hold. It seemed to be more important that they should be consistent and reliable, and some workers were well liked by their clients even when the clients felt disappointed that more practical help had not been given.

In view of the importance to the clients of being cared about as people rather than cases, social workers were asked whether the parents 'mattered to them', and whether they thought the parents thought they mattered to them. It is interesting that this question, which was immediately comprehensible and relevant to the parents, often needed clarification for the social workers. Some clearly felt that there were un-professional implications if they said yes.

Social worker: 'Mattered to me? We were all chuffed together when things were going well. They knew I cared. There *was* an emotional sharing, but only emotions relevant to the case were shared.'

Social worker: 'I get very aggravated by him. I find him difficult, and have a low opinion of him. If he were hurt, I would feel guilty. I feel more for some clients than others. I hope it doesn't affect my work. I am very careful.'

Social worker: 'I am professionally prepared for things to go wrong with him. That's why I don't get too bothered by him. He's not just a casual caller, though, as some clients are.'

Others were more positive:

Social worker: 'Yes. The situations where I can actually achieve something are those where I can use something personal.'

Social worker: 'They matter more, partly because of the time I spend with them. They are pretty exhausting and demanding, but I am aware of having quite an affection for them.'

Social worker: 'Some of my cases, I could say they didn't matter much to me. But I was really ever so fond of Emma. She could have been a friend.'

In eighteen cases the social worker said the parents mattered more to them than most of their other cases; in one case, less; in six cases, about the same. These answers were often related to the length of time the social workers spent with the families, and to their and their children's vulnerability. Families which had fewer problems and made fewer demands, tended to matter less. On the other hand, those who mattered most were often those where there was least chance of 'success'.

Thirteen of the twenty parents interviewed thought they mattered to the social workers, two thought not, and five did not know. Often the clients based their answers on whether they seemed to understand how they felt, or whether they provided an appropriate service.

Mother: 'She suggested things we hadn't thought of. You don't feel as if you are always begging. She took us more as people, not just another case.'

Mother: 'We got more friends in the end. She did care because if she said something, she would do it. It wasn't a false promise.'

Father: 'He went to great lengths with his court report. He came to show it to us first. He really cared about us all, and wanted to get the children home.'

Mother: 'They've got to get involved to understand the situation. Once we thought he had run away. The social worker got onto them the same night and came round that night and said, "Don't worry, he's still there." He seemed more like one of the family. Although he was so busy, he always seemed to have time.'

The sense that on the whole the social worker cared about them led some of the parents to be more accepting of social workers' inadequacies, or to lay the blame for them not being able to help on the 'system', or on excess of work:

Mother: 'If somebody comes up to me and says they are going to do something in a fortnight, well, I want it done in a fortnight. But he does care about us. He is doing his best.'

Mother: 'Matter? Sometimes I go up there and she says "I'm busy." I feel she brushes me off sometimes. But she does care. I know that much.'

In other cases the social workers had never established with the family that they cared about them or could understand their feelings, and often this was related to the initial handling of the investigation leading to care proceedings, and to an inability to combine a supervisory with a caring role.

Mother: 'He was all talk. All he wanted to know about was whether we hit him. He didn't care about us. He said he would help us with our financial problems, and then he didn't turn up for weeks. He was no help at all. He didn't actually say no. He just kept putting it off.'

Mother: 'Some of them think they are one above you. They think you are a bit thick. She patronised us. She had great difficulty grasping our problem. She would have been lovely with old ladies or with someone who was how she expected us to be - totally inadequate.'

The study, then, confirms the importance of empathy in establishing a relationship through which help can be offered, and suggests that with some of these clients, whose self-esteem has

Chapter 6

been almost inevitably damaged by the need for statutory intervention, the establishment of such a relationship can require considerable time and skill. Some social workers had, as seen above, emphasised their controlling and supervisory role to the extent that they had seemed not to care for the parents at all. There were other cases where the social workers had denied their statutory role in the initial stages, only to exercise it later, much to the anger of the parents. This was especially the case when children came into care voluntarily and it was subsequently decided to take court action or parental rights; or even, as in two cases, where parents were persuaded to part with the children 'voluntarily', when the social workers had every intention of taking statutory action once they were in care. Hence the stress which the parents and some social workers laid on the need for honesty. In some cases, decisions made after the children were in care meant that the social worker could not avoid appearing to have deceived the parents, but sometimes in such cases the parents could accept that the deception was not deliberate. Sometimes this need for honesty from the social worker was related to being kept informed about how their children were progressing in care, and about the timing of return home.

Mother: 'The welfare said, "After you have had a rest, you can have the children back." That put me against the welfare. I think the welfare do good, but the way they do it is bad. They told me to have a rest and I believed them. They conned me.'

Mother: 'They didn't bother about my feelings. I thought something funny was going on because they didn't tell me to get any clothes for the baby. She came that day and said you can get him dressed because we are taking him away to a foster home. I turned against her after that.'

Mother: 'When they went away, I was relieved, I had asked for help. I've since learned they would have taken them with a court order. I was very bitter when they took the parental rights. They were not honest.'

Mother: 'The children have been told things which were not true. They were told they would only be there for a few weeks, then they were told they would never be allowed to come home.'

Mother: 'The social worker is in a difficult position as mediator. I thought she was less than honest before Jim came home. She tried to influence our opinion as regards the foster home. To tell us everything was all right when it wasn't.'

Mother: 'He was coming home, and then he wasn't. I was angry with the social worker. I said, "I can't keep hanging about, either I have him home or I don't".'

Mother: 'I like this social worker. He tells you things.'

In order to clarify further the nature of the relationship between social workers and parents, the parents were asked how they viewed the social worker, and what role he fulfilled for them. Social workers were asked how they thought the parents viewed them, and what role the parents saw them as fulfilling. The answers were complicated, as parents usually referred to more than one social worker, and felt differently about social workers at different times. The social workers also felt that their role, and the attitude of the parents towards them changed. A fairly common pattern was for suspicion and dislike before care to turn to resignation and suspicion or goodwill whilst the child was in care, and to goodwill and apprehension on the child's return home, turning to affection and acceptance if all went well.

TABLE 6.4 Feelings with which the parents viewed the social workers, according to the parents interviewed and the social workers

Parents viewed social workers with:	According to social worker (25 families)	According to parents (20 families)
Goodwill	13	11
Confidence	10	10
Affection	9	11
Acceptance	2	4
Suspicion	9	8
Dislike	6	4
Fear	2	2
Apprehension	11	7
Resignation	6	5
Confusion	5	2
Resentment	5	6

To summarise, there was some agreement between social workers and clients. Positive feelings were mentioned thirty-two times by social workers and thirty-one times by the twenty parents interviewed; feelings of acceptance and resignation eight times by social workers and nine times by parents; negative feelings related to authority, twenty-five times by social workers and seventeen times by parents, and hostile feelings (dislike, fear and resentment) thirteen times by social workers and twelve times by the parents. It must also be remembered that the parents were often referring to previous social workers. Sometimes each parent felt differently.

Mother: 'He couldn't get that close to us because my husband, he speaks his mind, and there was always that between them, her being in care. There was a sort of grudge there where he couldn't say, "Hello, how are things, sit yourself down". Now I feel I know him instead of just knowing his name and that he is the social worker. I suppose you would say goodwill, because he has tried to help Jenny, and he has helped, and very often it's been difficult for him because my husband got upset.'

Social worker: 'They were confused. I had to give evidence in court. They couldn't see how I could be their friend, as it were – come round and have a cup of tea. The meaning of someone standing there before strangers and detailing how you had not been looking after the child, when they had been visiting and not said what they didn't like. It was devastating, even though they knew before. We explained before, we have to do this to protect him. I'm sure they thought I should have stopped them getting to that pitch.'

Mother: 'One day it's sweet talk and drinking cups of tea, and the next they are accusing you of this and that and the other.'

TABLE 6.5 The role in which parents saw social workers - according to social workers and parents interviewed*

	According to social workers	According to parents interviewed
Parent for self	5	1
Parent for child	1	3
Aunt/uncle for child	1	2
Helper	16	7
Friend	12	9
Provider of material aid	6	4
Therapist	5	4
Inspector	8	7

* Parents and social workers usually gave more than one answer.

Table 6.5 gives the opinions of social workers and clients on the roles in which parents saw the social workers. Bearing in mind that only twenty families were interviewed, there is some agreement between social workers and parents. Although only one mother said she thought of her social worker as a parent, it was clear from the behaviour of the other four mentioned by social workers under this heading that they did cast the social workers in a parental role, and four of the five had been in long-term care.

Mother: 'She is more or less like a mother to me, not a social worker. I can't talk to my mother like I talk to her. I can always look on her as someone to go to, if I'm ever in trouble, and I don't say that about all the social workers. I think low about social workers but you can't think low about her. We have our little joke. I say I want to be adopted. I say, Mary (social worker) can adopt me. So I go to the Welfare, and I say, larking about, "Hello, mother". She turns round and laughs and says, "Go on".'

Social worker: 'She was just like a child saying, help me, cuddle me, I can't stand this life.'

Social worker: 'The basic thing with her, she needs mothering. I'm not sure that I'm the ideal person to give her that.'

Social workers tended to under-estimate the number of times they were seen as officers of the court or the department, and, perhaps more interestingly, they under-estimated the importance which the parents attached to their work with the children. An indication of the fact that some social workers were seen as friends was that

seven of the parents called the social worker by their first names.
Mother: 'He was like a friend, because he would pop in and sit and listen. And if he said he was going to do something, he got up and did it.'

Father: 'I just go and see the social worker for company. I can manage my money all right, and my rent is paid direct.'

Social worker: 'I am a therapist to some extent, but she is very anxious for me to be a friend. It is difficult because it seems such an unfair thing to do. You march in. They accept you as a friend, treat you as a friend, and it can't be mutual. They want you to be godparents to their children because they have nobody else. I am very involved with them. I *can* sit back and look at it, but it is a struggle.'

Sometimes the parents would be angry with the social worker in his parental role, or resentful, and this could lead to 'acting out' behaviour which could harm the child, such as sending children down to the department alone in one case, with a neighbour in another, asking for them to be taken into care. Social workers cast in this role also felt the stresses it placed on them in the context of a large caseload.

Social worker: 'Jim is at risk because of my lack of time. This is really a family service unit case. She knows I will try to be there if she really needs me. But sometimes she comes down so often, I have to tell her to go away. I'm afraid one of these days I will misjudge it. Also, I am not firm enough with her over Jim. I haven't the time to pick her up consistently.'

Several social workers emphasised the importance, for balanced judgment, of good consultation and supervision for the social workers in such cases.

Casework and supportive help

Table 6.1 shows that twenty-two families were receiving supportive visits, and that casework help was offered to nineteen families. There was considerable discussion with the social workers as to what sort of work should be included under which heading, and the table can only be taken as a rough guide. The question about supportive work was qualified by 'diffuse work, whether or not based on a casework relationship, which was aimed at keeping the family functioning as well as possible without actually aiming for major changes in behaviour'. Casework was qualified by 'relationship therapy (verbal or non-verbal), or functionally specific work which aimed to achieve change by following a plan'. Many of the social workers were diffident about describing what they were doing as casework, often because the verbal, interpretive element was not prominent in their work. In most cases the pattern was for the work to be mainly supportive, but with brief spells of more or less intensive, and more or less planned, casework. It was interesting that in some cases where the social workers were not too sure whether the term casework was appropriate, the description by the clients made it fairly clear that it was. (3)

Social worker: 'I really feel rather hesitant about calling it casework, whatever I was doing. I don't think I had anything so grandiose as a plan. I talked to her a lot about her background and the effect it had on her. I worked with them together about the way they handled Philip.'

Mother: 'This social worker I've got now, she sees me about once a week. She's nice. She sort of understands. You can say anything to her because she listens. The others, you can't sit and talk to them. I can talk about my problems now. I couldn't explain things to the others.'

Social worker: 'Mostly casework. They knew their problem was emotional rather than financial. It was one of those rare cases where the emotional stands out loud and clear.'

Social worker: 'She was a withdrawn person, with persecution feelings at times. I was working with her to get her to look at employment, and at the relationship with her family. We weren't necessarily focusing on John, but on how she saw their family life.'

Social worker: 'She was learning about how to express herself verbally, instead of just "acting out".'

Table 6.3 shows that seven of the families interviewed thought that casework was the most important form of help offered, in that they valued most the chance to talk about their problem and to work towards an improvement in the situation. Usually there was an unexpressed understanding between social workers and parents about this. In ten of the twenty-five cases there was some more specific contract between them about the goals to be aimed at, and the means of achieving these goals.

Social worker: 'I use a reality therapy approach with the parents as well. They know I will help them provided they are straight with me.'

One mother, having said how much she appreciated the chance to talk regularly about problems, said about previous social workers who seem to have offered only support or supervision:

'I used to think to myself, "What's the point? You only sit there and ask how everything is going on, and have a look at the baby." Waste of time, her just coming for a chat.'

In other cases, though, an interpretive approach was not appreciated:

Mother: 'He didn't help at all. Everything you say, he made two meanings of it.'

Mother: 'I can't sit and talk to her. She keeps chiming in every time and argues with you.'

Usually the casework goals centred around child care, or personality problems, but in four cases there was a more systematic attempt at marital therapy. Some parents clearly required the focus to be on themselves rather than on the children, but in other cases there was some confusion that someone who originally had a supervisory child care function had turned into a marital counsellor.

In two cases parents were ambivalent about this form of help, and felt to some extent pushed into it because of the hidden or open threat that otherwise their children would be removed:

Mother: 'The marital business, I objected to it, but I put up with it.'

Father: 'We had no choice. If things hadn't been sorted out, they were going to take her completely. We wouldn't have any choice. We were told that.'

Sometimes the casework help was offered jointly with other workers, such as a residential social worker, the head teacher at a special unit, or a voluntary worker at a battered wives' hostel.

Social worker: 'Getting him into school had been a tremendous success in the first two years. My work was linking that into the home. Using the changed situation to try to improve what was going on in the home. Trying to get a mutual acceptance between husband and wife and Terry. In a way, there was guilt too because their task had been taken away from them. There was guilt that the school had succeeded.'

Usually casework help was offered in conjunction with supportive help, although in two cases the social workers said that they were offering therapy but not support. In four cases they were offering supportive visits but not casework, and in another case they were offering support to the parents but casework only to the child. In one case it was felt that neither casework nor supportive help were needed by the parents, but only casework help for the child. The social workers thought that supportive visits were the most important form of help in nine cases, and the families in two cases. This discrepancy was perhaps due to the fact that in some cases, although still talking about problems with the parents, social workers had come to the conclusion that they were unlikely to achieve change and were concentrating on support and/or supervision.

Social worker: 'After making various attempts to deal with things in depth, I've come to the conclusion that all the other pressures and demands, and the way that one's time is worked out, make it more realistic to use that time on other cases. And also the family's inability to cope with that anyway. It's a fairly limited objective, but it seems to achieve at least that limited object.'

Social worker: 'If my plan had any validity, it would have been a long time before they could be independent. I was thinking in terms of ten years' solid parenting.'

Social worker: 'I tend to focus on delinquency. But mostly I tend to be supportive. It turns out more supportive, whatever I aim at. More controlling, advice giving. I would like to say I do casework, trying to show them what is the problem, and how they can overcome it, but I have more or less given that up.'

Social worker: 'She wants you to be there. She wants to talk about her feelings but basically she wants to know that you are there.'

Some of the casework could be described as family groupwork, or family therapy, and sometimes residential workers, foster parents, teachers, and senior social workers were involved. There were few opportunities for the parents to take part in groups, to a large extent because of the rural nature of the area. Two groups for mothers were run by social workers, one in a child psychiatry department, and one in conjunction with a playgroup, and four mothers attended. Another was gaining a great deal from the group support in a hostel. Only two parents commented, both favourably, but one social worker described her attempt to introduce a mother who was suspected of harming her child to a group as unsuccessful.

Social worker: 'I took her to the group, but she didn't like it because she said people there had problems and she didn't. Jill played up when she wanted to leave, and she couldn't cope with that.'

Mother: 'I went to a group. You talk about your own problems. It's hard to say if I found it useful. I can talk to a crowd of people, all mothers. We had the same problems. We all talked to each other.'

Supervisory and protective visits

Since all the children were either on supervision orders or care orders, where the social workers had parental rights and duties, it is not surprising that supervisory visits were mentioned in all but three cases. It is perhaps more surprising that they were not mentioned in three cases, and that they were seen as the major form of help in only three cases by the social workers. This is in part explained by the length of time many of the children had been at home, so that the social workers were in several cases confident that the children were no longer at risk.

The question of authority has been touched on before, particularly with reference to the relationship between social workers and parents. There were two main aspects to this authority; the first (the rather negative one, as far as the parents were concerned) of statutorily removing the children, and the power to do so again; and second, the supervisory or parental aspect of the duties imposed by the court or the social services committee. There is considerable discussion amongst workers in this field about the possibility or desirability of the therapist also being the person responsible for removing the child, should it be necessary to protect him in this way. Most of the social workers interviewed thought these roles should and could be combined, and there were examples of their having been successfully combined. One social worker thought that her work was easier because she had not been the one to initiate care proceedings:

'I'm sure it's easier for me not being the social worker who took him away. I took him over a month after he came home. They had won.'

Others who took over similar cases thought it made things even more difficult in that they had to decide whether to let the traumatic incident remain in the background, known about but not talked about, or bring it out into the open again.

Social worker: 'If I had gone in on their terms, we could have had a nice friendly relationship, but for the first meeting, I thought it important that the official side of it was clear. I found it very difficult, but I thought I had to do it. He said, "I hope you are not going to be like our last social worker. I'm not going to have interference." I felt right from the start that we had to establish the fact that unfortunately I sometimes had to say and do things they might not like. It was pointless to base my relationship on a collusion. He got extremely angry, then apologised, then got angry again and didn't apologise. After that, whenever I called he shut himself off, or if he was there, he stood and showed me the child and said, "Look, he is all right, isn't he?" I remember I went one day, and the radio was playing, and I heard an angry voice and a door slam. She came and opened the door to me and went back into the kitchen and I followed. In a few moments he came out, and I said, "Hello, are you well, as you are at home?" and he said: "I am quite well" and slammed the door again. And about two minutes later came back again and said, "Now you can see him, you can see he is all right," and went off and slammed the door again. The air was blue.'

This comment shows how much anger there can be, and I did feel that some of the social workers tended to under-estimate the feelings of the parents. Almost all the parents I spoke to, even several years after the event, could remember in great detail the date and time of day, and what had been said. They may have chosen to put their anger on one side and to get on with the social workers; they may have come to see that what had happened was in their own and the child's best interests; but they certainly had not forgotten the pain, and the anger.

It is relevant here to consider more fully the nature of parental anger, as the skill or otherwise of the social workers in working with angry parents coloured their perceptions about whether these parents might be able in the future to offer good enough care to their children. It was suggested in Chapter 4 that in some cases parental anger was an almost inevitable result of the clumsy and insensitive handling of the original investigations and removal of the children. Several parents complained of lack of honesty on the part of the social worker about what was likely to happen; of twisting of facts in the presentation at court; of breaches of confidentiality without their permission having been obtained and without any explanation as to why it was necessary to pass on the information; and, most of all, of being left alone without help as soon as their children had been removed, sometimes not knowing even where they were.

Some degree of anger when a child is compulsorily removed is almost inevitable if there exist any feelings of attachment between the parents and the child. As Olive Stevenson (1968, p.12) put it, for all parents 'reception into care breaks the primitive tie which can be seen in all species of animal, in endless variety of pattern'. One need only look at the work of the National Association for the Welfare of Children in Hospital, and read Margaret Drabble's (1965) 'The Millstone', to realise that for 'normal' families to demand, sometimes aggressively, to have a say about the way their child is cared for in hospital and to be with him as much as possible, is considered acceptable and indeed commendable behaviour. As indicated in Chapter 4, most of these parents did not deviate from the norm in terms of their perceptions of the needs of their children, and therefore it is to be expected that they would want to see as much as possible of them, and that some would react aggressively if they were denied access to them.

On the other hand, Chapter 4 also showed that several of the parents had themselves experienced depriving circumstances as children, which may have led to the mental illness and relationship difficulties which were noted, and to immaturity which was likely to show itself as anger at times of crisis.

We have to deal with parents at every level of emotional development: so that we may be working with people who behave like adolescents - stormy, rebellious, up against authority; or like 3-year-olds - unable to tolerate much frustration, demanding of attention and affection; or even like babies - this last often the most difficult - people who have never formed the capacity to see others as really separate from themselves, who have never learnt, as the baby does in the first year of life, that there is someone who can be trusted to stand them' (Stevenson, op. cit.).

More recently several workers in the field of child abuse (Baher et al., 1977; Roberts, 1978) have discussed the extreme difficulty for social workers of relating to some abusing parents whose behaviour is characterised by a lack of trust (and the consequent need to be in control) and at the same time by infantile dependency. When this combination of dependency on the worker and inability to trust him occurs, it inevitably leads to 'testing out', threatening and aggressive behaviour such as threatening to remove a child from care, or, if he is back home, to harm him again; or in some cases to behaviour which is designed to disrupt the placement.

As they have been constantly let down by those close to them, they don't expect anyone to be consistent and reliable.... The attitude of mistrust is a very difficult one for workers to deal with as the parents expect criticism and rejection. They also tend to resent anyone in authority (Roberts and Lynch, 1978, p.118).

It is not surprising that some of the inexperienced workers investigating some of these cases were unable to face these angry feelings, and retreated into an authoritarian and apparently uncaring role.

For the skilled workers there were fewer problems arising from being in at the start of an investigation and some advantages. The paramount need to protect the child, the state of shock of the parents, and even the anger itself meant that by frequent contact over the emergency the social workers and parents got to know each other. Some, having protected the child, did not force the issue about exactly what had happened for several weeks, and in four of the seven cases where children were in care because of suspected ill-treatment there was never any admission that the parents had been responsible.

Social worker: 'You do need to take your time, before you actually put it into words, "We believe you have damaged this child". I think they did keep a little bit of dignity that way. When I eventually said it, she absolutely relaxed and was so relieved that it was out in the open.'

Where the social workers lacked skill or experience, and particularly where there was a great deal of emphasis on finding out who did it, it was difficult for them to get beyond the initial anger, and some never did.

Mother: 'She just talked and listened, and it was always the same things she came back to: "Did you hit her?" She kept on and on about the same thing. When she lost at court she didn't like it. You could see it in her face when she came out of court.'

In some cases the initial removal, or removal after a child had been back home on trial, came after lengthy attempts to keep the family going; and on at least four occasions it was part of a casework plan and the intention was to return the child home as early as possible, with the hope that the authority which the care order conveyed would induce the parents to behave more reasonably to the child. One of the social workers wondered, however, if it was reasonable to expect the parents to understand the subtleties of such a plan, and could understand that they might not appreciate its therapeutic value for them, even if they did appreciate its necessity for the child.

Social worker: 'We thought very hard before we took care proceedings, and in the end allowed our hands to be forced (rather too late, some people would say), because we didn't want to use care proceedings as a threat. This was a problem because no doubt they were perceiving it as a threat. We are perceiving it in a rather grandiose casework way as authority. People find it hard, however much you try to explain the difference between a threat and parental authority – I can't let you do this. That was my problem when I was visiting them during the "home on trial" period. Because they went over what I said to them when I left them, and they saw it as a threat. So perhaps they didn't tell me things about their feelings about the child, and the tensions, in quite the same way they did before. But the relationship was of three years' standing. I at least was able to read between the lines and after I had been there about an hour they would begin to think, this is the woman we knew three months ago, and it is the same woman. It came up as a barrier. They knew I was a social worker. This social worker/authority bearer/friend relationship is a difficult one. I had a clear idea what it was about, it was my job. But they saw me as an entity. If they have not had good parenting and are not sufficiently integrated to know, because they have never experienced it, that authority and permission can come together in the same person – I tried to do it, but it might not have come off, and one could argue that they were more confused than ever. I think it's too basic. In a way the work I was trying to do with them, they couldn't benefit from, and I would have done better to cut my losses earlier on.'

The problem of authority was further complicated by the social worker's actually having parental responsibility for children home on trial, and the parents having the day-to-day task of caring for them. Even if the parents had agreed to the child's going into care in the first place, and there were none of the problems of resisted removal referred to above, this sharing of responsibility requires considerable skill and tact. Several of the clients were aware of this, and commented on the tact shown by the social worker. Most seemed well aware of the nature of home on trial placements.

Mother: 'Legally, I don't have very much right to her, do I? I've talked to him about it. I do know he had more hold over her than I have. But she knows that if she does anything wrong they will take her away again, and that's good for her.'

It is interesting in this respect that seven of the twenty parents interviewed thought that supervisory visits were the main form of help offered, and in fact there were some very positive comments about its value. Some social workers stressed very strongly their supervisory or protective role.

Social worker: 'My most important work was my responsibility under his care order.'

Mother: 'Yes, I know I matter to her. I know she is keeping an eye on me.'

Mother: 'He doesn't know me very well. I consider the main part, if a child is being put back home is to watch that everything is going smoothly.'

Mother: 'I saw her more as a supervisor. I didn't view her as an interfering old so and so. I used to see her as a person who was doing her job, checking up.'

For some parents, though, it was, as one social worker put it, 'difficult to hold the idea of how someone can share the parental responsibility and yet walk out of the door and leave him there'.

There were certainly difficulties for some of those parents whose own insecure background led them to be fearful of losing control, and yet these were often the cases where the children were most vulnerable. To find a middle way in such cases was difficult and some social workers aroused a great deal of resentment. There were several cases where a strongly authoritarian line, with the social workers not making allowances for and working round the parents' anxieties and fears, led to threatening behaviour from parents; in particular, threats to take the children out of care. In other cases social workers were more able to handle this resentment.

Social worker: 'There are times when it is used as a weapon, and we have to go through the fact that I do have responsibility, and that is part of my role. At other times, when she is afraid I will stop visiting her, she is pleased to be told that I have got to visit her.'

Social worker: 'I discussed it with them first so that we all knew where we stood, but I don't see any point in harping on it.'

Mother: 'She never put me under pressure, she never made me make a decision. If I made a decision, I made it, not she led me to it.'

Social worker: 'They are aware that if I wanted to I could wield a big stick, but I don't operate that way.'

In some cases the social workers had not succeeded in combining a caring role and a supervisory role.

Mother: 'We never really hit it off with her because she seemed to be looking all the time for trouble.'

Mother: 'He never once pulled her dress up to see if there were any marks. Once she was in bed and I said, "Shall I bring her down?" and he said, "No, leave her!" This one goes up to her room to inspect her. Makes me feel like a criminal.'

Father: 'He once started laying the law down. I got snotty about it then. He put me in that mind. He seems like a military sort of person, "I'm the man and you will do as I say". Definitely a court officer.'

Some social workers found that there were problems in combining a supervisory role with that of the therapist, although they could more easily combine supportive and supervisory roles.

Sometimes social workers who started with a mainly supportive role found that things were not going well and they had to change the emphasis to one of protecting the child.

Social worker: 'My role changed from being initially a casework and supportive one, to one of saying, "You know there were bruises on his body". I could sense that she felt she was more and more under the spotlight.'

Social worker: 'I was visiting frequently because they were having a tough time, but in a way the frequency of the visits was getting disturbing. They were seeing it as more threatening than helpful. We had moved back from the therapy bit to the supervisory bit.'

For some of the parents the threat posed by the supervision order or care order was either a constant or an intermittent but serious cause of anxiety.

Mother: 'If she came round one day, and being as they are on supervision decided to take them, then I would turn against her. I mean they are clean and fed. What does neglect mean anyway?'

Mother of a child back in care: 'I said, "What would happen if we went and got her out?" She said, "They take them and hide them away, regardless of whether it hurts them!" Another mother wrote to her MP and she lost her visiting rights because she created a fuss.'

It was particularly galling for parents to feel that important happenings concerning their children were no concern of theirs.

Mother: 'No, they didn't care about me, because when I told them that somebody had tried to interfere with my little girl, they turned round and told me that the people shouldn't have told me, but should have told them. I flew up in a temper. I'm only their mother!'

Chapter 6

It is generally acknowledged, except perhaps by some magistrates (see the report into the circumstances surrounding the death of Wayne Brewer, Somerset County Council, 1977), that even with the very strong powers of a care order, and much more so with the powers conveyed by a supervision order, if a child is in the care of the parents he can only be adequately protected if there is some willingness on the part of the parents to seek help when things get difficult. It seemed important to ask, therefore, whether the parents were honest with the social worker when the child was at home, or whether they tended to hide their difficulties rather than risk the child's being removed again. This question was related to the relationship between social worker and client, and whether the parents could trust the social worker to act in their own best interest. This clearly involved a capacity to understand that the social worker's paramount responsibility to protect the child, whether from ill-treatment or from becoming further involved in delinquency, did not preclude his concern for them and their own needs. Table 6.6 collects the views of social workers and parents on the degree to which parents were able to be honest with the social worker.

TABLE 6.6 Parents felt able to be honest with the social worker, according to the social worker and the parents*

	Always	Usually	Sometimes	Probably not	No	D/K
According to social worker	4	11	6	6	0	2
According to parent	14	1	7	0	0	

* The answers in a few cases include different responses from the mother and father. As with the question of relationship, there was considerable change over the total period of involvement.

It may be that the parents over-emphasised to me their willingness to tell the social workers of difficulties, but I think that the discrepancy between the social workers' and parents' answers is due to the fact that the parents who were feeling that all was going well when I interviewed them had forgotten occasions when they might have concealed things. From comments of social workers and clients it was clear that at the time when honesty was most essential (before the child went home, and in the early days after his return), it could least be relied on. The willingness to be honest was sometimes not related to whether there was a good relationship with the social worker, as clients were conscious that the decision about removal did not lie with the social worker alone. In such cases fear of the child being taken away was stronger than the need for help with whatever was causing the difficulty.

Mother: 'Was I honest? If I was asked a question I would never lie. I would evade. I did used to hit him again when he came home. Till I'd got him in my routine. He was at risk, because

I hated him. I resented him for what he'd done to me. I felt
he'd made me ill, not that I'd hurt him. I knew as long as there
were no marks on him, then I would be all right. And I never
told my social worker. I knew she would take him straight back.
I knew that. I was horrible'.

Stepmother: 'At first I used to do my best so that he would
think I was suitable - he wouldn't think I was too young and
that. She did play me up quite a lot at first. I didn't feel
able to be honest at first in case he would take her away. Now
I feel more secure.'

The parents who were more likely always to be honest were those
with older children.

Mother: 'You can be honest with her. I'd tell her if he was
doing wrong. I told her when he hit me once.'

In between these two extremes was a large group who were sometimes
completely open about their difficulties and sometimes not.

Social worker: 'She is confused in her feelings. She wants to
trust me, and can't quite. Always, when anything happens to
one of the children she tells me, in a way for reassurance that
I don't want to take them away.'

Social worker: 'She is usually honest, except she has this thing
of being ashamed when she does something we won't approve of.
The department is her moral guardian, so that she won't be
entirely honest.'

Social worker: 'They will tell me half a story, the half which
will influence me most. I still don't trust them. I am aware
that they are conning me at times.'

Social worker: 'At times she would refuse to open the door to
me. She didn't want to be honest with me. But at times she was
very honest.'

Most of the families had no real reason not to trust the social
worker, but those who had felt let down by having matters which they
thought were confidential brought up in court, were constantly
struggling between their fear of this happening again, and their
need to trust the social worker so that they could be helped. These
were sometimes the families who had the greatest fear of losing
control of the situation, and yet the greatest need for casework
help, and a dependable relationship through which they could grow
into more mature parents.

Mother: 'She cut down visiting. And one day she came and I
said, thank goodness you have come. I've got more problems than
I can cope with. Now, if I didn't have confidence in her, I
wouldn't have said that. But then again, you are openly honest,
you tell them everything, and you realise that your honesty has
led to some misunderstanding.'

Father: 'They would rake up everything they could find out about
our past. If you conversed with her, she would take things out
of context. When this court thing came up they were quoting
things I'd said when I was upset, things which I didn't mean.

Sometimes we talk things out, and react, and things look pretty black, but once we have talked about them, we feel better. But if the social worker is a bit of a worrier, she goes back and makes a report. That is all written down.'

Mother: 'It doesn't make much sense. They are trying to help. You tell them what's wrong, they go up to somebody higher up that doesn't even know you, and they start making orders. Above your head.'

Mother: 'It doesn't stop me getting help, even though I know I risk them taking her back. If anything happened and I got upset, I would phone him, order or no order. I would hate to think I hadn't got him. That's what hurts. You have got to think before you say anything every time.'

These comments show the complexity of the social worker's task in these cases, and the problems of minimising the risk to the child. An inspectorial role, without the provision of a helping relationship for the parents, clearly failed to offer protection for the children and tended to lead to the 'drawing up of battle lines', and considerably increased anxiety. Yet even a very good relationship with the social worker in some cases did not lead to complete honesty, though it did in others.

TABLE 6.7 Social workers thought children would tell them if things were going wrong at home

	Too young	Yes	Probably	Sometimes	Probably not	No	D/K
Number of children	5	7	5	1	11	3	2

Social workers felt even less able to rely on the children telling them if they were suffering. All the children who were seriously at risk and those who were eventually removed again came under the headings 'too young', 'probably not' or 'no' in Table 6.7. The most frequent reason why the social workers thought that children would not tell them if things were going wrong was that the child didn't want to go back into care, but also mentioned were loyalty to parents, and fear of parents.

When the problems of offering adequate protection to the children in these circumstances were put to the social workers, they were often, though not always, aware that they could not rely on the parents or children telling them of mounting problems. However, those with good relationships with the parents did feel some confidence that this allowed them to pick up hidden messages, both in the behaviour of the children and the parents.

Social worker: 'He makes his probem fairly obvious. Several
    times he has collapsed, drunk, in my office.'
For younger children there were other checks at school or at the clinic. None of the children, even those who were removed, suffered serious physical harm, and in most of the cases where it was necessary to remove children again, the social workers managed to do this and yet retain their relationship with the parents.

Advising and controlling

Mayer and Timms (1970, p.88) found that 'clients welcomed the idea of receiving suggestions, advice, and recommendations from the worker', and also that 'guidance was offered on a wide range of topics'. Sainsbury (1975, pp.79-86) found that 'workers exercised firmness and set limits' in twenty-three cases out of twenty-seven, and that 'this seemed to be compatible with close relationships', and not to lead to long-term resentment. In my study the findings were similar. Social workers regularly gave advice in twenty cases, and did so in such a firm manner in fifteen cases for it to come under the heading of controlling. However, in no case was this the main form of help offered, according to either parents or social workers, although in five cases social workers thought that the parents thought it was. To the question, 'Are you ever firm with the parents, strongly advise them to do or not do something?' the answer was 'Yes' in twenty-one cases, 'Sometimes' in one case, and 'No' in four cases. Several social workers linked this with the parental role they adopted with the parents, although some said they were pushed into this role more often than they liked.

 Social worker: 'Firm, yes, often. I can't think of specific occasions, that's just the role he puts me in.'

 Social worker: 'I suppose a social worker never likes to feel they are being directive and giving advice. Sometimes I just treat her like a child and give her a ticking off. It's very difficult not to. Last week I was giving her two choices, largely because I could not make up my mind, but it was impossible not to prompt her to some extent to the direction I was moving in.'

Several of the social workers were very conscious of the power over the parents which the care order (and, to a lesser extent, the supervision order) gave them, and saw dangers in some cases (especially with the parents who had been in care) of encouraging excessive dependence and in others of arousing resentment. Thus comments such as 'Yes, but as little as possible,' were common. On the other hand, social workers did seem to like working with care order cases, and definitely preferred care orders for children who were at home to supervision orders, largely because of the power the care order conveyed. Some found that, attempts at therapy having failed or got as far as they were likely to get, controlling became their main function.

 Social worker: 'In the end, they were not using me for help with their marital problems but to give advice about child care, and to control.'

The above comments refer to advice and control directed towards the parents. Social workers, usually with the approval of the parents and often at their request, exercised control over the children, as will be discussed later when social work help to the children is discussed. Again there were obvious dangers in undermining the authority of the parents who, care order or not, had day-to-day control over their children.

 To summarise, although there was reluctance in some though not all cases to exercise authority, and although it was rarely seen

as the main form of help, one could certainly not describe this as
non-directive casework, and comments such as 'Controlling? Yes, ad
nauseam', were common.

The reactions of parents to a directive approach varied and were
summed up by one mother: 'Advice is good if it is good advice'.
There were probably more adverse comments than seem to have been
encountered by either Timms or Sainsbury; but this is not surprising
as both these previous studies were of social workers in voluntary
agencies who were less likely to arouse resentment because they did
not have statutory powers. As indicated earlier, fear of not being
in control was a very strong characteristic with some of the parents
and the mere knowledge that the social worker had the right to
exercise control, even if he did not use it, was enough to cause
anger and resentment. The resentment was not only expressed by the
parents who had personality difficulties, though, and one could
argue that it was a perfectly natural reaction of parents who loved
their children, felt that they knew what was best for them, and
were no longer the sole, or even the main judges of this.

None of the families completely objected to being given advice
by the social worker. Of the twenty interviewed, seven complained
about inappropriate advice or direction on occasions, usually from
a social worker whose work in general they did not find helpful,
but they also gave examples of helpful advice. Even those who
clearly felt constrained and worried by the existence of a court
order were at times ambivalent, and conceded that it could be an
advantage to have a social worker who would at times exercise
control, and give advice. When the children were in care, far
more resentment was expressed about social workers controlling
visiting. In most cases, once the child was back home it seemed
possible, provided a good relationship had been established, for
the social workers to keep a balance between giving enough advice,
but not undermining the parents' sense of being in control.

Mother: 'When she said I needed a break, I was against it,
but she talked me round. She didn't say, "Well, you have got
to have a break." She was more understanding as a person.'

Mother: 'The first time he came, he got my back up, telling
me what to do. I don't like strangers telling me I am
neglecting my child.'

Negotiating, advocacy, legal advice

In Chapter 4 the problems of the parents were discussed, and in
eighteen of the cases the social workers were involved in negotiating
with other agencies on behalf of the parents to help to alleviate
their difficulties. Most frequently mentioned in this context were
the supplementary benefits department, and housing departments, but
also mentioned were schools, lawyers, the police, and employers.
In the five cases where advocacy was mentioned, this implied that
the social worker strongly argued the case for his client with
another agency, a tribunal, or in court.

Social worker: 'There was a terrific amount of negotiating
with other agencies and other people. I have intervened three

times in court personally, at a level far beyond just a social worker's report.'
In almost all cases social workers gave legal advice on occasion, and usually they also helped clients to contact a solicitor. Some social workers thought that in some cases it might be unhelpful for a solicitor to represent a child in court, as it was feared that, if the offence were of a trivial nature, the court might see this as a hostile act on the part of the parents and be less sympathetic.

Practical and material help

In Chapter 4 we saw that the majority of parents had a wide range of practical problems, and that the position, both in terms of housing and income, was improved for several of the families at the end of the study. Tables 6.1 and 6.3 show that, although practical help was rarely seen as the main form of help either by parents or social workers, it played a large part in twelve cases, and was not mentioned at all in only five cases. As well as the more obvious ways of helping with rehousing or housing transfers, money, and clothing, social workers had also been involved in mending electrical appliances and other practical tasks. Certainly the image was far from that conveyed by Wootton (1959b) and Sinfield (1969) of the caseworker who fails to recognise the practical needs of his clients.

However, there were certainly cases where the social workers did fail, much to the annoyance or disappointment of the parents, to help with practical problems. In some cases they had failed to notice the problems, but in others they had not offered help because either they knew there would be no resources to meet the need, or that this sort of help was not approved of in the area where they worked. There were marked differences between areas; for example, in the payment of fares to visit children in care. When asked if the social worker had helped them, nine of the families interviewed immediately thought in terms of financial or material help, as opposed to emotional support or therapy. Seven parents expressed dissatisfaction about the lack of practical help, in three cases this being related to expenses resulting from children being in care, rather than family needs in general. The others either were satisfied with the practical help received or did not expect any. On the whole, parents had a low level of expectation of help from the social workers; or, in a few cases, had other sources of help.

Mother: 'I think, if we had asked, he would have helped us. But I'd never be that short, and if I was, I would ask my mother.'

Mother: 'No, I wouldn't ask her. She can't. Those sort of people, social workers, they can't. They are just for the children. We manage. We go without ourselves to let the children have it.'

Father: 'They never offered to pay the fare. I was out of work at the time so it was hard to get over there. But I wouldn't ask.'

Mother: 'I got in a bit of a muddle, going over there and ringing up. That got me in debt with the rent. When he came home, he hadn't got a coat to go to school in. I had to get one out of the club. I got into debt because he lost a pair of trousers and three jumpers and his anorak there. I was that relieved to get him back, I didn't mention it.'

Parents were asked if any form of practical help could have helped them to keep their children at home in the first place. Here again they tended to be undemanding, and to say no. This was especially so with fathers on their own with children. When prompted as to whether a home help, day nursery, or daily minder would have made things more possible, the usual reply was that it was thought of but there was no day nursery available, or the home help hours would not fit in.

Father: 'A home help? That wouldn't work. They suggested one, but then they couldn't find one. Wrong area.'

Only two families had complained about the lack of resources, both to their MPs about housing. Where parents were dissatisfied about the level of practical help, this tended to be because they had felt humiliated at having requests turned down, or because they had thought that the social worker should have been sufficiently sensitive to take a hint about their difficulties without forcing them to ask.

Mother: 'They very seldom say, "Have you enough money?" The other one used to. She used to say, "Show me your purse. I want to see you have enough money for you and the kids over the weekend." With the others, I won't say they won't help you if you are short, but you have to ask.'

Mother: 'A friend took my money and I phoned them. My own social worker was on holiday. I said, "I've got to pay people." He said, "You will have to leave it." He never bothered to find out if we had any food or anything.'

Mother: 'I only asked him once, for help with the fare. He said no. And I never bothered again. That's lowering your dignity.'

Other parents had a different story to tell:

Mother: 'There was that trouble over the rent. I was so upset. I cried. She took me for a cup of tea, and then took me down to social security and sat with me.'

Mother: 'If I asked, she would have done anything. She took me in her car when I had to go to hospital. I thought a little job would have helped, so she got me one. She even got me a holiday at a home for tired mums. But I didn't go. She was very kind.'

Mother: 'The times I have been down to the social services department, and I've never come away empty-handed. Well, I appreciated it, because I hated asking for money.'

Two forms of help which were little used, and which social workers said they would have used more had they been available, were voluntary help, and family aides or home helps with special skills in helping families with child care problems, or able to work longer hours to help single-parent families where the parent was in work. There was also a serious lack of day care, although where it was mainly a question of giving a parent a break, playgroup fees were sometimes paid, and transport provided. Volunteers were also used to transport children to summer camps. One of the important ways of offering practical help was to arrange for some of the children to come back into temporary care for brief periods, either to give the parents a break, or if they were ill.

The place of financial aid in social work is the subject of debate, with something of a swing away from the original welcome given to the power to give assistance in cash in the 1963 Act, and Section 12 of the Social Work (Scotland) Act. When they made an early study of the workings of the Act in England, Heywood and Allen (1971) found that there were considerable discrepancies in the way that social workers used their powers, largely depending on their own views and management policy. There was a strong tendency to use material aid as a casework tool, and at times as a means of controlling behaviour. More recent discussions on the subject have shown that the uncertainty about how the powers should be used continues (Newman, 1975; Jordan, 1974; Lister and Emmett, 1976). 'A Cash Code for Social Workers' (BASW, 1977) comes down strongly against the giving of financial aid by social workers except in very narrowly defined circumstances. As part of the DHSS sponsored study of local authority social work practice, Michael Hill (1978) found a wide range of views and practices in relation to the giving of financial aid, but concluded that for most workers this was an unpopular aspect of their work. In this study social workers were asked general questions about their views on the giving of financial and material aid, and also whether they thought that extra financial help would have been beneficial to the particular child we were discussing.

All the social workers said that it was sometimes necessary to give financial or practical help to parents to help them to resume care of their children; but some wanted to see the initiative taken by the parents, whilst others thought that the families might need help initially before they could start making their own efforts. Their comments included:

'I give practical help as necessary. Basically I don't believe in handing out unless the people are quite incapable of solving the situation without. I prefer to help them to cope with their own situation - to enhance their own self-management. I don't think handouts do any good really.'

'If you give them some encouragement and help, it might spark a lot of things off.'

Others related giving or withholding practical help to an initial diagnosis as to whether the children should go home.

'If you have planned for good reasons that the children should go home, yes, it is right that you should encourage them. But some parents who don't want children home but can't admit it, need practical reasons as excuses.'

'If they are not able to give the basic physical and emotional care, I don't work towards rehabilitation, but if they seem capable of trying, they often need practical help. I really do feel that changing the social environment does effect change. For example, families with marital problems can have time and energy after rehousing to start sorting out some of their other problems.'

One social worker gave a more pragmatic reason for limiting the amount of practical help given, although she nevertheless gave a great deal.

'I've been trying for months to get the housing department to do essential repairs. They tend to take the view that because she gets a lot of social work help, she is somehow less 'deserving'. I am required to get her standards up, whereas if I weren't visiting, they might have done the repairs by now.'

When asked if they thought that long-term financial help to low-income families would help to diminish neglect, only one social worker thought it would not do so, though others supported Bill Jordan (1974, 1976) in saying that such help should definitely not be administered by social workers. Several commented on the Finer report (HMSO, 1974) on single-parent families, and thought that something on the lines of the suggested 'Guaranteed Maintenance Allowance' would be an important step in reducing the stresses which sometimes led to neglect or delinquency. The answers to the question about the relationship between low income and neglect showed a fairly wide range of views.

'Of course it would help. It's just a question of paying people enough to live on.'

'It would be better if social security paid more than a bare minimum. I don't like getting involved in financial matters, but we are forced to do a lot of negotiating with social security. If nothing else, helping to get a decent level of income helps to show we care.'

'I'm not denying the value of practical help. I think social workers should help, but I don't think more money alone would stop neglect in any family.'

'More money could improve the standard of living and take some of the pressures off.'

Despite a general feeling that financial help was 'a good thing', when it came down to the individual cases we were discussing most social workers were not so sure that it would have made any difference; and, as we saw from the comments of the parents, some had failed to pick up and act upon requests or hints about practical help. Although eleven of the social workers talked about helping families with budgeting, only in four cases was there any real sign of success, and comments such as 'not seriously', 'periodically', and 'I tried but gave it up' were often added. Even with weekly visits there was not felt to be time to achieve much here, and some thought that this was an area where a family aide might be helpful in certain cases. Some workers related a reluctance to become too involved in budgeting to their belief that income was too low to allow for a reasonable standard of living, and that the somewhat haphazard spending patterns of some of the families were a not unreasonable response to inadequate income. Others thought that by helping with budgeting they risked undermining the parents' sense of self-worth.

>'Sometimes we have given her financial aid which I am supposed to supervise. On the whole, she manages fairly well, but she does sometimes mis-spend it, I have come to take the view that within limits she should be allowed to do that, and I don't supervise too closely. It is an area of controversy, and there have certainly been seniors and area officers who have thought I should. It is a role she half expects, and we could easily control her to a considerable degree. But if we do, how does she establish her independence?'

Some of the social workers of parents who had been disappointed by the lack of practical help made the following comments:

>'She behaves as if she is badly off. She is always making demands.'

>'Although she exists on a fairly low income, they haven't got any real financial problems.'

>'I must admit, I didn't think about help with clothing.'

In contrast, some of the social workers saw maximising the parents' income as a crucial part of their work, and put considerable effort into persuading management and other agencies of the need. One worker who complained of the difficulty of getting money under Section 1 of the 1963 Act gave as a reason for not applying for the discharge of a care order that this was the only way to make sure of being able to give financial aid.

>Social worker: 'It seems to me a valid use of care orders. I don't think care orders should just be seen in terms of residential care. It is important that the children are clothed well, that they do get holidays. It is very useful for this sort of thing that the children are in care.'

>Social worker: 'They constantly need understanding financial help, and the DHSS use their special welfare officer with them. I have managed to convince them that the family's efforts to keep going are genuine, and they are extremely generous.'

One further aspect of financial help is the question of parental contributions to the maintenance of children in care. Parents are assessed to contribute on the basis of a means test, whether the children are in care voluntarily, or against their parents' wishes. Only six of the twenty-two families whose children were placed away from home did in fact contribute. One was assessed to do so but refused to pay, and contributions were eventually waived, and in fifteen cases a 'nil assessment' was made. Social workers and parents were asked if parents ought to have to contribute, and here social workers and parents tended to differ in their views. Only four of the parents interviewed thought parents who could afford to contribute should do so, if the child was away from home against their wishes. On the other hand, ten of the social workers thought the parents should have to pay if they could afford it. Eight social workers thought they should not pay unless they wanted to do so, other than giving up the family allowance (child benefit), and some thought they should keep the family allowance if children were going home frequently to visit. Two thought that this should be a social work decision. Only one worker was aware of problems resulting from this, but three of the parents who were assessed to pay expressed strong resentment to me.

Social worker: 'They refused to pay. It was a gesture of defiance. I think we should have a completely free child care service.'

Father: 'We did pay, but it got us in debt, and we objected to it. It came as a shock when they said we had to pay £5 a week on top of the cost of visiting, and we still had to clothe him.'

Social worker: 'I've known families where it's been important to contribute. I think there should be a basic commitment to contribute.'

Mother: 'Yes, you should have to pay if you can afford it. I mean, our social services can't keep on forking out. It costs more to keep them in care than it costs you to keep them.'

Social worker: 'It always seems to be rather a stab in the back. On the other hand, there is an importance to parents in feeling there is something they can do. I expect some of the discomfort is facing up to when we remove children. We feel responsible for the pain inflicted, and having to go back and say you have to pay is facing it again. It is important to keep some discretion.'

Mother: 'No. As far as I am concerned, they took them, they can pay. I did pay to start, but then they twisted things so many times, I gave up. I think he has now decided to let us get ourselves sorted out. I would have paid if it had been voluntarily, short-term care, but why should we when we want them home?'

Social work with the children

The main focus of this study was on the help offered to the family as a whole. However, the main focus of the social services involvement with these families was the children, and this was clearly perceived by parents and social workers. The principal form of intervention in twenty-two of the twenty-five cases was the provision of substitute care, which was discussed in Chapter 5, and will be looked at in the next chapter. The social work and other help offered to the children when they were at home will be considered briefly here.

There were considerable differences between the ways the social workers talked about their work with the children. For some, the whole of their work with the family was based on a plan aimed at achieving the best possible pattern of life for the child. For others there was less evidence of a plan, and of assessment of the child's needs. Sometimes plans involved a close relationship with the child, and a combination of casework help and the provision of other experiences to enrich is existence. For others, the plan was to help the parents as much as possible, and be a friendly presence in the background for the child in case difficulties occurred.

Social worker: 'I have a fairly close liaison with the school. I'm deliberately keeping a low profile on the children until something changes. I hope I am getting to know the children well enough to be able to respond more helpfully to them in a crisis.'

Social worker: 'He mattered to me more than other members of the family because of his care order, and because he was the one at risk. It wasn't a matter of trying to drive a wedge between him and his family, though. I think any social worker runs a risk of doing that when he removes a child.'

Social worker: 'My role when she went home was supporting her in the home, looking for any signs which might suggest rejection by either parent, and looking for any lasting psychological problems which might come out at a future date.'

Other workers, whilst recognising the emotional significance of the parents to the child in their care, had decided they were going to achieve little with the parents, and were aiming to supplement, or sometimes to counteract, what they provided. This was particularly so with the older children.

Social worker: 'All you can hope to do with this sort of family is to give the kids something which they will remember and absorb, and perhaps use later on in life. It's wrong to take away what the family means to them. But legally we have got to try and get these kids to conform, so that they don't set themselves up against the law.'

A great deal of thought in some cases went into long-term planning, and the social workers were consciously modifying their role at different times, stepping up their own importance to the child at times of change, and then emphasising the role of the parents, caretakers, or teachers at other times.

Social worker: 'Because of the foster parents' attitude, things were more difficult for her. They weren't preparing her at all. The foster mother was hanging on with both arms. It was me who was doing the preparation. They were tugging from the other end. She started to show behaviour difficulties then, but through seeing her, and explaining to her, she had a bit of trust in me, and this seemed to help her through. There was a stage when she wasn't speaking to the foster parents. You could see her withdrawing and migrating to the other family, even at one stage withdrawing within herself. The foster parents were saying, "We are worried, what are we to do?", and I was saying, "Well, she is really withdrawing from you. She is wanting to break that bond, and she isn't finding it easy".'

In several cases the chance to make a relationship with a child whilst in care was capitalised on when the child came home, and this was something which several parents thought to be valuable.

Mother: 'You see, she knows him. He is the only one, really. He's been the link between her foster parents and us. She trusts him. He cares all along. I think, as far as he is concerned, we are just parents. But Angela is Angela. He really cares about her. I think he got attached to us, but his job is mainly the child.'

Social workers were asked whether the children mattered to them as individuals, and whether they thought that the children thought they mattered to them. As most of the children were not interviewed, this was an attempt to assess whether the relationship was a meaningful one for the children. Social workers thought that they had managed to convey that they cared about them to only twenty of the thirty-four children. Thus, although some had a very good relationship with the children in their care, a sizeable minority did not. In some cases the children had been away from home since the worker took over the case, and the main relationships were with the caretakers, but on the whole the social workers who did not think they had a good relationship with a child were uneasy about this. Some thought that more time would help; others that the uncertain legal position of a supervision order made it difficult; and others that a child's apprehension lest they once more remove him from home made him wary of them, and disinclined to trust them.

Roberts (1978), Roberts et al. (1978) and Baher et al. (1977) have called attention to the need for continued help, both in groups and individually, for children who have been exposed to traumatic circumstances. The fact that, for whatever reason, many of the children did not have a close relationship with the social worker lends support to the view that for every child placed at home on trial an adult should be identified who knows him well enough to detect signs of stress. This could be the family social worker, but if he is unable to play this role, a teacher, a health visitor, the residential worker, intermediate treatment worker, or foster mother; or in some cases a friend or relative could do so, as they in fact did for some of the children in this study.

Table 6.7 showed that nineteen children wouldn't, or probably wouldn't, tell the social workers if things were going wrong at home, or were too young to do so. Table 6.5 showed that there was some discrepancy between the social workers' views of their role with the children and the views of the parents, in that the parents saw the social workers as having an important role with the children, whether supervisory or therapeutic, in fourteen cases (out of twenty), whilst the social workers only mentioned this in seven cases (out of twenty-five).

Social worker: 'If you are doing child care work, you have not to let yourself be given too many cases, and make the time. You have got to have that commitment to the child. You have got to put yourself out to build up a relationship. There has got to be something there, if you have to move a child. You can build up trust, and this will be reflected if things go wrong. They will come back to you.'

Social worker, about a 6-year-old: 'She desperately needs help in sorting out her feelings about her mother and foster parents. She is a bright enough child, and I see her often, but I still don't know her well enough. She doesn't trust me.'

Social worker, about a 7-year-old: 'After nearly twelve months at home, he just about manages to speak to me. He is scared stiff I will take him away again.'

Mother of a teenager: 'The social worker didn't really know him. I think if she is going to make decisions about him, she should get to know him better.'

Mother of a teenager: 'Sometimes, if she is in a bad mood when he calls she isn't very sociable with him. She likes him though. I hope she gets somebody as good when he leaves.'

Social worker about a 10-year-old who went back into care: 'He's a child who tends to clam up. He can be as "dumb as a dodo" and remain like that for several hours. I always think we under-estimate the confusion we might cause with children when we are trying to relate to a child and his mother, and there is a bad relationship between them.'

Social worker about a 5-year-old: 'I explained to the foster parents that there were things I needed to talk to her about. Really I wanted to get her to talk to me, to know me as a person. Now she sees me as a friend, as her chum. She is always pleased to see me, and we have a chat about school, about what is happening. She can talk to me, she is able to look into her problems, perhaps fantasise a bit.'

The above comment moves one neatly from the question of relationship to the therapeutic use of that relationship. For the majority, the relationship, where it existed, was mainly supportive, although at times of stress or change there was more interpretation to the child. Casework with the children was, however, mentioned in eleven cases, and in some cases this was the main form of help offered to the family. In some cases too, the children were involved in the family therapy.

Social worker: 'I used reality therapy with him. This is what he needed, a close relationship but no mincing of words. We would agree on a contract. If I break that contract, it is up to him to take it out on me in some way, and vice versa. He had the intelligence to understand what we were working at. When it broke down, and we had to take him into care, I felt unhappy for him - we were repeating a pattern. He respects me, and he thought he had let me down. But in a way, he was probably relieved, because the reality therapy was expecting a lot of him. I took him to visit first, and then I took him. I still saw him every fortnight, and he knew I was at the end of a telephone. The contract was still there.'

Mother: 'I said how she was behaving, and he used to have a long talk with her on her own, just to see how it was. I wanted him to see her on her own. She might not have come to me and told me. She doesn't come right out and say, "This is wrong". She is very close with him. If there are any problems, she will say what's on her mind to him.'

Mother: 'Yes, she did help him. She used to talk to him on his own. I thought she was there to help him, rather than order him about. She wouldn't do that.'

Social worker: 'My role with him was that I knew what his family was like, what he had to go through when there were severe traumas at home. It was emotionally very violent. He needed someone else who was experiencing it. He could draw on that when talking to me. I took an interest in how he was getting on at school, relating what was going on at school with what was going on at home. Getting this sort of communication going was difficult, because he used to leap out of the window when he saw me coming. I wanted him to see me as someone who wasn't completely authority and against him. Sometimes it would take a long time to explain to him why he had to have a medical examination, for instance. I suppose you could say I was a guiding influence who had some understanding of what he was going through. The main therapeutic role was with the school.'

Although the supervision order or care order is made in respect of the children and not the parents, social workers were more often firm with parents than with children. To the question, 'Are you ever firm with the children?' the answer was 'Yes' in fourteen cases, 'Sometimes' in six cases, and 'No' in eleven cases. Three children were too young. Social workers tended to prefer to reinforce the authority of the parents wherever possible, rather than imposing their own authority, although they were sometimes called upon to back up parents.

Social worker: 'I always saw her at home, though the first time I made her come into the office, in order to make sure she knew I was in control.'

Social worker: 'I tended to feel he was at home with them, so he was their responsibility, and I was just over-looking.'

Social worker: 'It is a question of striking a rather dodgy balance between accepting John's point of view, and not undermining mother's authority.'

Mother: 'I think he sat there and talked to him. I mean, we talked to him, but you get anybody like that talk to him, and he could explain what would happen if he got taken away next time. In the end he seemed to get in into him that he wanted to stay out of trouble.'

With the younger children, especially those who would not tell the social workers of problems, they had to rely on their observations of the child's behaviour and appearance.

Social worker: 'I see her at home as often as possible. She is not frightened of her mother. She is very physical with her.'

Social worker: 'From being a fairly happy-go-lucky lad, a bit attention-seeking, he changed in the space of weeks to not saying anything. He almost became completely mute. It was quite frightening.'

In a few cases more intensive help was offered to the children, either in groups, or at residential camps with a therapeutic orientation, or, for one younger child, at a day nursery. As already mentioned, some children went for holidays with previous foster parents. One social worker had attended an adventure training holiday with a boy, and this had allowed him to strengthen his relationship with him.

Social worker: 'That't the thing with Peter. He's very conscious of his family's low status in the area, and he doesn't like it much. He enjoyed the adventure holiday. I stayed down for three days with him. He started to model himself more on me. He did smarten himself up a lot.'

Several workers said they would like to make more use of groups but there were problems about organising them, especially in rural areas. One social worker who would have liked to see more choice in the sorts of group experience available, felt that he could not introduce children who had not shown any signs of delinquency to the existing groups or camps because they might be influenced by the others. Since the interviews on which the study was based were carried out, there has been an expansion in the availability of group experiences through intermediate treatment schemes, and this has been greatly welcomed by the workers with whom the study has been discussed. It was clear from the comments of parents that they too would welcome such experiences for their children, and appreciated this sort of help when it was offered.

Two social workers were involved in the task of keeping children in contact with the parent who had left home, and with whom the parent they were living with no longer had contact. The children I spoke to had little to say about their social workers except that they liked them. They were apprehensive about changes of social worker, and both families I spoke to agreed about what makes a good social worker:

'I like social workers because they help you to get home.'

CONCLUSIONS

Clients' and social workers' satisfaction with the service

When asked whether they were satisfied with their own work, as opposed to the total service offered by the department, (4) social workers said they were in eleven cases, fairly satisfied in nine cases, and not satisfied in five cases. The discussion around this question was related to Sainsbury's (1975) assessment of 'good' and 'successful' social work. Some workers thought they had done all they could, but could not be satisfied because the outcome had not been successful. Others were satisfied with their work if they had done all they could, even if the placement at home had not been a success. Others said they were satisfied with their work because they had been able to make time to work to a plan, and offer a dependable relationship, but several of those who were not satisfied or only fairly satisfied related this to not having the time to do more. Some who were not satisfied said that they had made a decision that this was not a high priority case, or that they were not likely to achieve change, and were not investing the amount of time which would be necessary if they were to feel satisfied with their work. The decision to spend time or not was usually based on the degree of risk to the child, and was in some cases related to the fact that the situation had improved appreciably before the worker took over the case. Some of the social workers' comments were:

'I find the time at the expense of other people. It is a high priority on my caseload, and I give them more time than anybody else.'

'I'm fairly satisfied, because I've accepted that we are not going to bring them up to the standards that society wants. I've modified certain things, and we have given the lad a lot that he will remember and hopefully use later.'

'I'm fairly satisfied because I can rely on Mr Smith to come in to see me if things aren't going well. If I had to initiate more, it wouldn't work, because of the pressure of my other work.'

'I'm fairly satisfied. But I think one has to accept that this mother is going to be very dependent for a period of years, and I can't be consistent with her because of my caseload, and the demands she makes.'

'I'm not satisfied, because I judge satisfaction in terms of success. I'd like to see more change in John's behaviour.'

'Yes, I'm fairly satisfied. I expect there are things I don't see, because I don't look hard enough, and I don't want to see, because I haven't the time to deal with them.'

'Yes, I'm satisfied. I changed my goal in order to move him from home, and move him in the best possible way.'

'It broke down completely after two years of intensive casework. It would have happened sooner without, and possibly the child would have been less disturbed. It meant that both parents came to depend heavily on a social worker, and the effect of that may be that now they will turn easily to a social worker when they need help. Before this, they were very hostile to social workers because they had been let down so often. Although, for a while, they were very angry with me, she still writes me lengthy letters. Is it effective? Or is it worth it? It wasn't effective in keeping the child at home, but it might have been worth it for the parents to achieve a good relationship after so many destructive ones.' (This mother subsequently had another child, having moved to another part of the country, and continues to need help.)

TABLE 6.8 Parents and children satisfied with the social work help offered according to parents and social workers

	Yes	Fairly	No	Don't know	Too young
Parents (according to social workers)	8	11	4	2	-
Parents interviewed (20)	11	8	1	-	-
Children (according to social workers	13	13	2	3	3

Table 6.8 shows that nineteen of the twenty sets of parents interviewed were either satisfied or fairly satisfied, and that the social workers under-estimated satisfaction. In only two cases did social workers think clients were satisfied when the parents themselves were only fairly satisfied. It must be remembered that several of the parents expressed dissatisfaction at the way previous social workers had handled their cases.

Mother: 'Yes, she has helped. She has done a lot of harm, but then, she has done a lot of good. I wouldn't like to be without her.'

Mother: 'I won't say he is really the sort I can talk to. Rather reserved. But he can do his job all right.'

Father: 'When I started with the welfare, I had a terrible time because my mother was against them, and I was against them because I had it pushed into my head that they were no good. But me and this one get on all right. But let's get this straight, he isn't doing me any favours. He's for the children. This has been going on for three years now. I was against them then, and I'm still against them. But they've got to do a job, and I just follow along with them. There are some people you can get on with, and some people you can't.'

Mother: 'I was lucky, I know I was lucky. I had a good social worker.'

Mother: 'He is the only one who cared. He *was* the only one who cared. He did everything I asked, he was the most wonderful social worker.'

To conclude, whilst there were cases where, on the social workers' own admissions, the service was less adequate than it might have been (especially in terms of the help offered directly to the children, and to children, parents, and caretakers at the time of placement), there is no evidence to support the view that local authority social work with children at risk is of a generally low standard, and much to support the opposite view. These families were all, at least at some stage, offered a dependable relationship by a social worker who was more likely than most to be qualified and experienced, and to be putting them high on his list of priorities.

Chapter 6

What is not clear is whether there was something special about these parents or children which led to their being offered a high level of service, and which, in turn, led to the children returning home; or whether the return home of the children and the high priority in agency terms which this gave to them caused the social workers to put in the skills, energy, and deep concern which clearly characterised much of the work with these families. This question will be considered in the concluding chapter.

In Chapter 1 the difficulties of assessing the effectiveness of social work were discussed, and it was suggested that, alongside attempts at more objective measures, the views of the consumers should be sought. In this study the parents were asked if they thought things were better, worse, or about the same for them as compared with the time immediately before the children came into care. (The situation in respect of the children was discussed in Chapter 5.) Twelve of the twenty sets of parents interviewed thought that things were emotionally better for them, seven thought they hadn't changed much, and one thought the family was emotionally worse off. There was considerable agreement between the answers of the parents and the social workers, who thought that, of the twenty-five families, fifteen, including some cases where the children were back in care, were better off emotionally; there was no change for eight families, and two were worse off. (The only families which were thought to be worse off emotionally were the two who still maintained they had been wrongly accused of ill-treating their children.) Most of the parents who said that things were better for them thought that social work intervention had contributed to improvements, either directly, or by giving practical help which had led to general improvements in well-being. However, it would be impossible to say in a study of this nature what part social work help had in fact played.

Some general comments on social work with children at risk and their families

This chapter has not attempted to say how social workers ought to help families with children at home under statutory supervision, but to describe the help they actually offer, and their own and the parents' views about their efforts. To some extent it covers the same ground as Mayer and Timms (1970) and Sainsbury (1975) in that it is looking at family social work, but it differs in that it focuses on a statutory as opposed to a voluntary agency, where one would expect pressure of work to be greater, and where the staff are likely to be less well qualified, less experienced, and less specialised. The clients also differed in that they could not opt out of contact with the social workers. Despite these differences, the findings were remarkably similar, although, as one might expect, more clients tended to have complaints about the service than was the case in Sainsbury's study of the highly specialist family service units.

It is also interesting to compare the findings with those of Glampson and Goldberg (1976) in their study of a sample of local authority clients in Southampton, where the findings about client satisfaction are similar, but where there are some interesting differences in the comments of clients, as well as similarities. The parents interviewed here, like clients in Glampson's study, seemed to want 'trained professionals rather than practical universal aunts with little specialised knowledge or training' (Glampson and Goldberg, 1976, p.12), and there were also indications of a desire from some for 'real involvement in the social services', which was exemplified by their willingness to tell me what they thought of the service so that others might have an improved service. Like Glampson's consumers these parents also stressed the importance of a pleasant personality, and the ability to empathise. On these two characteristics of good social workers they all agreed, though on details such as age and life experience there was not the clear picture which emerged from Glampson's study. Although a high degree of professionalism was achieved by some of the untrained workers, they too saw the advantages which training might convey, and some qualified workers expressed a strong desire for more training in this very demanding work, especially in view of new legislation.

Unqualified worker: 'You want to give the client the best service you can offer. No, I'm not satisfied with my work with the family. I can't offer them the best service when I don't know what there is to offer.'

On the question of changes of worker this study tends to agree more with Sainsbury's findings that 'no special advantages in the quality of relationship or outcome of work accrues from avoiding changes of worker' (Sainsbury, 1975, p.100), rather than Glampson and Goldberg's comment that change of social workers caused client dissatisfaction. Clients did complain about very frequent changes, and gaps without a social worker at all were damaging, but the anxiety about a change was sometimes compensated for by the new worker seeing things through new eyes. Also, for those cases where the help was not satisfactory, a change of worker offered the chance of an improved service. The quality of the help offered was the important factor, not the age, sex, or permanence of the worker. It may be that frequency of contact is a significant factor, and families who are visited often as in this and Sainsbury's study are less affected by change (so long as it does not occur too often and is well prepared for), than those such as the elderly and handicapped who tend to be visited less often.

Glampson and Goldberg found that satisfaction decreased as the length of contact with the department increased, and suggested that this finding supports Reid and Shyne's (1969) work about diminishing returns from long-drawn-out casework. There is some support for this in this study, in that those whose contact with the social worker was fairly brief and not very intensive tended to say they were satisfied. On analysing the tapes, and the tone of what was said, however, in some cases the apparent satisfaction was based on a low level of expectation, rather than a real easing of their problems. Those who had been in contact with the department longer, including those who received a high level of service, tended to complain about aspects of the service, but this could, by taking account of other parts of the interview, be linked to social work help leading to an increased awareness of what the possibilities for help might be. In other words, social work help had lifted some parents' horizons above the very low level of expectation they had originally. Because of the small size of the sample these comments are only tentative. However, the study does suggest that there is room for discussion of the impact of organisational change and new developments in social work theory on work with children at risk and their families.

In Chapter 1 mention was made of Goldberg et al.'s (1978) observation that less severe family cases tended to be closed at intake, and that perhaps it might make more sense to invest more time and skill in helping such families earlier rather than later. It was noted in Chapter 6 that in this study several families were known to the department before the crisis which led to care, but that a comprehensive preventive service was not offered. In the early 1960s the sort of long-term supportive social work role pioneered by the family service units began to be taken on by child care officers, and preventive work began to assume a prominent role in the statutory services. This development was stepped up after the passing of Section 1 of the 1963 Children and Young Persons Act, and some children's departments took on specialist family caseworkers to undertake work with children and their families in their own homes. The extent to which positive programmes for improving the quality of life of children at risk were involved, as opposed to merely preventing them from coming into care, is not clear, but several of the social workers interviewed who had been child care officers before reorganisation expressed the view that the upheavals of the two major reorganisations had made it difficult to continue this sort of work.

Others suggested that although pressure of work had a part to play, supportive help to vulnerable families tended not to be offered because of changing 'fashions' in social work theory. In particular, the emphasis placed on short-term, task-centred work where a contract has been negotiated with the client tended to mean that open-ended supportive family social work was difficult to justify, and that workers were under pressure to close cases if they were not able to achieve defined goals. It may be that this was the result of a rather naive interpretation of task-centred work. The advantages of this approach for families of children at risk have been explored by Goldberg and Fruin (1976, p.7):

> Less misunderstanding and a greater sense of achievement for both client and worker ensue if aims are specific - preferably agreed between social worker and client - relatively modest, and capable of achievement.... Greater clarity about the aims and functions of the intervention may help to demystify the comings and goings of social workers whose presence is imposed on the client.

In their most recent paper on social work in long-term teams Goldberg et al. (1978) comment (p.285):

> It is worth noting the relatively favourable outcomes of work with families where the material problems were tackled as the most outstanding ones. Would casework aimed at more specific and concrete targets also repay in emotionally disrupted families who are often beset by many practical and environmental problems?

However, writers on task-centred casework make the point that:

Chapter 6

Some situations are so complex that it is difficult to know where to begin, and where to go. Nor are social work aims in the social services always associated with dynamic change in the short run.... Nor can there always be agreement about the aims of intervention between client and social worker, since, in a statutory setting, the social worker is often called in without the express consent of the client (Goldberg and Fruin, 1976, p.7).

In her chapter on social work activities in the recent report to the DHSS on work in local authority social services departments, Elizabeth Browne (1978, pp.114-23) found that social workers used the terms 'crisis intervention', 'contract', and 'task-centred' very loosely, and referred to the difficulties in formulating agreed goals in certain cases because of the range and complexity of the clients' problems. She commented that it seemed not to be understood by some social workers and managers that task-centred social work was intended to be used selectively. Anne Vickery (in Specht and Vickery, 1977, p.130) comments that some clients 'need time to gain trust in the social worker before they can agree about the need for change and its goals'.

From the comments of the social workers interviewed in this study, it seems that preventive services may not have been offered other than at a very superficial level because of a lack of understanding that time might be needed to build up trust before goals could be defined. Hence, some clients felt they were 'brushed off' when they approached the department for help at an earlier stage. Once trust had been built up, as happened at a later stage, and usually after statutory intervention had become necessary, several of the parents interviewed did appreciate the task-centred approach.

It may well be that recent developments arising out of work with abusing parents will lead to a renewed interest in prevention and the development of skills in early intervention. The identification at an earlier stage of families who may abuse their children, which has been noted by Clare Hyman (1978) in a study of the work of the NSPCC special units, and the work at the Park Hospital (Roberts, 1978) have again led to calls for the development of preventive services:

It will be clear that many families in which abuse occurs are families which have for a long time been in need of help. It is therefore important ... to formulate one's goals not in the negative terms implied by the concept of 'prevention' but in a detailed positive programme which aims to improve the family's whole pattern of interaction and quality of life (Lynch and Roberts, 1978, p.124).

If everyone is to be encouraged to identify the child at risk as early as possible, then there should be the knowledge and resources available to provide effective help once the identification has been made (Roberts, 1978).

The comments of parents and social workers reported in this chapter have indicated that intervention, whether at an early stage or when statutory action becomes necessary, requires a high degree of skill and commitment of time and emotional energy. If relationships of trust are to be built up social workers must be able to accept and see beneath the complex and painful feelings, and particularly the anger and resentment, to whatever positive feelings exist for the achieving of goals which will either allow the child to stay or go home safely, or have a stable and secure future elsewhere.

Chapter 7

DECISION-MAKING AND PLACEMENT POLICY

Social worker: 'Intensive support was given for two years. But things got worse. Both children came back into care and the family is broken up. And when you look at the degree of emotional disturbance Wayne had when he came back into care finally, it's then you look back and say, I wish we had more sophisticated tools for telling when things will just not work out. I had more confidence in their ability to cope than was justified. My initial diagnosis was wrong.'

It is unfortunately usually in the context of placements (whether with the family or with substitute caretakers) which have not worked out well, that we discuss how mistakes can be avoided, and search for 'more sophisticated tools' to aid diagnosis. (1) It is always easier to say why something didn't work out, than why something else did, and none of the social workers was as specific as the one quoted above about why placements went well. Yet in several other cases which on the surface seemed to differ little from the one quoted above, the placement seems to have been reasonably successful. We usually look at mistakes which returned children home wrongly, but how many mistakes have resulted in their being wrongly separated from their families and remaining in long-term care? (2) This chapter has no prescription for making the right decisions, but seeks rather to clarify how decisions about placement are actually made. Since this study was undertaken, several publications have attempted to give practical guidance to social workers on positive planning for children in care or at risk in their own homes. In particular 'Good Enough Parenting' (CCETSW, 1978) and the 'Guides to Practice' (ABAFA, 1976; 1977a; 1977b) use case material to clarify the issues and explore alternative courses of action.

Several major decisions about placements were made about these children during the period studied. Should the children be placed away from home? Was court action necessary, or would the children and parents work voluntarily with the social workers in the interests of the children? If court action was necessary, should a care order or supervision order be recommended? If a placement away from home was necessary, should it be long-term or short-term? How much contact should there be between parents and children? Where should the child be placed in care? Should he return home, and when? Should he stay at home? When should the care order or supervision order be revoked? Another important decision, which none of the parents seemed to be aware of, was whether the child's name should be placed on, or removed from, the register of children at risk of non-accidental injury or failure to thrive. In looking at how these decisions were made, there seemed to be four main aspects to consider: the attitudes of social workers, parents, and caretakers and the way these attitudes affected the work of the social workers; the reactions of the parents and children; the resources available, either to keep the children at home, or to care for them when away; and the management and legal considerations.

ATTITUDES AND THE WAY THESE AFFECTED SERVICE OFFERED AND DECISIONS MADE

In Chapter 1 mention was made of the view that social workers strive to keep children at home with their natural parents, or return them home when this is not in their best interests, because they put too much emphasis on 'the blood tie'. In a lecture to a BASW conference in 1975 John Howells put this point of view.
 The first misconception is that which is concerned with the so-called mystical bond between parent and child.... The second common fallacy is that no other bond can be as satisfactory as the natural bond between parent and child (Howells, 1975).
 At the same conference Olive Stevenson (1975) also commented on this issue:
 Social workers in child care have never used the 'blood tie' as a basic assumption of practice. It has become confused in the minds of the public, and some professionals who should know better, with the emphasis which has grown in social work since 1948 on the creation and preservation of a child's sense of identity through knowledge of his origins and of the correction of his fantasies about his real parents through exposure to reality.
 In trying to assess how the decisions were made in these cases to return the children home, or to leave them there, it seemed important to ask to what extent decisions were influenced by the theories of child care, maternal deprivation and separation which were discussed in Chapter 1, and in particular to ask what weight was placed on bonds between natural parents and children. Several questions were asked about this, and often there was a lengthy discussion about the issues raised by the questions.

General attitudes and consideration

The workers were asked if they used any rough guidelines as to the sorts of family where they would tend to work towards rehabilitation, or not to work towards rehabilitation, and if so, what sort of families in each case. All the social workers said that they did not categorise families in terms of the original reason for care, and that they were principally concerned to assess the nature of the relationship which existed between the child and his parents, and also the capacity of the parents to work towards improving the situation which led to the need for statutory intervention. There was some agreement about the sorts of family where rehabilitation might be less likely to succeed, and workers said they would be particularly cautious where the parents suffered from personality disorders; where their inability to cope was to the detriment of the child, and they seemed not to have the capacity to make progress; and where the parents were too damaged or too deprived to recognise their children's needs.

In discussion, few of the workers referred to the theoretical work on the subject outlined in Chapter 1, (3) nor were they particularly dogmatic in their attitudes. Some were conscious of the debate about the 'blood tie' and the effects of separation, but on the whole the influence of child care theory on their own basic assumptions about the relative importance of different factors lay somewhere beneath the surface, and decisions were based on what Olive Stevenson (1975) refers to as 'practice wisdom, a mixture of knowledge and skill derived from training and experience'. Here are some comments from the social workers:

'... It's a subjective judgment based on objective observation over a period. Are the family asking for it anyway? Having satisfied myself that what they are saying and what they are really meaning are the same thing, I would work accordingly. I wouldn't take circumstances prevailing at the time of reception into care, and even still prevailing, as necessary reasons for not going home....'

'On the whole I would work for rehabilitation. I suppose there would be some where I wouldn't, but I haven't come across them. If the parents say quite openly that they don't want the child back, I wouldn't, but I wouldn't necessarily take that at its face value.'

'In some cases, you can see a terrible emotional death within a family with quite high standards. If there is nothing there, then I wouldn't work towards rehabilitation.'

'I would work for rehabilitation with families where the ability to change is there within them. It doesn't depend on the symptoms or the injury. I would want definite guidelines from the parents and the older children about how they can see me and use me. I am looking for the families where one can sit down and say, "Where have we got to?" A family whose communications systems are not so alien to the outside world. It would be difficult if one person is very much in charge and would never accept the involvement of anyone else in that situation. It isn't a question of whether they share my values but whether we can work together, whether they could all adjust to the idea of the child coming home, and the child wouldn't be totally mystified at the idea. But it requires skill. The way the social worker puts it could completely turn people off the idea of co-operating. The skill is in observing what is going on in a family, and how new events change situations.'

These comments show that there was a range of opinion, in that some would lean more towards rehabilitation than others, but that all stressed the need for change and involvement on the part of the family. This comment of one of the mothers sums up the usual attitude.

'They knew what I was like and I thought they were against me from the way I lived. On the whole, I think they did want me to have him back, but it was up to me to change.'

In discussion on the concept of the 'blood tie' there was a fairly wide range of views about its relevance and meaning, though all except two social workers considered birth identity to be a factor of some importance. Some discussed it in terms of the extended family, and wanting to place siblings together, or place children with relatives. The very fact that all the children except two were at some stage away from home indicates that however important the tie between parents and children was thought to be, other considerations overrode it at times. The comment of Olive Stevenson quoted above sums up accurately the views of the majority of the workers on this issue, in that most thought that the significance of the 'blood tie' was not necessarily that the child should live with his natural parents but that he should know who they were. There was little support for the view of Goldstein et al. (1973) that ties with parents should be completely severed, even for children in long-term care.

In most cases we were talking not about the 'blood tie' alone, but about a combination of a relationship through birth, and bonds which had been established with natural parents before a child came into care. This was clear from the fact that the adoptive parents were referred to as if they were natural parents, and there was in none of these three cases an attempt to establish contact with the natural parents. Opinions varied from ' "Blood tie"? I just don't think it is a valid concept,' to 'Oh, yes. I find it incredible why anybody thinks the "blood tie" isn't important.' For most, opinions lay somewhere between these two points of view.

'I'm more and more convinced that in some cases the "blood tie" isn't desperately important. Sometimes the personalities of parent and child are so opposed that the "blood tie" isn't important. It depends very much on personalities.'

'I wasn't aware of placing weight on the "blood tie", but the fact that I worked on the assumption that they should go home indicated that really I did. I don't think about it all that much. I suppose it is of most importance to the parents.'

'I think the "blood tie" is a valid concept. It is the area with older children where I try to find out what they feel. I'm impressed by the problems we have with long-term foster children, and the children coming out of residential care at eighteen, in terms of identity. Quite often it is a major factor in their problems. It isn't overriding, but it is one of many factors.'

'I think we all define the "blood tie" differently. I think the child has a special bond with his parents, just because they are his parents, and not because he likes them as people. The "blood tie" is important if it is important to the child. I would almost always want to place a child near his parents.'

'The "blood tie" is significant to the children. They want to know who their parents are. I have come across it too often to ignore it. Almost every child I have worked with, even after years away, they might not want to go home, but they want to know who they are. I certainly think it is important to maintain relationships. I think it is important, too, going home, because you see it so often - you say kids don't know what they want, but they do want to be at home, whether objectively it's in their interest or not. That's why it's so difficult. You can't be glib, and say you are acting in the best interest of the child if the child doesn't want what you are offering, and wants to go home.'

Foster mother: 'I don't want to adopt them. I've no right to take them completely away from their parents. But they need to be cared for and protected until they are old enough. You can bring up a child for somebody, but you must always leave it open for them later to decide. Don't forget, I was a foster kid, you are always looking for your parents. You always want to know who they are. I'm not going to say that will make your parents love you, but it is important to know them. At least if they do know, if there is any reason why they shouldn't go back to live, at least they can find out for themselves. I have had girls here who don't know where their parents are, and that is terrible.'

These comments show that the social workers were concerned to know what the significance of the birth relationship was for the child and his parents. The parents were not asked a direct question about the 'blood tie', but were asked if they would consent to adoption if it were not possible for the child to return to them. All the parents interviewed except one said they would not consent to adoption, and it was clear from their comments that the 'blood tie' was very relevant to them.

'Why did I have him back? I don't know. Because he was mine, and because he *was* mine, and what gave *them* the right to take him away.'

On the other hand, most of the parents also spoke of the bonds which grew from caring for the child, and a mother who had had two children placed for adoption at birth commented about the two in care:

'No. I would never consent to their being adopted. Because I had them since they were born. I had them live with me. Ten days in hospital is too long. I only had my last baby two days in hospital and I discharged myself.'

The question of bonds between parents and children was seen by social workers as being more important than the 'blood tie' in deciding about placement.

'The "blood tie" is important to the child in terms of its own identity. It may be because of our society that it is bound to be important for the child as he grows up. But it wouldn't necessarily mean that it was paramount. Much depends on the strength of the relationship.'

'If the child obviously warms to the mother, relates to the mother, that would be an extremely important factor in whether you let a child go home, even if there is some degree of risk.'

'There do seem to be important ties between parents and children, that is, psychological parents, whether adoptive or natural parents or even grandparents. The ties which exist are more important than the actual "blood tie".'

Some social workers made it clear that they were also concerned to assess the potential for making relationships, and that they would consider returning children to parents even if, as with some of the younger children, bonds had not been formed because of early separation. This was particularly important where step-parents were involved.

'If there is a relationship, or the possibility of a relationship, that can be rewarding to both of them, it is worth passing through all sorts of difficulties. Housing, financial, and right through child care methods.'

'It's the potential for bonding, whether you feel that there is the potential for growth in the relationship. I wouldn't place any weight on the "blood tie" if I thought there was no chance of a relationship being formed.'

Stepmother: 'The main thing he had to think about me was whether I loved her, and short of having had her, could be her mother.'

The third important question to which social workers sought an answer when deciding whether rehabilitation was a goal to be pursued, and which most mentioned, was whether the child would be safe from physical harm, and whether the emotional care he would receive at home would be, in Winnicott's terms, 'good enough' (1971). Here the question of the age of the child was seen to be important, when the possibility of physical harm was being considered.

'One is looking at the relationship between the parents and the child, but one is also looking at the parent's capacity to parent successfully.'

'She so clearly wanted to go home, and the parents were consistently working towards it. She was no longer a little tot, and we thought as the school was also keeping a watchful eye, that we could take a calculated risk.'

'I thought she had a fair bit of insight, and was beginning to really care about him, but I wasn't sure whether she had the strength to cope with the demands of a disturbed child.'

'The welfare of the child was the important thing. She always came first. I don't think the rights of the parents ever came into it, and I don't think they ever should in cases as nasty as this.'

It is perhaps in this area of assessing whether the care which the child would be given if he stayed at home or returned home would be good enough that the social workers agreed least amongst themselves, and it was here that the weight they placed on the importance of birth identity probably unconsciously influenced the decision about how hard they would work to help to make home standards acceptable, and the degree of risk which they would find tolerable.

These differences of emphasis are reflected in the literature. Several of the writers in 'Good Enough Parenting' (CCETSW, 1978) stress the need for parental care to be supplemented, sometimes over prolonged periods, so that they are enabled to meet their children's needs. Other writers in the same publication, and the writers of the ABAFA guides to practice (1976; 1977a; 1977b) emphasise the need for a thorough assessment of a parent's ability to give good enough care as early as possible so that long-term plans can be made if parents are unable to meet their children's needs. The two approaches are not mutually exclusive, but do represent real differences of emphasis which are likely to be reflected in the nature of the social work service offered. This issue is returned to in the concluding chapter.

The skill and sensitivity of the worker in seeing through the immediate distressing circumstances to what might be possible, and getting below the surface of what the parents and children were saying, as discussed in Chapter 5, to what they were actually feeling was crucial, as was the capacity to empathise with those particular parents. Some of the social workers talked of instances where they had asked for cases to be transferred to a colleague because they had felt that someone else might be able to get through to the parents where they had failed, and that every effort should be made to improve home standards before the necessity for long-term care was accepted. Families, too, were conscious of these differences between social workers, especially if the arrival of a new social worker led to a change of plan. Two families in particular thought that a label had been put on them, and that because they had been unable to cope in the past, or at a particularly stressful time, it was assumed that they would never be able to cope. They were particularly suspicious of case records in this respect.

'Jim told me only last week, he said the thing that hurt him most, when he had been there about two weeks, and asked the social worker when he could come home, he said, "There is no question of you going home. You have got to stay here." He told us he wanted Jim to forget his family ties, and also it was abnormal that he was so upset being parted from us. Very probably, if that social worker had come to us fresh, as we are now, it would have been all right. It's just that he saw us when we were down. He seemed to make a lot of assumptions about us which we were for ever correcting. Because I had been in a convalescent home once after I'd been ill, he immediately moved that up to I'd been in care. When this new one came, we think, from her attitude to us she must have read something about us in the reports. She found we were quite different from what she expected.'

Father: 'What happened, when the court case was over everyone thought they had better not come near me. You see, to the welfare, I am a bad case, let's put it that way. They were all for my wife, they thought I was the wrong party. Now they have seen what has happened, and they have changed right round.'

This last comment illustrates that in several cases where the parents were separated the social workers were assessing two possible homes for the children, and two sets of ties.

A major influence on the decision for children who were no longer infants was the attitude of the children themselves, and it was clear that most of the social workers interviewed were already doing what the 1975 Children Act requires them to do, namely to 'ascertain the wishes and feelings of the child regarding the decision and give due consideration to them.'

Social worker: 'David made it clear that that was what he wanted, that he was determined to come home, and was desperately unhappy in care. Also he wasn't so damaged as came over at first.'

Social worker: 'I am still not sure about rehabilitation. He has a relationship with his parents, and they want him home. But the child isn't pressing for it. When he is home, he says he wants to stay home. But there are a lot of indications that he wants to stay in the foster home as well.'

When children had returned home, if home circumstances gave cause for anxiety, it became particularly important for the social worker to assess the child's views.

'When they go for holidays to the foster home, they are excited and pleased to go but also quite pleased to come home. If the children said they would rather be away, I would think again, so I discuss it with them.'

'I would like to get him out of the home again. I don't think he should have gone back. But I will only do it with his agreement, and he doesn't show any desire to even consider the idea.'

As was seen in Chapter 6, most of the social workers put a great deal of emotional energy into their work with the parents, and several said that they were influenced by pressure put on them by the parents, but even more so by a very strong desire to help them to care for their children, and thus avoid for them the distress of long-term separation. (In none of these cases did parents overtly reject the children, though some of the parents who had left home may have done.)

Again opinions varied from the worker quoted above who placed no weight on the rights of parents to the following:

'I find it difficult in this case because I am so much more influenced by the parents than by the child.'

'I suppose this sort of family typifies the whole controversy about the "blood tie". You have two really deprived people who really wanted to make a go of things. They know all about their deprivation. They knew why they behaved as they did. but that didn't stop them. They wanted to change, but, in the light of hindsight, they didn't have the capacity to change. Nothing had

gone right for them. A handicapped girl, and a chap brought up
in children's homes. They had a child whom they didn't think
they would be able to have because of her handicap. They were
homeless at the time they had the child. It seems that society
owes them the chance to be able to hang on to their child and
make a go of it, and owes it to the child. Because if there is
a hope of somebody maintaining their birth identity successfully,
I don't see why they should be deprived of that. It is a very
serious thing to do, to deprive somebody of their birth identity.
If it is done, it must be because there is no alternative.'

Thus it can be seen that the social workers' attitudes were shaped by several factors, and that the relative weight given to any one factor varied with the case and the attitudes of children, parents, and caretakers. (The attitudes of caretakers will be discussed later.) The comment quoted below is fairly typical of how the various factors were brought together.

'Yes, I suppose the "blood tie" must affect my thinking. These
children have other relationships, but I see the relationship
with their mother as the most important. I tend to think it
might have had a quite serious effect on her if they had stayed
in long-term care. If the children were removed from her now,
she wouldn't have anything. Despite the deprivation of the
home, they seem to want to stay there. They seem to have kept
their ability to make relationships and they probably could be
satisfactorily placed in a foster home. It is a dilemma,
especially with a younger child. When you take an older child
into care, its chances are perhaps not so good. But with a
younger child, you can easily find long-term foster parents,
who would perhaps adopt him. That might give him a much better
chance than he would have in his own home. That is the dilemma –
why let them go home? It comes back to seeing the parents as
individuals. The children have rights, but the parents have
rights too.'

The attitudes related to cases

How then did these various views affect the social work help offered, and the actual decisions made? In some cases there was no conflict. The child wanted to go home, the parents wanted him home, and the parents could provide, with or without help, care which was considered adequate. It was where the different factors were in conflict that decisions were most difficult, as when children wanted to go home, but the parents were unsure, or seemed unable to improve the standard of care offered, or when a child had ties with foster parents and natural parents, and where both were able to offer good care. The two major decisions about placement were whether and where to place a child away from home in the first place, and having done so, whether to work towards rehabilitation. Whatever the views of the social workers about rehabilitation, they were clearly prepared to take children into care if they thought this was necessary for the child's welfare, and to overrule the wishes of the parents. One of the reasons for social workers recommending care orders was so that they would have the power to intervene and insist on improved standards of care.

'The care order was to introduce an element of control. Even as we were getting the care order, the intention was not that he should remain in care. We hoped that the parents would respond to the intervention of court proceedings and of us saying, "This far and no further. We are going to take extra responsibility for your child, so that if there are similar circumstances again, we can intervene immediately."'

In this case return home was clearly planned even before court proceedings, but this was not always the case. Social workers were asked if they always worked for return home, and they said they did (or the information was available on file where other social workers had taken the decision), for twelve children, but not for sixteen children. For the remaining six the end of a period of assessment was awaited before any plans were formulated. It was thought that the parents always wanted the children to go home in nineteen cases, and eventually after they had been away for a while in four other cases. With five children one parent wanted the children home, and the other one didn't, and the parents of six children tended to change their minds. Thus, despite the importance which most social workers placed on the relationship between the child and his parents, in the cases of sixteen children they originally expected care to be long-term, and worked accordingly. In another three cases, social workers who had returned children home as part of their original plan changed the plan to work for the child remaining in long-term care when it became clear that even with the sanction of court action, the child's welfare was not adequately safeguarded when he was at home.

Social workers were asked if the parents and children were actively involved in the decision about whether the child should return home, whether the eventual return was planned, and what most influenced them in deciding to let a child stay at home, or return home. All the children except the six who were too young were actively involved in the decision, and all the parents, although in four cases this was not until the children had been in care for some time. In three cases the active involvement of the parents was with the court and solicitors, and in opposition to the plans of the social workers. Although initially the plan had been for sixteen of the children to stay in long-term care, eventually the home placement was part of a plan for twenty-six of the children. It was precipitated by the breakdown of a placement in one case, and was the best option available in two cases, it being thought that all the placements in care would be unsuitable for the children, and possibly more damaging than remaining at home. In one case a holiday at home proved so successful that it was thought that rehabilitation should be attempted, and in three cases courts returned children to their parents quite unexpectedly, so that there was no time to plan the return. These findings tend to contradict a fairly widely held impression that most children who are at home on trial are there because no suitable placement is available. However, the picture might have been different if children over sixteen had not been excluded from the study. Table 7.1 shows the answers to the question as to what influenced the social workers most when they decided to let the children go home.

TABLE 7.1 Influence on the social worker's decision to let the child stay/return home

	Number of children*
Positive improvement at home	16
Positive improvement in the child	3
Child's unhappiness in care	3
Pressure from the child	7
Pressure from the parents	15
Unsatisfactory placement in care	4
Lack of suitable placement in care	3

* In some cases more than one answer was given.

The role of the social workers in weighing up these various pressures was clearly of considerable importance. To give but one example, they could take at face value the parents' reluctance to visit, seeing this as a sign of rejection; or they could encourage visiting by talking about the reluctance, and arranging transport. Thus some workers actively set out to create the conditions where return home might be possible, whilst others waited to take their cue from the parents or the children.

Social worker: 'My goal was to get them into decent housing, and to give them the vast amount of support they would need to look after a young baby.'

Mother: 'I went over their heads. I went to my MP. They didn't want me to have a house until the children didn't want to know any more, or something like that.'

Mother: 'I don't think he wanted us to have her first. Well, I think the social worker was considering how she actually felt. And I think at first he thought she would be better off with the foster parents.'

The reactions of the parents were obviously of some importance, and may well have been one of the most crucial factors influencing why these children actually went home. In Chapters 4 and 6 the reactions of the parents when the children went into care were discussed, and certainly they did seem to demand a high level of service from the workers, and demand to be kept in touch with their children.

The way the social workers reacted to this pressure was interesting. In some cases the pressure was clearly not welcome, and seen as an indication that things would not go too well if children went home, and that the parents would be unlikely to 'co-operate'. In others the social workers seemed to have a greater understanding of the different factors contributing to the parents' need to feel that they could influence the situation.

Social worker: 'I was influenced by parental pressure, not because I was responding to the pressure, but because it would have hazarded the whole treatment plan if their ability to tolerate frustration had been stretched too far.'

Mother: 'I used to have him for weekends, and they had a case conference and she said, "No, not yet." So I said, "Right, that's it." I didn't go any more. Then I suppose she got a bit worried because I wouldn't go, and about three months later I said, "Right, if I can't have him, you keep him." I got headstrong and said, "There is no point in my going to see him. I've had enough. Either I have him, or I don't. I can't hang about." I wouldn't have done it when it came to it, but I did say, right, have him adopted then.'

Social workers had another very difficult decision to make if the child had formed an attachment whilst in care, and in most cases the tendency was not to reintroduce parents once ties with natural parents had been broken. This was not the case with any of the children in the study, but there were cases where the child had divided loyalties, and the social workers were asked how their decision about whether a child should return home was influenced by the substitute caretakers, and whether, in the case in question, the caretakers wanted the child to go home. In some cases a different decision was taken about children in the same family because some of the children had developed strong ties with foster parents.

'The three oldest children had had time to grow with their mother, and develop a relationship with her. But the youngest two had precious little contact with her. I've made a lot of attempts to try to get her to build a relationship with them, but she finds it difficult. I would need to be more sure of how she would cope before I considered moving them from their foster home.'

'If there hasn't been continuing contact over a period, I would cease to work for rehabilitation, as it would cease to be a positive thing. That's why I was struggling to maintain the bonds between him and his parents.'

'I made a lot of assumptions about rehabilitation being possible, and ignored the extent to which placing a child in a foster home, and the developing of ties, interferes with the possibility of rehabilitation. I had seen it as something to do with the parents, and ignored the fact that one has to be looking at how the child is developing, particularly a small child.'

Assessment of the bonds with the foster parents was not simply a question of counting how long the child had been there. At least one of the children referred to in Chapter 5 who had been placed for some years seems not to have established very strong ties with her foster parents, and in two other cases the workers were unsure of the depth of the relationship.

'What worries me with him, his foster home has great security for him, and he is very close with the children of the family, but I'm not sure if there is any real bond with the foster parents. I could make a good argument that his long-term interest will best be served in care, but I don't feel happy about him staying in this particular foster home.'

TABLE 7.2 Foster parents/houseparents (principal placement) wanted child to go home

	Number of children
Always	5
Eventually	8
Attitudes varied at different times	3
Ambivalent	6
No	5
Don't know	3
Not placed away from home or hospital	4

Table 7.2 gives the answers to the question: did the foster parents/house parents want him to go home? Most of the social workers said that they were influenced to some extent by the views of the caretakers about whether the children should go home, and several parents commented that they thought that the social workers were unduly influenced by the foster parents.

Mother: 'The foster parents' opinion is always considered in a better light than yours.'

No matter how much they were influenced by the opinions of the foster parents, there was general agreement that the role which the caretakers adopted towards the child and his parents was extremely significant in influencing whether rehabilitation was possible. Fifteen of the social workers said that the way the caretakers fulfilled their role was very important in determining whether a child returned home, four said it was important, and one said it was not important. This leads on to a consideration of the sorts of placement available, which will be discussed in the next section; but it can be noted here that social workers felt that their decisions were constrained by the lack of suitable placements in care. Workers thought that six of the children who were in care at the end of the study could probably have been successfully returned home had different placements been available for them when in care, and that two of the children who were placed not very satisfactorily at home could have benefited from being in care in the right sort of placement.

'Even if one just looks at it in terms of enabling the child to return home, if the substitute parents can't accept it, it puts the child in a position of emotional conflict which is very difficult to resolve. It's a factor one has to take into account, and may have to overcome.'

'It makes a terrific difference if you have a unit which is, as in this case, geared towards the child going home. That influences everything that is going on in the situation. It's important to know what expectations the child has been surrounded with. If they think your parents are a rum lot, it's never going to work when you go home. Even if it is never said directly, you have to take it into account when you are thinking of the child going home.'

'You cannot make a decision that a child needs care in a vacuum. You have to believe that you can offer something better. One is often trying to make a good casework job of a "Hobson's choice" situation.'

RESOURCES

Resources available for prevention

The first important question to ask about resources is whether their availability could have prevented care or court action in the first place. The parents thought that removal from home could have been avoided for about a third of the children, whereas social workers thought it might have been avoided in only four cases. Social workers and parents were asked if any form of practical help could have made removal from home unnecessary. In only one case did the social worker think that practical help, in this case housing, would have helped, and even here in combination with a great deal of casework help. Of the parents who thought that care could have been avoided, two thought that this would have been possible if a place in a battered wives' hostel had been available for them and their children, two thought that day care for the children would have made care unnecessary, and two thought help to achieve a change of school would have been sufficient. The most striking thing to me about the answers of the social workers and parents to this question was how undemanding both groups were about what should be provided. It seemed fairly clear to me that a battered wives' hostel and good casework support could in fact have prevented seven children from being away from home for a total period of twenty-two years, and that a combination of day care and home helps with flexible working hours could have either prevented care for four children, or allowed them to return home much sooner. In other cases, although practical help such as day care could have prevented the need for removal from home, the parents would not have accepted it, or awareness of the possibility came at too late a stage to prevent the crisis which led to care. This was a point made by some of the social workers. In one case of suspected ill-treatment, day care was offered to the parents but they would not agree to the child going. In another case a young mother thought, with hindsight, that she might not have become so depressed if she had been able to go out to work with the children being placed in a day nursery, but said that the thought never occurred to her at the time.

It was fairly clear in these cases that resources alone would not have prevented reception into care, and that considerable casework help would have been needed. But in the light of hindsight, and in view of the fact that some of the children stayed in care for several years and were the ones who were eventually caught up in 'tug-of-love' situations, such an investment of time and resources would have saved a great deal of unhappiness, for children and for foster parents as well as the parents.

 Father: 'David was only eight months old. There was no day
  nursery or child minders. Social services tried all they could

to help overcome the problems. They couldn't find anyone to
look after the children during the day. So they went into a
private foster home, and when the custody case came up they made
a care order. —They did as much as they could to prevent it.
The facilities just weren't there, no day nursery or anything.'

Mother: 'After I left him they had to go into care because I
couldn't look after them and go to work as well. They just went
away because I didn't have anywhere else to live.'

Stepmother: 'I think, the way things happened, it happened
that she was taken into care. A man has got to work. He wasn't
happy when she came into care in the first place. He did go to
pieces a bit, but they could have helped him to move near his
parents. He had to live with another bloke. Perhaps if they
had offered a house and a day nursery near his family he could
have coped. But they don't, do they?'

One of the very strong impressions to come out of the study was
that of the extreme vulnerability of families at the end of a
marriage, either through death or separation, and the need for a
sensitive social work service to be offered very early on. A
father whose problems with his older children seemed clearly to
date from his inability to recover from the death of his wife
commented:

'About four months after, a welfare worker, I suppose she was,
came round and told me I didn't need to work, I could claim
from the social security. I could have stayed at home. They
left that rather late, I thought. I didn't want to work day
and night. The welfare system, they don't seem to realise that.'

Again, in the light of hindsight, it is easy to see that sensitive,
practical and casework help at that stage could have helped this
family, whereas when serious problems with the children developed
two years later, too much damage seemed to have been done to
relationships within the family for the social worker to have much
chance of success.

In another case a mother stated that she would have accepted the
child going to a day nursery voluntarily, without the need for
court action and care.

'They could have got a day nursery instead of care for him.
They got one when he was in care. I would have taken him
willingly.'

In three of the cases where day care could have been used instead
of full care, the social workers felt that the separation had done
serious harm to the relationship between the parents and the child,
which had added to the problems of rehabilitation. Such cases
would indicate that serious thought should be given to the introduction of a 'day care order', a suggestion which has been made
by Bob Holman, instead of a full care order, or to the more frequent
inclusion of special requirements for day care in supervision orders.
This point is returned to later in this chapter.

On the need for battered wives' hostels mothers commented:
'If that hostel for battered wives had been there that would
have been all right. Because he couldn't have gone there to

get me back. There was nothing like that then. I went to a place where I could only keep the baby and the others were taken into care.'

'This incident happened when he beat me up. He was at the end of his tether, and we had to get them away. I'd already rung the welfare and they wouldn't do anything. So I thought I'd ask a policeman. They will do something. They got social services to get me in bed and breakfast. They tried the battered wives' hostel, but it was full. If I'd gone there then instead of bed and breakfast, I don't think I would have gone back to him, and the children wouldn't have gone away.'

In Appendix I and Chapter 6 reference is made to 'intermediate treatment orders', and to the fact that no supervision orders with intermediate treatment clauses were made in respect of these children. It was also noted in Chapter 6 that social workers and parents felt some dissatisfaction at the service offered to the children, and that little use was being made of group work with them. Three of the children whose parents thought removal from home was not necessary were older children, and five of the older children were away for only a period of assessment. On talking to the social workers and more especially to the parents it seems clear that in four of these cases it was obvious from the start that the children would go home, and one can therefore ask whether the assessment could not have been done with the child in the home; also, if a residential placement was thought valuable, whether this could not have been made available, either as part of a scheme of intermediate treatment or in a treatment setting rather than an assessment setting. As several of the children concerned had to travel considerable distances to an assessment unit this question is particularly valid.

Mother: 'No, I wouldn't have agreed to a foster home. She wouldn't have stayed anyway. She knew that she was only going away for a short time.'

Mother: 'We wanted him to come home, but they said he had to wait for a case conference. He didn't mind, so long as he knew he was coming home.'

The other resources which could have kept some of the older children out of care was the provision of a school environment which could help with their difficulties.

Social worker: 'If the (special) school had taken him without a care order, the care order would not have been necessary. I see this not so much as a "home on trial" placement, but as a special treatment being offered on a day care basis. Our commitment is so small compared with the absolute routine commitment of the school. Without that it would all collapse.'

Resources for children in care

As mentioned above, one of the factors influencing whether children were placed away from home, and then whether rehabilitation was possible, was the availability of suitable placements. In Chapter 5 details were given about the placements, and it was noted that, although on the whole parents and social workers were satisfied with the care offered, only for eleven of the children was this the placement which the social workers would ideally have chosen. It was also noted that few parents visited the placement before the child went; and although half of the parents were involved in the decision about placement, one wonders about the value of this involvement if they had not visited the placements being discussed. It was clear from this study that parents did have very definite views about placements, and this was one of the areas about which those interviewed had most to say. Eight of the children had experienced both foster and residential care, and in other cases parents had been involved with both sorts of care because of placements of other children in the family, or when they themselves were in care. Thus several of those interviewed were able to make comparisons. Before looking in more detail at the comments about foster and residential care, a few general points should be made. The main general complaint of the parents was about a lack of planning, and the consequent need for changes of placement. Several parents commented that they had not been unduly worried about the initial choice, as they had thought it would be only short-term, but that in retrospect they thought the social workers should have talked to them more about the pros and cons of different placements.

Mother: 'They knew I couldn't say much about their being moved, because I was in hospital. It was "I'm glad you came in, Mrs B., because they are being moved tomorrow." The reason they tell me they do this sort of thing is so the child doesn't get attached to that particular woman. But they were moved so many times.'

Father: 'We took him over to the children's home. We didn't visit before. It was only a temporary arrangement, so we thought.'

Stepmother: 'I can see the sadness of the situation from the foster parents' point of view, which is why I say it's the social services' fault. In a case where a child is so much wanted, especially in a case where a parent has fought to keep him - it makes me think they didn't believe him when he said he wanted him back. If they had nothing else, it should have been a children's home. If they knew what the problem would be, they should have said, why not a children's home? I think in retrospect he (husband) would have preferred that. I know they asked for his approval, but with a visit for tea, you can't tell. At the time he was very grateful, and when he saw things going wrong, he didn't like to ask for a transfer.'

As mentioned above, most social workers were not satisfied with the choices available to them. Some seemed to have a sense of impotence, and this in part may explain the fact that the quality of social work help, in terms of preparation for care and pre-placement visits, was so often found wanting when compared to the recommendations in 'Foster Care: A Guide to Practice' (DHSS, 1976). As seen above, it also led to some children remaining at home when perhaps they could have been helped by the right placement in care; and some felt that there was little point in having good assessment facilities if the placement recommended was not going to be available. Others would have liked to see assessment facilities for younger children so that the reactions of children and parents to separation could be considered before a decision was made about the sort of foster care required. The following comments represent the more general views of social workers about placements.

'I like to know the unit, and how they are going to react, before I place a child. I think the problem is that you can try to specify what particular home you would like, but the chances of the child going are limited, and also the chance of the child going at the time you want.'

'I'd rather have the right children's home than the wrong foster home. I think the wrong foster home is more damaging because the relationships are much closer. But I've been very fortunate with foster homes. I've got some placements I'm very happy about.'

'A good foster home, or a good children's home, can make rehabilitation possible. You are putting in loving care and security, and all the things the child has been missing. We've not got enough of the right sort of foster parents and children's homes.'

Foster care

In Chapter 1 the discussion about 'professional' foster parents, or, in Holman's terms (1975) 'exclusive' and 'inclusive' foster care, was summarised, and in Chapter 5 it was noted that both social workers and parents, whilst having a preference for foster care for young children and sometimes for older children, stressed the importance of placements where the natural parents were able to play as full a role as possible in the lives of their children. A study of foster parents conducted in 1974 in the authority concerned found, in common with most similar studies, that the majority of the foster parents in the county at that time did not see themselves as performing a professional role. (Only 20 per cent of those interviewed considered that visits by parents helped them in their caring role, and two-thirds saw themselves as more like parents or adoptive parents to the children.)

Thus it is not surprising that social workers were not often able to place these children whom they wanted to rehabilitate in foster homes which they thought were ideally suited for them, and that in some cases children were hurt by the conflict between natural and foster parents. Most of the social workers interviewed had experience of working with 'professional' foster parents and expressed a strong belief in the value of such placements, and the fact that they could be found. Parents, too, were well aware of the advantages to their children of this sort of placement. Relating this to the discussion in Chapter 1, it would seem that, rather than accept the suggestion of Shaw and Lebens (1976) that departments

should accept the reality that most foster parents want to be
substitute parents and work accordingly, the social workers and
parents would want more efforts to be made to recruit 'professional'
foster parents; and that if this is not done they will be reluctant
to place children in foster care if return home is a possibility.
Several of the workers expressed interest in the Kent 'Family
Placement' scheme (Hazel et al., 1977) and would have liked to see
such a scheme in their own area.

Only two foster parents were interviewed specifically, but the
study has been discussed at several foster parents' groups.
Although foster parents commented about the strains which this sort
of role places on them, several of those I spoke to thought it was
not impossible to share the care of the children with the parents,
and several regularly do so. What they did strongly ask for was
recognition of the difficulties by social workers, and particularly
for support from the social workers in drawing up clearly understood
guidelines about visiting with the parents. A study of foster care
in Portsmouth makes this point very strongly.

This means much more than simply encouraging the natural parents
to visit the foster children, which can create strong tensions.
Ideally it could involve drawing up a plan or a contract, when
boarding out appears to be appropriate, in which the rights and
duties of each party are clearly stated. A point of central
importance is that nobody should be kept in the dark, with a
mounting suspicion that they are deliberately kept out of the
decision making. For everybody's peace of mind, the roles,
rights and responsibilities must be clarified and agreed upon
(Portsmouth Fostering Study, 1973).

In the majority of the placements in this study, this did not
happen, but it did in some, and in some cases parents and foster
parents were involved in case conferences.

One final comment, before I give the views of the parents and
social workers, is that this study reinforces Jane Aldgate's (1978a)
findings that in some cases, and those involving the most vulnerable
children, there is a need for the same long-term 'professional'
foster parents to provide substitute care for some children (perhaps
at intervals or perhaps giving day care) until the children are old
enough to cope on their own. At least twelve of the children in
this study in groups A and B had very strong bonds with their
parents, and yet the parents' problems were such that it was almost
inevitable that these children would need to spend time in care in
the future. In most 'professional' fostering schemes (Cooper, 1978;
McWhinnie, 1978) the task is seen as short-term care either offering
therapy (usually for older children) or an assessment setting.
The professional role of supporting the parents, and supplementing
what care they can offer (as outlined by Rowe, 1977), perhaps over
a lengthy period, is provided for in only a minority of schemes.
Although in theory 'traditional' foster parents have fulfilled this
role, in reality, as several studies have shown, they have done so
reluctantly; and it may be that 'professional' long-term foster
parents should be recruited for this particularly vulnerable group
of children. The Berkshire scheme, as outlined by Cooper (1978),
seems to fulfil this role for children of all ages:

Professional foster parents are not regarded as surrogate parents, but encourage the children to keep in touch with their natural parents who have complete access, the hope being that the children will eventually return to their own homes.

Children in single-parent families were particularly vulnerable. In Chapter 5 it was noted that only six children had returned to the same foster home when they came back into care. When this sort of arrangement was available to a family, the pressures on all concerned were considerably less, as the damaging effects of care are either minimised or more than compensated for by the benefits which the foster parents can offer.

Because parents and social workers had a great deal to say about foster care, their comments are included at some length.

Social worker: 'The initial placement is tremendously important, especially in situations like this where the outcome is uncertain. I remember thinking for most of the time when he was in and out of care, wouldn't it be helped by the right sort of home. He needed a granny figure, someone who would love him, and care for him when the parents were having their bad spells, where he would feel at home. Foster parents who would daily and nightly care, and yet be prepared to relinquish him to his parents, but continue their interest while he was there; who would have cared for him as somebody else's child, but be prepared to consider in the future a more ongoing relationship as a long-term foster child. He was in three different foster homes, because we could never get him back into the same one.'

Social worker: 'When he went home, the parents still felt they could turn to the foster mother. It allows one to feel happier about his going home, knowing that there is the foster mother in the background.'

Foster mother: 'He has been back several times. She just rings up and says will I have him for a night or something, because they are going out. I don't ask questions, and she knows I am there. I pop round from time to time, when it is his birthday, for instance.'

Foster mother: 'Teenage is a terrible time, for some mothers and daughters especially. If it would help to keep them together, why shouldn't a girl come back here for a while. If you can get to their mothers and talk to them, let them know you've had teenagers, you know what they are like. It's O.K. so long as the foster mother doesn't try to take over. You must never do that. I really believe in the foster mother, the parent and the social worker working together. Your job is a lot easier if you do that. The thing is, I've got my social workers behind me. I couldn't do it if I didn't have good social workers. I love my job. It's just what I want to do.'

Social worker: 'It is very difficult when you get foster parents who are hostile to natural parents, or the other way round. If you are trying to rehabilitate and you can get the foster parents to work with you it makes it so much easier. Sometimes I return children when I am doubtful, and I probably wouldn't have done if they had been suitably placed. Given a choice, I would rather use foster parents than residential care.'

Social worker: 'The right foster parents could have helped with the parents' problem, their deprivation. They had no reliable parent figures of their own, no extended family. They needed foster parents who, whilst being warm and friendly, would manage not to get involved in their marital problems. It would have had to be somebody very professional.'

Social worker: 'I see a place for different sorts of foster parents. These foster parents were very caring and good with the parents, in an intuitive sort of way. It was natural.'

Social worker: 'Really, he would be better in a foster home where there could be sharing over a long period with the parents. The hostility between them makes it difficult for him. But this has gone on for so long now that he has spent a lot of his life in this home, and I can't think it right to move him.'

Social worker: 'The attitude of the foster parents influences our decisions because it influences the child's development in the foster home, so you have a law of diminishing returns. If you have possessive foster parents who want to hang on to a child, and convey it to a child, if you let that happen for long enough, inevitably you are influenced by the wishes of the child, and you have to stop thinking in terms of the child going home.'

Social worker: 'They wanted to adopt him, even to the point of assuming this *was* their child, and telling the people on the estate that he was theirs. When he left, they couldn't accept it, and didn't accept till the day he was going. What hurt most, they refused to speak to him from that day, even though they often see him. They cut him off completely, after having had him for four years.'

Social worker: 'As it became clear to the parents that the foster parents didn't want him to go home, the parents started to pick holes in the foster home, and started insisting that he should go back home.'

Social worker: 'She does go to see her parents, but there is no attempt on the part of the foster parents to present the parents to her in a nice way. There is never any question, when she gets home, of "Hello, did you have a nice day?" It's always, "Right, off to bed".'

The parents and children liked foster homes mainly because they thought that it was better for their children to be in a family environment.

Boy, aged 9: 'The foster home was best. There was a man and a woman there. Just two housemothers gets boring. In the foster home you don't always have to eat your dinner, and you can go down the road.'

Mother: 'Another thing. Not every child likes children's homes. I should know. I've been in enough myself. A children's home isn't like your proper home. If they had more people who were willing to take foster children in a family, you will find a child takes more to that. I wouldn't let my child go into a children's home. I think they should shut them all up.'

Mother: 'I liked the foster home best. At the children's home, they wouldn't let us take her out down the park. But the foster mother was so nice and understanding.'

Mother: 'The foster mother was a very calm, capable person. They said they were very sorry to lose her, but glad she was coming back home to us. I'm glad she was in a foster home and not a children's home, at least with those particular foster parents.'

Mother: 'He used to call them mummy and daddy. They did really love him. I didn't mind at the time because I couldn't give it to him.'

Difficulties between natural parents and foster parents arose mostly over differences about how the children should be cared for (and especially about discipline); because of what natural parents saw as possessiveness on the part of the foster parents; or because some of the more immature parents were excessively critical.

Father: 'I used to pay maintenance, and buy her clothes. But even if we were taking her out somewhere special she would just be sent out in her ordinary clothes.'

Mother: 'Yes, I would say they had good care. I don't approve of the way they got hit, though. He never cleared his plate up one morning and he said he got slapped across the face. Now that got me mad. I went to the welfare and they said all kids tell fairy stories.'

Mother: 'Now, I can see it was the best place, but then I didn't because, it's a horrible thing to say, she wasn't very clean. I say a lot of things when I'm in a temper that I don't really mean. I think I finished her off. I think she never fostered any more. I think I did it.'

Stepmother: 'At the beginning, he did not feel it was a bad placement because he was so glad that there was somebody to look after her. But then things started going slightly off, like when he went to visit at his usual time and they would say, "We are just going out." And they had known for two weeks that he would be going at that time.'

Mother: 'I have rather strong views about foster homes. They are fine for long-term children where the children are not wanted, and I am sure there are many of those, but to me, Pat has always been wanted. What she had was a substitute home, and what she needed was a foster home where we could still be involved. Basically this was the problem, but lots of other problems followed from it.'

Father: 'It's easier when they are in a foster home where they call them auntie and uncle, but as soon as you attach the title mum and dad, then it gets difficult.'

Mother: 'I don't want to go and see him because of the mother and father bit. I cannot go up there. I will never stand for it. The welfare must have given permission. I went mad and went to the welfare and said will you stop that, but they wouldn't because they didn't want to stop it, and I haven't been back since.'

Stepmother: 'When they got Bill to call him "other daddy", that really hurt. And he came home literally in tears. When the children were placed, their daddy was there, and the foster mother asked the social worker what they should be called, and the social worker said mummy and daddy, of course. At first he was angry because the other foster mother had been auntie. But he was resigned, because he was relieved that somebody was going to feed her and care for her because he couldn't. I don't think he thought any more about it until she came out with this "other daddy", and then he sat there and howled.'

Most of the parents, even those where there had been conflict, were conscious of the difficult role the foster parents were asked to play, and felt some sadness for them.

Mother: 'I don't know if they wanted him to come home. It must have been difficult for them. I suppose they wanted to keep him - that's obvious. She must have worried about him when he came home.'

Mother: 'You can't ever hope to get a foster mother and a parent of a child to see eye to eye. You are always going to have something between you. I thought when Jean came home, I'll try to get friendly, go round and visit. But the foster mother wouldn't have it.'

Mother: 'I think she did a good bit for him though. I wouldn't like to really crab her. I can understand how she felt. I got a bit upset with her in the end because she got so upsent and it turned to anger, and she really took it out on the child. I did feel sorry for her though, because she really wanted to adopt him.'

Residential care (4)

Feelings about residential care, whether positive or negative, were less strong, and fewer children had residential placements. In Chapter 5 it was noted that most types of residential placement were included in the study.

The general impression from the social workers was that professional foster parents would be their first choice for the younger children, and for some of the teenagers; that residential care was preferable to the wrong sort of foster home, even for some children under five; that observation and assessment centres and the larger children's homes offered a high standard of care but that there was need for more, and more varied, residential provision for longer-stay children, or for those who needed special help. The difficulties of finding the right residential placement at the right time were frequently mentioned, and three social workers mentioned that one of the reasons why they recommended care orders rather than supervision orders or voluntary care was that this was the best way of obtaining a place in the appropriate residential setting. The shortage of long-stay or treatment facilities may also explain why, as mentioned above, several of the children placed in assessment centres were not really there for the assessment, as this could have been as easily done in the home setting, but for their therapeutic value. The danger of this approach was that children who had been given a great deal of help in assessment centres in some cases returned home too soon because they had finished being assessed and no other placement was suitable, or were placed in a setting which had less to offer them, and consequently felt let down, thus diminishing the value of the previous placement.

> Social worker: 'He didn't want to go, but when it came to it, he accepted it. I took him to see the place beforehand, because he was very anxious. He hasn't got a lot of confidence. I think that helped him, going away. There is a very warm atmosphere there. He was there for six months, at the assessment centre. He really improved. He was able to relate to people his own age - be a person in his own right as opposed to being a part of the tribe. He really began to take a pride in himself. But, despite my battles, he went from there to one of the old-style community schools. Everything that the assessment centre gave him he was stripped of. His smart new clothes were taken away, his hair cut, his pocket money reduced, the responsibility taken away from him. If he hadn't gone to the first place, he could have coped better with the second. The last thing he said to me on the phone before he ran away was: "I'm not going to stick this. You can't expect me to stick this." I didn't want him to go home from the assessment centre. I hadn't wanted him in care in the first place, but I could see by then that he was gaining a lot from it, and yet keeping the tie with home. We must give him something to build on, and maybe he will be able to make the break, and be more acceptable to society than his family has been.'

Slightly to my surprise, only one of the parents of the older children thought that residential care should have any punitive aspects, despite the fact that several of the parents were angry with their children for the worry, expense and embarrassment caused by visits to court. The parents very much appreciated the caring approach, especially of the assessment centres where high staffing levels allowed their children to be treated as individuals.

> Mother: 'No, they weren't too easy with him. I think they were strict in their way. But they were like parents to him. Oh, they definitely cared for him. If it hadn't been for the man in charge, he would definitely have gone missing.'

Mother: 'Yes, they were kind to him. They knew how upset he was.'

Mother: 'The housemother was like a mother to him, and even after he left I used to phone her up. She used to always want to know how he was getting on.'

Father: 'I asked him if he would like to go there. We went to see it. He said it was a nice place, he didn't mind. The day we took him there he started to cry. I said, "Don't cry, son, it's only nine miles away." But then he went to that boarding school. It was too far for us to get to see him. He didn't like it, and he was always ill there.'

On the whole, parents were less happy with the care offered in the smaller children's homes (though there were exceptions to this), usually because they did not think they and their children were treated as individuals. Less favourable comments from parents about residential care were:

Mother: 'He is not allowed to ring me and write me letters. It made a big difference when he was at the other place, knowing that if he was upset, he could ring me.'

Mother: 'She was upset there because some woman cut her hair short right up to her ears. Out of spite, she cut it right up to her ears.'

Mother: 'The last children's home they were in - I can understand parents going and whisking them away. The children are very rough, swearing, and the staff always seem to have such loud voices.'

Boy: 'I don't like this place, it's boring. You can't go out to play when the grass is wet. You have to eat your dinner. Your are not allowed out of the walls. Some of your friends just come to the gate. They aren't allowed in the garden.'

VISITING

Some general comments about visiting

Because of the significant relationship between parental visiting and children returning home noted in several studies, the issues surrounding visiting were explored at some length. It was noted that the parents in this study did visit their children more regularly than is usually the case with children in care, but that very few of the parents enjoyed visiting and most found it a painful ordeal. One of the strong impressions with which these interviews left me was of the strength of the determination of most of these parents to retain contact with their children, so that despite finding visiting difficult, they continued to do so. Although several of the social workers did encourage parents to visit by taking them, paying fares and talking about their feelings, several also commented that the parents needed no encouragement. Indeed, in several cases they were

positively discouraged and the fact that usually some time elapsed
before the first visit, and that few pre-placement visits were
made, seems to confirm that the social workers were not very actively
encouraging visiting, at least for some families in the early stages.
Parents were more likely to enjoy visits to residential than foster
placements, and only one parent positively enjoyed visits to a
foster home, although in other cases it was made clear that the
foster parents were encouraging, but the lack of enjoyment was due
to the pain at seeing their child away from home. Parents commented
that the residential workers were more likely to welcome and encourage
visits than the foster parents. The determination to visit despite
the difficulties may well have been one of the crucial factors
leading to these particular children going home. Comparing the
parents with those in Rosamund Thorpe's (1974a, b) study (many of
whom did not seem any less capable of caring for their children in
objective terms, but whose children were still in care), my own
study would give some support to the view of several writers that
if more help were given to parents to overcome the very real difficulties of visiting, more children could successfully return home.

With children on care orders because they were suspected to be at
risk from their parents, there were problems for the social workers
in deciding to what extent the visits should be supervised. It has
been noted above that some of the parents in their anger did threaten
to take children out of care. In such cases social workers usually
got round the difficulty by taking the parents for the early visits,
and trying to be as unobtrusive as possible; but from the comments
of the parents it was clear that this supervisory role was often
resented. Most of the social workers interviewed were no longer
supervising visits at the later stages of placement, and felt it
important to show trust in the families. Both of the foster parents
interviewed felt that this was a difficult problem, but that they
too had to show the parents that they trusted them if they were
going to be able to help them at all.

Foster mother: 'He said, 'Do you have to sit with us?" "Oh, no,"
I said, "I've just got to go to the post with a letter. You
keep an eye on him for me whilst I pop out to the Post Office."
I dashed there and back with my heart in my mouth. But it was
very important to him to feel he wasn't being watched.'

As mentioned above, social workers thought that the attitude of
the substitute caretakers to the natural parents was extremely
important, and they quoted examples of how their work had been
helped or hindered by foster parents or residential workers. The
writers of 'At Risk' commented that in their study 'complaints about
practical arrangements and material details were frequent, as the
parents had a strong need to retain some control over their
children's lives'(Baher, 1977, p.119). It has already been noted
that this applied to some of the parents in this study, but only in
one case did the social workers discourage visiting because of the
disruptive effect such behaviour could have on the placement, and
in this case the children were taken home to see their parents. In
another case the social worker encouraged visits, but at the same
time had to limit their frequency because of the foster parents'
inability to tolerate frequent visits. Although all the social

workers said they encouraged parental contact, only one worker mentioned paying the fare, despite the fact that several of the parents had long distances to travel, and were known to be in financial difficulties. However, in eight cases the workers regularly took the parents to visit, though it must be said that in two of these cases it was under pressure from the parents. Six social workers said they encouraged parents to visit by talking about their anxieties, and seven by telling them that it was important for the children that they should visit.

Visiting children in foster care

It was noted above that parental visiting was positively encouraged in only six of the foster home placements, and that a neutral stance was taken in the rest, or that attitudes varied. Although none of the foster parents was thought to discourage visits actively throughout the placement, several began to do so as time went on, and especially as it became clear that the child was likely to go home - sadly for the children, the very time when positive relationships between parents and foster parents were most essential. As a study in the same county showed that only 20 per cent of the foster parents interviewed thought parental visits were helpful, it may be that there was some hostility below the surface in those cases where an apparently neutral stance was adopted, and that a more positive attitude could have made the experience a more agreeable one. On the other hand, most of the children in foster care were younger than those in residential care, and the experience of seeing their children looked after by someone else was likely to be more painful if the children were younger. Also the parents and foster parents knew that the children were there because of something the parents had done, or not done, rather than because of some problems with the children, which was more likely to be the case with older children; and this inevitably coloured their attitudes towards each other.

Social workers rarely had difficulty in persuading parents to visit, and in some cases had to curtail the frequency of visits at the request of the foster parents. In several cases they got round such problems, or the pain for the parents, by taking the children home to see their parents, and several of those whose children rarely visited them at home said they would have preferred this.

'They didn't need particularly encouraging to visit. They were quite keen to go. I think they felt very much it was a question of behaving properly. That if they behaved properly and did the right things, they would get him back.'

'They didn't visit often. They felt very angry and threatened. They wouldn't have enjoyed visits anyway, because of the Place of Safety Order. On the previous placements, when it was voluntary care, visits were less of a problem. Over the period of the court case I couldn't get them to visit at all. They had so little self-confidence in any case, that seeing some one else coping well shattered them. They tried to avoid it. They

used to pretend they would go next week. They knew that they
should, and in a sense wanted to. Also, there were so many angry
feelings that there was a real worry about them taking the child.'

'The involvement would have been greater had it not been for the
attitude of the foster parents. He looked upon the foster mother
as something of an ogre, out to get him: "You didn't turn up,
you so and so," so he was afraid of her and tried to avoid the
contact. The foster parents were not able to understand at all
the needs of the natural parents.'

'The foster parents don't recognise the need for visits, but they
wouldn't mind if they didn't think the parents were trying to get
him back. He quite enjoys it when he goes home, but doesn't like
the parents to visit him there, because he senses the hostility.
They discourage visits subtly, like always telling him what he
has missed by going hom to visit.'

'They can't recognise that whether the child goes home or not,
he needs to be in contact with his parents. Their attitude tends
to be, we are not having our weekends messed up by parents
visiting.'

'You see, I don't think they ever did figure that the father
would remarry, and settle down again. They did really think
that she was theirs, so they didn't mind him visiting at first.'

'In a way they enjoyed the visits, because the foster mother took
on a maternal role. But they also found it very upsetting and
she was very nervous with the foster mother.'

Some social workers worked very hard to try to support the foster
parents in what they accepted was a very difficult task, but there
was a strong feeling that once a wrong placement had been made,
little could be done about making visiting easier. Perhaps worse
still, it was obvious that resources were such that social workers
were still making placements where visiting would be difficult and
knew they were doing so. One worker commented about 'Foster Care:
A Guide to Practice' (DHSS, 1976) that it was all very well, but it
didn't help if the right sort of foster parents were not available.
The professional foster parents who were available, and this refers
to some who were professional in attitude although this was not
always recognised in the way they were rewarded, were greatly valued.
It is interesting that with these foster parents the standard of
social work support as measured against the guide to practice, in
terms of pre-placement visits and support to the foster parents, was
higher.

Social worker: 'The most important part of my work was the work
with the foster parents. The parents wanted me to exert more
control over aspects of the foster care. In return the foster
parents were full of hostility towards the parents. Towards the
end of the placement, in order to reduce the strain which was
beginning to affect her, I had to ensure that the parents and
foster parents never met during the weekly visits home. They
just couldn't tolerate intensive parental contact. But they did

love her deeply, and despite the certain knowledge at the end that she would go home, they did not reject her. If she had been rejected (a not uncommon reaction in this sort of situation), a temporary move would have been inevitable and hurt her even more. Many hours were spent with the foster parents, particularly during the last six months of the placement, trying to cope with the expression of bitter feelings and trying to reduce the tension, for everybody's sake, but especially the child's. Fortunately they proved emotionally tough enough to withstand losing the child whom they had come to regard as their own.'

Foster mother: 'I've been lucky. I've got on well with most parents. If they come after me like a roaring lion I always say to them, "Let's sit down and have a cup of tea first." Parents are just as possessive of older children as they are of younger ones. Jenny's mother says to me, "You don't try to take her away from me." It's difficult, you mustn't try to take the mother's place, but you can't detach your feelings. This mother is just a kid. She is the one who really wants fostering. Sometimes it is a strain. But I like her, and I don't want to hurt her, because she is desperately looking for love.'

The parents' memories of visiting their children were often very vivid indeed. For those who found the visits painful, it was easy to see how close they sometimes were to giving up visiting, and hence to understand why some parents do not go to see their children. For others, visiting became less painful as time went on, and it seemed clear that these different reactions were influenced by the ability of the foster parents to make the visits positive rather than negative experiences. Some of the foster parents clearly took on a teaching as well as a maternal role with the parents. One area of difficulty mentioned by several parents was that of visits for the extended family. Several of the parents commented that they were asked to go on their own, but that they thought it was important for the children to see relations, and also sometimes they needed relatives to provide transport or emotional support. In other cases grandparents visited regularly and were welcomed. In some cases there were problems when parents were separated in that both parents wanted to visit, and were jealous if the foster parents seemed to favour one rather than the other. Others wondered exactly what the foster parents had been told about them, especially in the neglect cases. This is an area where social workers could have been more helpful to parents if they had been more explicit about exactly what the foster parents had been told. Some parents were angered because they learned that foster parents had talked to neighbours about their problems.

The parents' comments about visiting are reported in some detail as this was an area about which they had a great deal to say.

Mother: 'It was about three weeks before I visited. I had to make the first move, but I think they did want me to visit in a way. I was always taken by the social worker. In a way the foster mother thought I was a nuisance. I couldn't make conversation. I didn't know what to say. I think they wanted to keep him. I used to swear under my breath and think, you've got my baby and I can't have him. I stayed about twenty minutes. I played with him. Gave him a few things. You feel as if you are interfering. You think they look on you as somebody who can't look after children, as though they are watching you to see if you are going to drop him. In a way I enjoyed seeing him. But you get all confused, and the distance from here to there, and not having anywhere to go if you do take him out. And you think oh, what's the use. You just don't seem to bother any more. I thought, what's the point of going to see him if I'm not going to have him back. Somebody else is looking after him.'

Mother: 'Once I got used to it, I quite enjoyed it. Well, not exactly enjoyed. I didn't enjoy it. I liked going out to see her. I got tensed up every time before I went. I was resentful, not of them, they were very good foster parents, of the fact that I had to go to someone else. Somebody else had my child and I didn't think she had a right to her. Even at Christmas, we were not allowed to see her on Christmas Day. I think the worst thing, one day I said something about her medicine, and she said, oh, she was taken off that a couple of months ago. I thought, well, isn't it marvellous when your own child is taken off medication and you can't even know about it. We weren't told when she had to go to see the specialist and things like that.'

Stepmother: 'I think they bow down to the foster parents too easily by saying, "Oh, yes, only once every three weeks." He had to fight for the opportunity to continue that relationship. Not because of the department, but mainly because of the foster parents' attitude. If he had been allowed more frequent or longer access it would have been easier for them both to readjust when they came back together. It might have made things slightly more difficult when she was in the foster home, but in the long run, it would have been easier for both of them. The social services were at fault for not doing more research before she went. They thought she wasn't wanted. Or perhaps they were so taken up with the idea of having a little girl that they didn't really listen.'

Mother: 'I hated it. I used to think that she was watching me. And I couldn't express how I felt, because I didn't feel anything. I didn't play with him. She used to play with him. I went twice a week, but out of duty. I thought that I ought to, seeing as he was coming home sometime.'

Mother: 'I found her a very "aweing" lady. I took them sweets and toys. She used to always put them on a shelf, and they would always be still there when I went next week. It was very unpleasant to know your kids weren't with *you*. I had to pluck up my courage every week. I always got upset, you see.'

Father: 'I don't think they minded how often we visited, the idea was that we saw her so that she didn't forget us, but not so much as to upset her daily life.'

Father: 'When I used to go in they used to say hello, but I knew they didn't like me. I wasn't allowed to take them out. It was terrible. I just went over to see them and that was that. My wife's family were allowed to visit, but my mum wasn't. My name was mud over there.'

Mother: 'I had to stop going to see the others. I was so mad. I just wouldn't speak about it. I used to go once a fortnight. Then they came and said: "You aren't my mum. That's my dad, and that's my mum." Their minds have been turned. The social worker wanted me to talk about it in front of the foster parents, and I just lost my temper and said, I'm off, because there would have been trouble, if I'd talked to them. Now every time I think about it, I just feel sick.'

Father: 'My wife was so upset about them being mum and dad, that when we had them out all day, she wouldn't go near to take them back, in case she lost her temper. She didn't want to know the people, and the next day, she just walked off.'

Father: 'They were told we had knocked her about, so we never told them anything, and didn't say a lot at first. They always used to sit in the room with us. They wouldn't go and get on with things and let us talk to her. I think they were told they had to. They thought we were going to pinch her back. We were supposed to be allowed an hour a week but they used to let us stay longer.'

Mother: 'The social worker took us out. I was glad of the introduction but not of him sitting there. He was there to see how I reacted, and he thought maybe I would get stroppy.'

Mother: 'I couldn't really talk to her. She never did condemn me. But everybody knew why she had got him, because she told everybody.'

Mother: 'Later on I took him out. They wouldn't let me at first. I had to see him in their house. We just used to all sit there. Not that she was nasty, because she wasn't. I just felt that she was.'

Mother: 'She is a perfect lady. We sat down, and we used to talk. I can sit and talk about my problems. I said, "Do you think I can take him out?" She says, "Yes, certainly!" She said, "He is under my roof, so I don't see why not." They were under her care, and she was responsible for what happened, that's what she mean.'

Visits to children in residential care

Parents and social workers had far less to say about visiting children in residential care. On the whole they enjoyed visits to the larger establishments, which with their larger staff were more able to find the time to be welcoming to parents. Smaller establishments sometimes presented the same problems for parents as foster homes, in that houseparents were more likely to feel that their routine was being disrupted. As many of the children in residential care were older, the children were not usually perceived as at risk at the hands of their parents, and thus more of them went home to visit, and parents did not have a sense of being watched. Some comments about parents' visits to children in residential care were:

Social worker: 'It was difficult to get the parents through the door. I wanted them to see what the place was about, and the houseparents tried to get them to come in, but they only once went in. Partly, Bill didn't want them in. He was ashamed of them. As soon as the car appeared in the road, he shot off.'

Father: 'We enjoyed visiting. You are left alone with your boy. Nobody stands over you. You have got your son as though he were your own.'

Mother: 'We used to make a family reunion of it. My other daughter used to go as well with her children. They let us take him out every week. Oh, yes. We did enjoy it. I rather miss it now he's back home.'

Father: 'The matron used to go up to his bedroom when he was upset and try to get him to have a cup of tea. She said, "We are ever so pleased you can come and see him. He looks forward to his phone calls".'

Social worker: 'The visits were difficult, because they were highly critical. Were they there to see the children, or were they there to work out their own feelings, to prove that they were not in the wrong? It didn't go down well with the houseparents. It upset the organisation of the home.'

Social worker: 'She didn't enjoy visiting, because she was embarrassed. It was so very difficult to communicate with him, and she does find it so very difficult to show any warmth towards him. I tried to encourage her to go. I offered to take her. But in the end, I took him home to visit her.'

Mother: 'The thing that got me. I was only allowed to visit once a fortnight. And then they didn't like it. Most of the other children didn't have visitors, you see. They weren't used to it. The social worker said, "Stay away for two or three months and let them settle".'

Father: 'At no time did she offer to take us except the first time when she said, "I must come with you!" She seemed to be spying on us all the time. I used to phone them up once a week, and they wouldn't let me speak to them once. I said why not, and they said the social services stopped it. The social worker told me she thought I might be running my phone bill up too much.'

Mother: 'She insisted on staying with us. We were ushered into the waiting room. The social worker sat there on sentry duty. The children were upset. They said it was because I had gone to see them too soon. It was nearly a fortnight before I was allowed to see them again, and they said that if I went to see them without their permission, they would tell the police.'

Mother: 'I visited every Saturday. I had to catch three buses. I used to leave at nine in the morning, and get back at nine at night. I was there two and a half hours and the rest of the time was travelling. They never offered to help with the fare.'

Mother: 'It was difficult getting there with the other children. We have to rely on people giving us lifts. They should try and have a mini bus. I've discussed it with other parents. We could all pay so much. I worry about it being so far. What would happen if she was ill. I suppose they would get the police to get me.'

Mother: 'None of our relatives were allowed to visit. The only way I can get the relatives to see the children is by getting them to drive me there.'

SOME ADMINISTRATIVE AND LEGAL FACTORS WHICH AFFECTED DECISIONS

The Juvenile Court and the social services committee

The cases of all except one of the children were at some stage considered by a Juvenile Court, or a Magistrates Court (Matrimonial Proceedings); and that one, together with eight other children from four families, was the subject of a resolution of parental rights by the social services committee (see Appendix I).

The reports for the court were prepared by the social worker in twenty-nine cases, and by the probation officer in five cases. Social workers and parents were asked if they thought that a court appearance was necessary, and also what they thought had been the effect on the parents and children of the court appearance. Social workers were also asked about their reasons for recommending different courses of action to the court, and particularly the differences they saw between recommending a care order intending to place the child at home, and recommending a supervision order. The advantages and disadvantages of the use of Section 2 of the Children Act as opposed to court action were also discussed.

Although in the majority of cases the social workers had initiated court action, this was not so in seven cases where action was initiated by the police, and in a further three where the custody of the children was decided by the court as part of matrimonial proceedings. With seven families the social workers thought that court action or the assumption of parental rights was not necessary, and in two other cases the workers interviewed had not been involved at the time but thought it probably could and should have been avoided. In twelve cases the parents thought that court action or a

Section 2 resolution was not necessary, in five cases they were not sure, and only in eight cases did they think it was necessary. (These included the three matrimonial court cases, a case of non-accidental injury, and four cases of delinquency.)

The main reasons given by social workers for initiating court action were: to get more control over a situation in order to protect a child; to be able to make consistent plans for him; or (usually in conjunction with the others) to have access to more resources, whether residential or financial. As mentioned in Chapter 6, the decision to go to court was sometimes very much part of a treatment plan which had been discussed with the parents, so that even if they did not agree they had been told that it might happen. In other cases, where a child had already been on probation, the parents could see that a progression to a care order was probably inevitable when a child re-offended. Sometimes, however, the decision to take statutory action came very much as a shock, and this was particularly so if children had gone into care voluntarily, and parental rights were assumed at a later date.

Mother: 'They thought it was very necessary for her to go away. I, no. At the time I did need a rest, because I had been up at night so much. It would have helped if they had offered to take her for a while for a holiday. That way they are not telling you you are useless.'

Father: 'They took the children away for a few days whilst we sorted ourselves out. They said they had to take a Place of Safety Order because that was the only way to get them into a children's home.'

Mother: 'I would have agreed to him going into care, but not a full care order. I would have left him till he was better, so there was no need for the court.'

Father: 'It came to court because my wife left me, and I was in a terrible state. They said, "After you have had a rest, you can have the children back." Then they took it to court. That turned me against them.'

Only one parent appealed against the decision of the juvenile court to crown court, where the original decision to make a care order was changed and a supervision order made. In another case, parents who strongly disagreed with the court decision seem not to have been advised that they could appeal, and so waited until the child had been in care for six months and then applied for a revocation of the care order. In this case also a supervision order was made. In one other case parents applied for revocation but lost their application, and in another case the original application for a care order was not granted, and a supervision order made. In the three cases where supervision orders were made when the social services department had asked for care orders, the work of the social workers was particularly difficult because of the resentment which the adversorial system of the court had helped to engender. In particular, if the parents are given the impression that the case being made was not proved, then the parents tend not to accept the need for the social worker to visit. In two of the cases the court did seem to be saying that there was insufficient evidence, in which case a supervision order should not have been made. It would be far more helpful for the social workers and families in such cases if the court, when making a supervision order, made it absolutely clear to the parents that even if they did not feel that a care order was necessary, they had found the child to be 'in need of care or control which he is unlikely to receive unless the court makes an order'. In contested cases it would be more helpful if the court were much more specific about why they were making a supervision order, and consulted the social workers about any special requirements.

Mother: 'The court didn't say anything about him examining her. He said he had to, but the magistrate just said, "If you need help of any sort, just get in touch with the social worker".'

Mother: 'The judge said the social services should never have taken him in the first place. They were in the wrong. So he gave him back to me with a supervision order.'

Social workers were asked if they welcomed the power of the court under the 1975 Children Act, to appoint a 'guardian ad litem' in care cases. A few knew too little about it to comment, one thought it was not a good idea, but the majority welcomed the idea, although wanted to see how it worked out in practice. One worker said she thought it essential that the 'guardian ad litem' should not be making recommendations in a vacuum, and should have a sound knowledge of the care resources available in the area. At the moment the court is required to appoint a 'guardian ad litem' only in cases of applications for the revocation of an order which the social services department is not opposing. However, the fact that in this study the court's decision to return three children home against social services advice seems to have been a reasonable decision for the child, does lead me to suggest that a 'guardian ad litem' should also be appointed to assist the court when the social services department is opposing either an appeal against a care order or a Section 2 resolution, or an application for revocation.

Apart from these three cases, and two others where care orders on delinquent children were made when supervision orders were recommended, the courts followed the recommendations of the court reports.

Supervision orders or care orders for children going home?

How then did social workers decide what to recommend to the courts for these children where home standards caused concern, but where they were hoping to keep the family unit together, or to work towards rehabilitation? As mentioned above, none of the supervision orders had a condition for intermediate treatment attached, and only one had a condition requiring the parents to give the social worker access to the child. When asked whether they preferred supervision orders or care orders for children who were likely to go home, all the workers said they preferred care orders, except for older children where offences were minor and home conditions fairly adequate.

'A supervision order is seen as a periodic reporting or checking up, rather than a full involvement of the social worker. A care order gives a sense of more fully sharing responsibility for a child, and also gives access to financial help. Supervision orders are all right for petty offences by youngsters but I find them quite difficult to work with in cases of child neglect. I don't think the courts are aware of the difficulties of social work contact with supervision order cases. The parent has more of a commitment to the social worker where there is a care order, and is seen as more involved with us in sharing future plans.'

'I'm not very keen on supervision orders. They don't give you the power to do anything other than visit. If a case warrants a care order, I would rather work with that. Supervision orders tend to be made in cases where voluntary help would be acceptable. If parents don't want the help, there is no point in visiting them, and if it is serious enough to overrule them, it is better to have a care order.'

'A care order "home on trial" sometimes is hard for the parents to understand. He's your responsibility, but we have to look after him. In some respects I prefer a supervision order when a child is at home - giving more power to the parents' elbow - but then you go back to the current climate. Where a child has been injured in the past, I prefer a care order because I know I can remove him immediately.'

'With a care order we act as the parent, and I make sure they have everything they need. Whereas with a supervision order, you have to make a much stronger case for helping with clothing.'

'I find it difficult to recommend a supervision order. I like to have all the resources of the department available for my work with the child. The removal from home bit of a care order is of secondary importance. The emphasis here tends to be, if one recommends a care order, the child has to go for assessment. I don't agree with that. I think it was a great advantage for him to be on a care order at home. Often they go straight to the assessment centre - one tends to visit once a month - and you are trying to build up a relationship! I was able to make a commitment to him, and keep that commitment.'

'A court's interpretation of a supervision order is so unclear. It is seen as up to the department how to interpret it, but there is always a slightly uneasy feeling behind it. Whereas, with home on trial, particularly if you are involved with the decision in the first place, there should be some contract between the worker and the family, as to what it means, what the conditions are. One is landed with a supervision order by the court.'

'Although she is on a supervision order, I don't see them in that context at all. I am there to help, and they see me as a helper rather than a supervisor.'

The parents could also see the value of care orders, but were worried by the power it gave the social worker to make decisions about their children of which they might not approve.

Mother: 'I don't mind the supervision order, because if anything goes wrong, say if he is ill or has an accident, I can get a social worker to help. If there wasn't a supervision order I couldn't just ring up, and say, "He's hurt, will you take me to the hospital?".'

Mother: 'It's different from probation because if you break your probation they either fine you, or put you back on probation. She's broken her probation three times. The care order is more serious. For the time being, a care order is better than a supervision order. She knows if she does anything wrong they will take her away. That is good for her. That does bother me though – legally. I don't have very much right, do I? I've talked to him about it. He has more hold over her than I have. When she is sixteen I'm going back to court to get it changed.'

Mother: 'I talked to the social worker yesterday about it. I said, "Once she comes home, I shall have nothing to do with you rotten lot." She said, "You will have to see me." I said, "Fair enough, I will see you, but I will want the care order changed to a supervision order".'

Mother: 'The care order is till he is eighteen. That sticks in your mind. As to the social worker coming, that doesn't worry me. I don't mind as long as Bill is at home.'

Father: 'How they explained it to me, he was in the care of the county, and if anything did go wrong, they could come and take him straight away, and we would have nothing to say about it whatsoever. I agree with it in a way, though.'

Mother: 'I never really think about it in that way. I think, he's mine, so the care order doesn't really bother me.'

10-year-old boy: 'A supervision order means you are under care, and if anything happens they come and take you.' To the question, "Is that good?" there was a vehement "No. The social worker came to check up on us."'

Mother: 'We still can't have her legally ours, not for some time. The social worker says she will do it. We could go to court now, off our own back, but we are more likely to get refused until she agrees. Which is fair enough. I will be relieved, though. Because, right now I know they can actually walk in if they feel like it, and maybe take her away.'

In only four cases (five children) had the care order been revoked, and one supervision order had been completed. In two of the four, revocation was against the advice of the social worker. There seemed to be a fairly general reluctance on the part of the social workers to apply for the discharge of care orders. On the whole this was because they felt that the parents did not really mind, and that the existence of the care order allowed them to continue to have access and to offer practical help. None of the workers was planning to apply for a revocation within the next six months; in thirteen cases they said they would oppose if the parents applied; but in four cases they said they would not oppose, but would not take the initiative. The social workers thought that all the parents knew how to apply for revocation of the order, and in fifteen cases they had discussed it, but in five cases they had not. Only in seven cases had the social workers advised the parents to discuss the position with a solicitor, but all said they would do so if the parents wanted to apply, and they intended to oppose.

Mother: 'I've never thought about getting it cancelled. Most probably, I would lose anyway.'

Mother: 'I shall be glad when the supervision order is over. Not so much now, because this social worker doesn't make me feel she is coming to spy on me. Even when it's finished, if I needed help, I would ask her.'

Social worker: 'She is quite capable of not letting me in. That's why I still need the care order.'

Social worker: 'I will apply for revocation when he comes to be settled, and has enough maturity to be independent.'

Social worker: 'I'll consider applying when things have been settled for about six months, when there is a sort of "jogging along" feeling.'

Mother: 'I now want to adopt my children jointly with my second husband. I want to get this care order off first. I can't go through it all again. I just can't.'

Mother: 'We will never be a happy family until we get the care order finished. With all this interference, this to-ing and fro-ing. At one time, the social worker always used to turn up at a meal time. Let's face it, the sooner we get back to normal, the better. You can't be normal like that.'

The comments seem to suggest that although the families were not too hostile to the care orders, there was more resentment of their continued existence than the social workers thought.

It may well be that there is a need for an order which falls somewhere between a care order and a supervision order precisely for that group of families which is the subject of this study. A full care order, with the possibility of the child being in care until the age of eighteen, and leaving a rather ambiguous situation when the children went home on trial, clearly caused anxiety, and was not really appropriate for a situation lasting for years. However, the supervision order was not thought by the social workers to give adequate protection to the child, or to sanction the intervention of the social worker to the extent which was felt to be necessary in most of these cases. The supervision order could be strengthened more often that it now is with intermediate treatment orders and special requirements, as for instance, that the child should attend day care. The name 'supervision order' itself gives a false impression to magistrates, parents and children of the nature of the help offered. It has been stated above that it is impossible to 'supervise', particularly young children, if they are in their own homes, and their parents are not willing to co-operate. The social workers wanted care orders so that they could help the parents to care for their children, and act immediately if the child needed protection. It would therefore seem that the present supervision orders with conditions for intermediate treatment could be used for children of all ages, preferably with the name changed to 'intermediate care orders', or 'home care orders' which would accurately convey the nature of the service offered. Such orders would give social workers access to the child and the power and indeed the duty to provide as much practical and social work help as would ensure that the child's needs were adequately met. It might also allow them, as does the present intermediate treatment order, to remove a child from home for a limited period, but would require them to go back to court if an extended period in care were needed. Since the study was undertaken more use has been made of supervision orders with intermediate treatment clauses, and this may have changed the attitudes of social workers to supervision orders for older children.

Assumption of parental rights

Nine of the children from four families were the subjects of parental rights resolutions by the social services committee. (See Appendix I for a discussion of this procedure.) With two families the children had been in care for some time under the voluntary provisions of Section 1 of the 1948 Act, and it was not until later that it was decided that it was necessary to assume parental rights. This is the usual way in which parental rights are assumed. In two cases, when the children were initially received into care, as their parents thought voluntarily, the decision to assume parental rights was taken straight away. In the one case it was felt that there was not enough evidence to take the case to court under the 1969 Act, and in the other case the parents were told shortly after the children went away that the case would be taken to court if they did not agree to the assumption of parental rights.

The decision to receive children into care voluntarily and to pass a Section 2 resolution immediately, rather than to make a Place of Safety Order on the children, and then apply to court for a care order as was done in other cases in the study, is a controversial one. To some extent in all these cases it was done with the best intentions of protecting the child, and avoiding for the parents a court appearance. However, in three of the four cases where parental rights were taken there was a deep resentment on the part of the parents, especially when they were taken immediately after the parents had agreed to voluntary care. In all four cases the parents technically consented to the resolution, but in reality three of them felt coerced. Also, even if they technically consented they all received a formal letter telling them of the reason; and all found the legal language, and lack of a chance to defend themselves, as hurtful, if not more so, than those parents who went to court. In one case, having already been to court and had identifiable details in the press, they did not feel inclined to appeal and risk a similar experience; and the other parents who considered appealing did not wish to risk the possibility of publicity. Also, both of these families did want their children to be in care at that time, and therefore did not want to go to court to ask for the resolution to be withdrawn if they were not actually certain that it was the right thing for their children to come home there and then.

Mother: 'We had to sign it, to agree to them taking parental responsibility. They forced the issue, and we had no rights. We asked for help, and the next thing, they brought the paper to sign over our parental rights. When it was pressed, it was said they were afraid we would go over and take her from the home. Which was complete nonsense, since we had asked for her to go there. They forced it, and there was no right of appeal, only by going to court. I would have appealed if I could have been sure it would be absolutely private.'

Mother: 'We got this letter about persistent and wilful neglect, which was absolutely untrue. It disgusted me.'

Mother: 'I had to go up to the office. The probation officer was there too. The social worker said, "Do you mind signing this?" I said, "What's it for?" and she said, "It's just to say he is going to be looked after for a little while." I signed, and that was the parental rights. They didn't mention anything about parental rights. They just waved it in front of me. I couldn't understand nothing. They didn't explain anything. They never said anything about going to a lawyer and appealing. No one gave you any advice or nothing. I like things explained to me. You know, what you are supposed to do and what they are supposed to mean. They didn't explain what it was all about till I asked my mother after he came home. She said, "They come round and keep an eye on you".'

Father: 'He brought this letter. I said, "Are you saying we have neglected them?" He said, "It's not that, but it's the nearest sub-heading we have got".'

Mother: 'I remember the social worker saying when we got the children back, if ever you get worried about things, ring up and we will come out and sort things out. So we had a talk, and he said, "I just can't stand it, you will have to get the children away for a while." He was really feeling ill, so I thought I would ring up and see what they had to say. They came out in the evening. They were very nice and reassuring. He said, "Would you like a break, perhaps for a month or so? Perhaps they came out too quick last time." He said, "You won't have to go to court, nothing like that. Just sign a form for voluntary care." So we did, and I talked to the children, and said, "Do you mind going away for a little while?" So they went. Two days later he came and said, "I've come for the children's clothes. We've decided that the children will benefit from being away for a long period." They were going to go to court, but then they called us to the office. They said, "We've got these forms, that will save you a lot of bother." We were a bit upset and we didn't see why we should have to go to court. They were so prejudiced against us last time. Having experienced the twisting of our case last time, we didn't know what they were going to drag up. They glossed over what we were signing. They said it didn't matter really as far as we were concerned. He didn't say anything about parental rights. It certainly was not clear to us at the time what we were signing, that it was till they were eighteen. I rang the solicitor about it. He said, "You have already signed that form now, it's too late to do anything about it now. You are better off under that than a care order".'

Mother: 'What I am saying, in the hope of helping people in the future, there should be a right of appeal apart from dragging people through the courts, which I think is a basic failing in the system.'

Reactions to court

One of the above comments shows that a court appearance could be a very unpleasant experience for some of these families, even though the Juvenile Court is intended to have a treatment rather than a punitive role. None of the parents in the study was prosecuted in the adult courts for an offence against the children, so that the comments all apply to the matrimonial courts or Juvenile Courts.

All except two of the parents interviewed found the court appearance upsetting, even if they had no complaint about how the court was conducted. Several parents complained about being 'made to feel like a criminal', and about the length of time they were kept waiting, thus missing work. Another complaint was of the number of court appearances for one case. In particular they thought that if a remand was likely, it should not be necessary for the parents and children to attend, if they accepted the need for a remand. Although no specific question was asked about family courts, my general impression was that the present formal court experience was seen as punitive by the parents as well as the children, and did not encourage a constructive attitude on their part so that the best plan for the children could be worked out. The following comments by parents represent the range of opinions about court.

Mother: 'The court? It was all above my head. I didn't really care at the time. The psychiatrist had put me on so many drugs. I remember the social worker saying, "You have to go to court. I will go with you".'

Mother: 'I admit that for battered babies and that, there has got to be court cases. But I hadn't hurt them, there was no need for a court case. Why can't they just sit and have a talk about the child, and about what is going to happen.'

Father: 'I went to court with him. I felt terrible. Shaking like a leaf. I am a big man, but anything like that, I break down easily. I didn't want him to go away. I could hardly say anything. They wanted me to say what had happened and bring back memories, and there are a lot of people in there, and he would feel silly. They took him out after a while, because I broke down.'

Father: 'You have three or four months waiting before you go to court. And this was for a pint of milk. It's enough to give you a nervous breakdown. I mean, if a child does something, you don't wait three months and then give it a smack. You lose ever so much time off work. I had to go three or four times. It's £10 a day. And they just mess you about. I was there thirteen hours over three days. You can't even go outside. You just have to wait. I'm already punished, and then I am punished again when I go in.'

Mother: 'I didn't agree with anything the court did. There is no justice in these courts. I think once you have been in trouble and you come up in court again, they think you are no good, and shove you away.'

Mother: 'We went to two courts, the first was awful. The second, the magistrates spoke to those boys very nicely. I think that gets further with the children. I don't think it helps to scare them.'

Mother: 'They were very understanding. The social worker came and made a report. She spoke for me, and said I was a good mother but they were out of my control. I was doing it for their sake, not for my sake.'

Mother: 'I felt terrible. My legs were like jelly. I didn't want to go. The social worker took me. When I went into the witness box, my legs were shaking. I felt on trial. The social worker came into the box and put his arm round me. It was upsetting when they said she would have to go away, but I got a fair hearing.'

Father: 'I had a solicitor. He was helping me as much as he could. Not just for the court. But how I felt. When I walked into court I was crying my eyes out. The magistrate said, "Instead of standing in the witness box, would you sit down, because you are in a state." I didn't get a hearing at all. The welfare was on my missus' side. And everything they said she agreed with. I didn't get a hearing at all. I think there should have been a paper shown to me for my rights, I understood nothing. My wife's solicitor had a go at me for about ten minutes. I didn't have a clue what he was on about. The magistrates had no chance, there was that strong pressure against me.'

Mother: 'We met the social workers in court. Three people sitting on a bench. Like Perry Mason. You don't think it is actually happening. The lawyer was a young chap. It was his first case of that sort. He did the best he could. We hadn't met him until we went into court. Before the court, one of us saw one chap, and next time we saw another chap, and we didn't even know the name of the chap who was going to be in court.'

On the whole, those parents who contacted a lawyer seemed to have been satisfied with the service offered, but in at least three cases they were wrongly advised, and there did seem to be a lack of expertise in child care cases, and also some uncertainty about whom the solicitor was actually representing. This is not surprising, as the solicitor in fact represents the child, the parents having no status in the court in care proceedings and therefore no right to legal aid. Since it is the parents who contact the solicitor on behalf of the child, they tend to see him as 'their' solicitor. The parents I interviewed did not seem to realise that they were themselves not parties to the proceedings, though some were made aware of the fact by the court. This question of separate representation for parents and children where their interests may conflict needs to be considered as a matter of urgency as the present situation is not satisfactory for anyone.

Father: 'I went in there and tried to say what the situation was, but I wasn't allowed to speak.'

It is in order to ensure that all concerned are adequately represented that these cases are increasingly being taken to the High Court under wardship proceedings.

Two further points were made by social workers and parents. Although the names of juveniles are not usually revealed by the press, the very detailed reporting of some of these cases was contrary to the spirit of the requirement not to reveal names, in that, especially in small villages, families were very easily identified, and parents and children suffered considerable embarrassment as a result of publicity.

Social workers and parents also commented about the way that the lawyers for the social services department sometimes made their case. There was some feeling amongst the social workers that the lawyers were sometimes not sufficiently 'au fait' with the intricacies of this sort of case, and that the way evidence was sometimes presented in court made their own task of continuing to work with the family considerably more difficult than it need have been. In Chapter 6 mention was made of the fact that some families were reluctant to tell social workers about their difficulties in case their comments should be repeated, sometimes out of context, in court.

Mother: 'I think they were twisting the evidence. When the social worker first came, he used to ask different things, and he would sit and listen. I said one day that our other boy was a handful. So when we got to court he said I couldn't cope with him either. At the foster home we weren't allowed to take her out of the house, and they always had her fed and changed when we got there. But at court the social services solicitor said, "You never even bothered to feed the baby or change her, or take her for walks." For months we had been trying to get permission to take her out.'

Mother: 'Our solicitor got on to the county solicitor before the case and they agreed about a supervision order. What got me at the court case, the social worker produced photos of me and inferred that the children had been beaten up like that as well. There was one tiny bruise on one of the children, but the papers next day said the children had been seriously bruised. If the reporters took it like that, the magistrate must have done. I never gave my permission for the doctor to give evidence about me. I was shocked at what was said about us. That's why I don't want to go back to court. I just wish to luck and chance it. I know it would be a waste of time. They would bring it all up again. Rather than lose face and give them back to us, they would just whisk them away. I complained to the social worker and the solicitor. They said there is nothing you can do about it now. Just be grateful you have got them home.'

Mother: 'They more or less ganged up on me. You know, when you have a child taken away and you get upset and say things you don't mean. Now the social worker wrote it all down. I don't think that was right, to bring up in court what I said when I was upset.'

Management and the decision-making process

As mentioned in Chapter 1, not only the social workers but also several of the parents were aware of the debate about child care policy and especially about non-accidental injury to children. Both felt that recent inquiries following the deaths of children had meant that social work with children at risk and their families was looked at differently from work with other cases. In particular, managers above the level of senior social worker were more likely to be involved in the decisions in such cases; and indeed the DHSS circulars on non-accidental injury to children have required local authorities to set up Area Review Committees, to arrange case conferences involving a wide range of professional opinion from outside the social services department, and to set up registers of families whose children have been non-accidentally injured, are at risk of being injured, or are failing to thrive. (5) None of the families mentioned the registers, and it was my impression that they were not aware of their existence, although I did not ask a direct question about them. However, several commented about the involvement in the decisions of others besides their own social worker and the courts, and especially about case conferences.
    Although there was general agreement that it was necessary for agencies to share information about families where the children were at risk, social workers had mixed feelings about whether case conferences, either those held within the department or the external conferences advocated by the Area Review Committee, should actually be making decisions about placement. The DHSS circulars and many writers on the subject suggest that decisions should be made jointly, but other writers, notably Howells (1974), urge strongly that the professional workers involved, in this case the social

workers, should be responsible for obtaining all the advice and information which is available, but should then make their own decisions and be held accountable for those decisions. The majority, but not all of the social workers interviewed, held this view, although most wanted the senior social worker to be involved in the making of the decision, especially for unqualified or inexperienced workers. Those parents who commented felt very strongly that the social worker should be the one to make the decision, or, failing that, that they should be allowed to put their point of view to whoever was making the decision.

Typical comments from the parents were:

'If they would just leave it to her, she knows what she is doing. I've seen the senior social worker once or twice, but he doesn't know me as well as she knows me.'

'The houseparents and the social worker would have let them home earlier. What they are battling with is the committee - who have never set eyes on us.'

'I would say the social worker wants to help. I think if it was left to people like him, the people in the lower ranks, making the decisions rather than the higher ups, if they could reverse the whole system, it would be a lot better, because they are the people who are actually in contact with us.'

'By the time it came back to court, I think they thought they had made the wrong decision. But they still opposed his going home. They were all there, the senior social worker, the lot. The social worker hasn't got any power at all. He has to go to his head and ask permission for me to do anything. I think the social worker should have his own responsibility. What is the use of the senior social worker making decisions when the social worker knew me all the way through.'

'They've got too much power up there. If they've got something on their minds, nothing will sway them.'

'The social worker just passes the report on to the others to read. You aren't a person to them.'

'By that time, all the higher ups had made up their minds. They don't know us, do they? The social worker came back and said, "Look here, I'm sorry, the seniors want to keep them longer, and want to put them under a care order".'

As mentioned above, the social workers' views were more varied, and even those who thought that they should ultimately make the decision were conscious of the pressures which the parents could put upon them. In Chapter 6 it was noted that the social workers did often care about these parents more than most of their clients, and several commented that this being so it was essential that they should have good professional consultation, as well as managerial supervision, which would allow them to come to balanced decisions. Most felt that the senior social workers were the appropriate colleagues to offer this, and that above that level the supervision ceased to be of value. One social worker who worked closely with a senior colleague felt that if both knew the family and were involved in the therapy, important decisions should be discussed with a third person, experienced in child care but not involved in any way with the parents or child. The findings of this study are in line with Olive Stevenson's report of attitudes towards work with cases of non-accidental injury referred to in Chapter 1.

> The social workers referred, not simply to the professional anxiety which such situations created, but to their fear of being found wanting and called to account (Stevenson and Parsloe, 1978, p.302).

The above comments of the parents and the social workers' views are echoed in her insistence on the need for professional self-awareness.

> Important as it is that the meaning and structure of accountability should be clarified, the agencies in which the social worker operates have also an obligation to provide an environment conducive to professional development, and supervision is an important element in that. For, in the last analysis, this is the best protection for clients and transcends formal systems of checks and controls, although these are needed as well (Stevenson, op.cit.).

Social workers were asked who made the important decisions about where the child should be placed, and whether and when he should go home? Most of the workers strongly stressed the importance of involving the child and the parents in both these decisions, although they felt that with statutory as opposed to voluntary child care cases the decision should be taken by someone from the department. To the question: 'Who should make the decision about child placement?' six said it should be the social worker; four said it should be the social worker and senior jointly; two said it should be the area officer, senior and social worker; one said that in cases of children at risk, it should be the case conference; and six were undecided, and said it depended very much on the case. The answers to the question as to who actually made the decision about placement of the children concerned, and whether the children should go home, are summarised in Table 7.3.

TABLE 7.3 Level at which decisions about placement and about return home were made

	Placement when in care	Decision to let child go home
Social worker	8	0
Social worker and senior social worker	11	14
Senior social worker	1	0
Social worker, senior and residential division	4	2
Departmental case conference	1	9
External case conference (N.A.I.)	0	4
Court	1	5
Don't know	5	0
	31	34

Although the court is not normally involved in decisions about placement of children in care, in one of these cases such a strong recommendation for assessment was made that this was not questioned. In two other cases the court made strong recommendations when making care orders for the children to be placed at home.

Social workers were asked whose opinion they thought carried the most weight in the decision and whether they agreed with the decision. Often the social worker interviewed was not involved in the decision about placements, but of those who were, most said they agreed, but three did not. Table 7.4 gives the answers to the question, about whose opinion carried most weight.

TABLE 7.4 Most influential person in decision about return home according to social workers

	Number of children
Social worker	10
Senior social worker	0
Area officer	1
'Very much joint departmental decision'	1
Parent	10
Child	5
Residential worker	4
Don't know	3

Most of the social workers agreed with the decision to return the children home, although in four cases reluctantly because in one case nothing better was available, and in the other three the parent was pressing very strongly and there were no good grounds to oppose. In three cases they disagreed with the court's decision to return children, and in one case a social worker disagreed with a court's decision not to return a child. Also, in two cases the social workers agreed with the decisions of case conferences to return children, but thought that the return was unnecessarily delayed. The following comments of social workers illustrate the wide range of views and rather mixed feelings about the involvement of senior management and case conferences in decision making.

'You need a lot of knowledge. You have got to have a person who can use a team approach, who doesn't want to go out on his own. But you have to be prepared to have views and give your views. I don't think any one person should struggle on his own. Last time I went to pass on a conference decision, I felt very angry and said I am not going on my own again. This happens all the time, the poor old social worker goes out to face it. The most junior person. I really felt the area officer should go.'

'The decision about home should be shared with the parents, the child, the social worker, and the foster parents. I don't find any level above that valid. You need a senior for consultation, but beyond that it becomes an institutional decision. I'd rather see social workers more experienced, longer trained, and accountable for those decisions.'

'The parents know that you have to go back, and they know where the responsibility lies, and I have had to explain why the pressures against him coming home are what they are.'

'You see, this is a N.A.I. case. That bears on the way I handle the case. My actions reflect the climate of opinion, the anxieties.'

'They send you out to make a decision on the spot. You decide what to do, and discuss it with the parents, and when you come back to the office, your decision isn't accepted by the powers that be. They say it won't do, and you have the job of going back and telling them that something else has to be done - take the child for an X-ray or something.'

Parents and social workers held the same sorts of view about external case conferences as they did about departmental hierarchies. Parents felt more hostile to case conferences than did social workers, but both thought that parents should be given the chance to be present, or to be told the lines along which the conference was thinking, so that they could at least give their views through the social worker if important decisions might be taken such as the assumption of parental rights, or the decision to oppose the child going home. Parents were very conscious of how important it was that the social worker should be able to put their views strongly if they themselves were not present, and in two cases felt that decisions had been taken due to a misunderstanding which they would have been able to correct had they been there. Parents felt that in some cases decisions were taken more in order to protect the agency from possible adverse publicity than to protect the child. Some social workers felt that there was a danger of inexperienced or unqualified workers being overawed by the senior people from their own and other agencies, and not putting their own views and those of the family sufficiently strongly. If the parents are not present, the social worker has a dual role of speaking for the parents in their absence, and giving his own professional view. Although many families would still need support if they attended, the social workers' role might be less ambiguous.

Social worker: 'The parents were involved in the case conference, and the foster parents. We thrashed out visiting in this way. We wanted us all to be saying the same things in front of each other, so that nobody could go back on it.'

Social worker: 'I went along to the second case conference with the explanation they gave, and was really put down by the doctors. I was made to feel very small. The difficulty was that I had no definite ideas because it was all so new. I was most submissive. But I suppose, on the whole, I agreed with the decision.'

Social worker: 'There was a risk that after all the work somebody would decide against her going home at the final conference. We made up our minds that we would appeal to the director if that happened. We would have been prepared to be persuaded at the conference by strong evidence. But if someone with very little acquaintance with the case had ruled the day, we would not just have accepted it.'

Social worker: 'I didn't agree with the case conference decision, but I didn't feel secure enough to stand against the majority. The parents still had, and have, very serious problems.'

Mother: 'It wasn't till I stuck out and said I wanted a case conference where I was present that I got to know anything of all this.'

Social worker: 'In theory a case conference should decide. But they vary so much. It depends who is there. Some are better than others.'

Mother: 'They said at the outset, our purpose is to get the child back home. But never at any time unless you make an absolute fuss are you involved in any case conference to consider the possibilities of how to get them back, what to do, how they are progressing. What really upsets me, unless people make a fuss, they just get downtrodden, overridden altogether.'

Father: 'Obviously it is better if the parents are there. They are controlling somebody's future and life without any reference to them. They didn't come to try to verify what was said at the meetings. If there is to be a case conference, then to avoid misunderstandings and misconceptions, and to try to get the parents to help to get the children back, they should be involved in the case conference.'

Social worker: 'They put forward at the conference, shall we say an obstacle race. For instance, they tend to say they must see a psychiatrist, to assess whether they are stable enough. They want to test the parents out; they erect barriers to test them out, which the social worker has to persuade them to comply with. Sometimes you get the feeling that you end up satisfying nobody, that is the sort of pressure which the social workers are under in N.A.I. cases.'

Social worker: 'They view me with apprehension. Because though I say I will try to achieve certain things I am governed by the N.A.I. conference on this case. Anything I want to do, I have to take back, so I can't give them a concrete answer. I feel as if I am carrying the committee on my back.'

Social worker: 'It's a rather emotional question for me, having been involved in case conferences and not really agreed with the decision. But I think N.A.I. cases are a separate category, though a lot of people don't agree with me. I think you do get pretty involved, and it can be a help to come back to a more objective case conference. But it is still hard, carrying out a decision you don't agree with.'

Chapter 7

Mother: 'The only time they should have a case conference is if the people concerned are there. They can say a lot of things which might be wrong, and we aren't there to put them right. It's treated with great respect by all the social workers. They are very aware of their high-ups. They seem to be afraid of them. The social worker was very upset. She said, "I'm sorry, I didn't know it was going to come to this." She had acted on her own judgment, and felt her judgment wasn't being trusted. She hadn't got the power that the social worker is supposed to have. She can do a certain amount. People up above only know what the social workers tell them about us.'

These comments show that the right balance between the helpful sharing of responsibility and encouraging the professional autonomy essential for building up a trusting relationship is perhaps more difficult to achieve than has been recognised, and support Stevenson and Parsloe's (1978) conclusion 'that we have a very long road to travel before we can claim to be providing a service in which the compassion of individual workers is contained within and fostered by, sensitive and efficient organisational structures' (op.cit., p.302).

As mentioned above, several of the parents interviewed had followed the debate about child neglect, and the changes in the law, and I conclude with some of their more general comments.

'I don't think the social workers are too worried about the children. I think they are too worried about their jobs, when it boils down to it. With the publicity and all that, if something goes wrong, they don't like to take the risk.'

'I'll tell you what the whole trouble is, it's because of Maria Colwell and Steven Meurs and the others, they are so absolutely terrified and frightened out of their wits that they have leant over backwards in the opposite direction. Anyone new is not given the benefit of the doubt. They are so afraid of public opinion, they have gone too far in the opposite direction.'

'I suppose the social worker and the senior decided that he could come home. But I pushed it. If I hadn't pushed it, I wouldn't have had him. I mean, I suppose nowadays they would say, "Right, that's it then, get him adopted." Because they daren't take that risk any more.'

'It's making the social worker's job very difficult because they are so frightened that in my honest opinion they are not giving parents fair and balanced consideration. What frightens me, the man in the street, once he gets into the grips of the social services, he wouldn't stand a chance, because he doesn't know what his rights are, how to make a fuss, how to stick up for himself and demand to be involved.'

'If you go to your MP and he can't do anything about it, there isn't much anyone can do about it. They are a law unto themselves. There is nobody else that can sway them.'

'I didn't know about social workers, I just didn't. I don't think
you should be punished. It's bad enough, you know, having to have
them taken into care. If I had gone to prison, that wouldn't have
done any good. I don't think the thought of prison would stop you
doing it. If you really do feel that desperate, that wouldn't
stop you. It's living with it. I have to live with it now. I
married again. I couldn't marry my husband without telling him
all about it. You don't know what it's like when it comes on the
television. Well, you can see, it brings tears to my eyes just
thinking about it. I know I've done wrong. You don't know what
it's like till it happens to you. And I know that I was one of
the lucky ones. I had a good social worker, and he got better
and came home.'

'This Colwell case has put people off asking for help. I should
never ask again.'

'I rang up to say he was knocking me about. They said that's not
their problem. They don't like getting involved. If it is
children, it's a different matter. It happened again, it was
shortly after Maria Colwell. They suddenly got very nervous and
did something. I was most surprised. We never expected all the
fuss. When we rang social services when my husband took his
overdose they just didn't bother. This Colwell thing keeps
cropping up. They say, "We know you don't bash your children,
but we have to be so careful." The social worker says we've
got caught up in the scheme, and it's worth getting us caught
up in it if it saves a few lives.'

'I don't think social workers should have too much right, too
much control over children. They need to have a certain amount,
so they can take a child out when it's harmful. But what they
consider is harmful, that child might not. There might be a lot
of love there. I've read several cases. One woman really loved
her children, but they had got her down, and they took them
away. I think the social worker's main job would be to help out
the child who is coming home, and the parents at home. I think,
in my own case, he did fairly well, but I still don't think they
should have so much say to take her away. I'd like it all to
stop, now.'

'When I read a report about the new act, I grew hot under the
collar and I was stamping mad for days. I wanted to write to
the papers stating our point of view. I think parents are going
to think far more deeply before putting their children in care.
People who have put themselves out to be in the know will do
everything they can to make sure their children don't go into
care. That might be the wrong thing, but in their view, it won't
be the wrong thing, because they will be keeping their children.
They won't be giving them up, with the possibility of giving them
up for ever. In our case, we had to give them up for a while
but we were not giving them up for ever.'

Chapter 8

WHO GOES HOME? SOME CONCLUSIONS AND SUGGESTIONS FOR AN IMPROVED SERVICE

WHO GOES HOME?

One of the questions which this study sought to answer was why these particular children went home. An authoritative answer to that question would need to compare the families with a matched group whose children had stayed in care, but this was beyond the scope of this study, and would have presented much greater methodological problems. (1) However, the findings here presented, especially if read alongside the larger-scale studies of children in care of Jane Aldgate (1978a) and Rosamund Thorpe (1974b), and the comments of the parents and the social workers, do give some indication as to why the children went home.

Three major influences on the decision to let the children go home or remain at home were noted: the attitudes of parents and children and their reactions to placement; the attitudes of the social workers; and the nature of the practical and emotional support offered and of the placement.

Of these three, the author concluded that the most important factor was the determination of most of the parents, and when old enough the children, to stay together as a family. Where social work plans changed, it was usually in response to pressure from the parents and/or children, or to the unhappiness of the children when away from home. What is not clear is whether the parents' determination to get the children back was more strongly related to anger at the statutory act, and a desire to vindicate themselves; to the parents themselves feeling strongly about the importance of the 'blood tie'; or to a very real caring about the needs of their children and worrying about the harm which could come to them in care. There was evidence that all these factors were present to a varying extent in the different cases. Whatever the reason for it, this determination made several of the parents overcome the pain, discomfort, and practical difficulties of visiting, and in some cases fight long legal battles or make strenuous efforts to improve their circumstances or behaviour to get the children back home. All the social workers stressed the importance of bonds existing between the children and their parents or step-parents, and of the likelihood that with help the parents would be able to provide good enough care.

However, comparing these interviews with those of Thorpe (1974a, b) with parents whose children remained in care, it seems possible that it was parental determination, rather than any obvious differences in personality or emotional stability making them more capable of providing good enough care, which differentiated the two sets of parents. Several of the parents did still have emotional problems when their children went home, whereas several of the parents in Thorpe's study seemed to be coping satisfactorily and unaided with other children.

It was noted that social workers varied considerably in the weight they placed on different factors, such as the relative importance of natural and psychological bonds, and the importance of contact with the natural parents. Although all the workers placed some weight on bonds with the natural family (or adoptive family for those adopted in infancy), all were prepared to place children away from home if they thought it necessary, and for nineteen of the children the original plan was for them to stay in long-term care. It was suggested that social workers' attitudes towards the importance of birth identity did influence the likelihood of the children returning home, in that it influenced the decision about the level of care which would be considered good enough, and the amount of practical help and emotional support which was offered to the parents.

The skill of the social worker in mobilising resources and in relating to the parents was also important, as was the availability of resources, and particularly of the right placement if the child left home. With the majority of these families it seems likely that the determination of the parents to keep in contact would have been there without social work help, and there were cases where they insisted on regular contact despite opposition from social workers and caretakers. In other cases it was clear that considerable help and encouragement had been given, and in others that if the worker had not adopted a more positive attitude in response to their pressure at a crucial time they might have given up the struggle. The fact that social workers gave considerable time and care to these parents meant that they were on hand to pick up indications of the possibility of a successful return home. With the low level of visiting to parents of children in care described in some other studies, there would have been no social worker around to notice.

Several of the social workers were actively helping with housing, employment, and in other practical ways, so that children could return to a more favourable environment. Again, if they had lived in areas of more acute housing stress where the social workers were unable to help in this way it is possible that some of these children would still be in long-term care.

These three factors seem to have had the major influence on the decision to let these children go home or remain at home. Concern was expressed that managers and case conferences might be over cautious about allowing children to go home, particularly those in the 'at risk' category. In fact, there was little evidence to support this view with these particular families, and parents, social workers, and sometimes courts, persisted in their plans for return home of the children, sometimes in opposition to the views of managers and case conferences. It did seem that in most of these cases it was the social workers, the parents, and the children who had the strongest influence on the decisions which were made, but there were indications that with less forceful social workers or parents this may not have been so.

SOME SUGGESTIONS FOR AN IMPROVED SERVICE

The methodological problems discussed in Chapter 2, and the fact that the points of view of managers, caretakers, and children were not systematically sought, preclude the making of strong recommendations. However, some views were held so strongly and consistently by parents, social workers, or both, that it seems important to make some suggestions based on these views. The suggestions refer to services to children for whom placement at home may be appropriate, and some may not be relevant to those children in care for whom return home is not thought to be a possibility.

Social policy and legislative issues

1 Lack of housing and low income, especially if income is irregular, still place extra pressures on vulnerable families, and housing and income maintenance services should be more responsive to need, especially in the early years of marriage when the first child is born. Housing is a necessary prerequisite for the return home of children; and if they do not go home, this should be for emotional rather than practical reasons (Chapter 4).

2 In view of the high incidence of physical and mental health problems amongst the parents and children, the role of the primary health care team in identifying early signs of physical and emotional neglect should be given more emphasis (Chapters 4 and 5).

3 More attention should be paid to the material and legal position of single-parent families, and the recommendations of the Finer Committee should be acted upon (HMSO, Cmnd. 5629.1). The establishment of family courts would allow for a more careful consideration of the needs of the children on the break-up of a marriage. More consideration should be given to the possibility of fathers being helped to care for their children, thus avoiding the prolonged stays in care before a father's remarriage, which caused such distress in two cases. Battered wives' hostels for victims of marital violence should be accessible in all areas, as should day care for children and domestic help for single parents at work (Chapters 4 and 5).

4 Courts should make more explicit, when making supervision orders in 'at risk' cases, that the case has actually been proved, especially if the parents and local authority disagree. They should also make more use of their powers to write into supervision orders specific conditions about access or day care (Chapter 7).

5 To avoid children staying in care unnecessarily because of an over-cautious attitude on the part of the local authority, and to give magistrates a second opinion when the parents and local authority are not in agreement, 'guardians ad litem' under the 1975 Children Act should also be appointed when parents are requesting

the revocation of an order and the local authority is opposing. If
a child is to be represented separately from his parents, the
parents should be parties to the court proceedings, and legal aid
should be available (Chapters 5 and 7).

6 There seems to be a need for an order somewhere between a care
order and a supervision order, precisely for the sorts of case
described in this study. In the short term more use could be made
of supervision orders with intermediate treatment provisions and
special requirements for younger children. In the long term it
would be desirable to introduce a new order which conveys more
realistically the 'shared caring' nature of the work actually done
in such cases, and also allows for immediate removal from home for
a limited period should this become necessary. Such an order could
be called an 'intermediate care order', or a 'home care order'
(Chapter 7).

7 The generally negative views about the Juvenile Court would
support those who would like to see family courts or something like
the Scottish panel system set up in England and Wales. This would
create a more positive environment in which magistrates, lawyers,
social workers, parents and children could reach decisions about a
child's future (Chapter 7).

8 In some parts of the country certain law firms and neighbour-
hood law centres have built up expertise in child welfare law.
This practice should be extended so that the quality of legal advice
and representation in court can improve (Chapter 7).

9 The spirit as well as the letter of the law should be observed
on the need for anonymity in Juvenile Court cases. The media should
be made responsible for ensuring that no details (such as the name
of the village in a close-knit area), are published which would
allow a family to be identified by neighbours (Chapter 7).

Management issues

10 Care orders should not be used or retained in force as a
means of obtaining resources, if voluntary help would be acceptable
to the parents and the child. This applies to places in residential
care and day care, and to practical and financial help. Interviews
suggested that insufficient funds were available under Section 1 of
the 1963 Act to help children not in statutory care, and that this
was one reason for not revoking care orders (Chapters 6 and 7).

11 Better guidelines should be given to social workers about
practical aid to help parents to visit children in care, and enough
money should be made available to pay fares, including in some
circumstances the fares of siblings or close relatives. This is
especially necessary if the appropriate placement is some considerable distance from the child's home (Chapters 4, 5 and 7).

12 The closeness of the relationship offered by the social
workers in the majority of these cases makes it essential in the
interest of objective decision-making and the offering of the most
appropriate service that professional consultation is available from
someone who is skilled in child care social work. This should be
seen as separate from management supervision, although it could be
offered by the management senior if suitably experienced (Chapter 6).

13 Careful thought should be given to the relationship between the social worker, the client, and management. Decisions should normally be made by the social workers (residential and field) who are in contact with the client, after consultation with seniors and other professionals. If, for any reason, the social worker is not the one making an important decision, the client should be informed of this and given the chance of putting his point of view to whoever is taking the decision, whether senior management or a case conference (Chapter 7).

14 More thought should be given to the preparation of cases for court, and the way in which confidential material, as contained in case records, is presented. The way in which this material is to be used should be discussed with the clients. Chapter 7 showed that in some cases anxiety about recording prevented some clients from making full use of the help which the social worker could have given.

15 More and more varied resources should be developed for children who need to be away from home, and these should be as near to the child's home as possible to facilitate contact with parents. There should be more use of foster care for older children; and for a small number of younger children residential placements should be available, especially for assessment where foster care is not appropriate or the reactions of parents are uncertain. Such provision could possibly be linked, as it is already in some areas, to a day care centre. Residential facilities for the whole family on the lines of those provided at the Park Hospital in Oxford should be more widely available. It may well be that for older children fewer assessment facilities, and more reception and treatment placements are needed. There is also a need for more placements for long-term care where the parents can be offered a friendly supportive relationship, and helped to retain a meaningful relationship with the children. Some of these caretakers, who would usually be 'professional' foster parents but could be residential care workers, should be available to keep in contact with the most vulnerable families when the children go home (either in a voluntary capacity or as family aides), and should be able to take the children back into full care for short or extended periods if this should prove necessary.

It was noted that most 'professional' foster parent schemes are for teenagers. This may be because the numbers of teenagers in care are increasing, and they are usually placed in expensive residential care. The placement problems of younger children are not so apparent as it is usually possible to find 'traditional' foster homes for them, especially if siblings are separated. Thus the pressure to recruit 'professional' foster parents for younger children is less. Those responsible for setting up such schemes and making decisions about priorities should be made aware that the placement of a child in the wrong foster home can lead to his remaining unnecessarily in long-term care, or to the considerable unhappiness of all concerned caused by a 'tug-of-love' situation (Chapters 5 and 7).

Social work

16 There is still room for improvement amongst social workers in

diagnosing and responding to the practical needs and financial problems of their clients. Perhaps because of their already low self-image resulting from the need for statutory action, most of these parents were reluctant to ask for practical help. At the same time they hoped that social workers would be aware of their needs, or at least acknowledge their embarrassment if they did ask for help and respond quickly and sensitively, even if they could not in fact meet the need. Social workers should make a point of asking parents if they need help to visit their children, and ensure that sufficient funds are available if the children are going home for visits. The desirability and significance to the parents of parental contributions towards the maintenance of children in care should be thoroughly explored when care is being discussed with them, and the legislation should be amended to make it more possible for the requirement to contribute to be waived if this is in the interest of the child.

17 More help should be given to establish a pattern of visiting which allows the retention of bonds between parents and children, and to support foster parents and residential workers in this aspect of their work. Pre-placement visits by parents and children, at which the routine of the children, the respective roles of the parents and caretakers, and visiting could be discussed, should be the rule rather than the exception. The question of confidentiality, and the extent of the caretakers' knowledge about the problems of the parents, should be discussed with both. Children should sometimes visit their families in their own homes wherever possible, and ways should be found of keeping the child in touch with the extended family.

18 The need for parents to be kept informed of what might seem to be small events in their children's lives should be acknowledged, even if the child is in statutory care. Whenever possible parents should be involved in important decisions about the child, and should be invited to attend all case conferences where important decisions are to be made, if not for the whole time, at least to give their views on important issues. If they do not wish to, or are unable to be present, the social worker should ensure that their views are clearly put to the conference, and that they know of the significance of the decisions to be made, and their legal rights. This should also apply to older children who may have a contribution to make to case conferences.

19 More help should be given, especially to unqualified or inexperienced social workers, with some of the more difficult aspects of work with children at risk and their parents. In particular there needs to be a greater understanding of why parents are reluctant to visit, and how they can be helped. Skills need to be developed in working with aggressive parents, and understanding the meaning behind the aggression, and in combining caring and child protection roles.

20 There should be more direct work with the children, and social workers should ensure that if they themselves do not have a relationship with the child which will allow him to talk about difficulties or allow them to recognise warning signs, such a role should be assumed by someone else, e.g. youth worker, teacher, volunteer, family aide, or day care or intermediate treatment worker.

More use should be made of groups, which should be more varied, and of short residential experiences shared by social workers and children.

SOME COMMENTS ON THE DEBATE ABOUT THE LEAST DETRIMENTAL ALTERNATIVE FOR CHILDREN IN CARE

The need for planning for deprived children has been emphasised by many writers, notably Rowe and Lambert (1973), Parker (1971) and the writers of the ABAFA Practice Guides (1976, 1977). Other studies have concentrated on children in voluntary care, or on children who remained in care; and this study, noting that almost a third of children in statutory care are placed at home at any one time, has given some thought to the situation of these children in the hope of throwing light on the reasons for home on trial placements and the problems which arise. It started with a review of the literature on the subject in the belief that common sense is not enough and that social workers must combine the empathy which, as this study shows, is so important to the parents, with a knowledge of what is documented about how a child's welfare can best be safeguarded. The 'experts' by no means agree, and, as Stevenson (1975) makes clear, 'in a field so uncertain and emotive, this is only to be expected', but, she goes on, 'everyone of us owes it to the children at risk to examine practice continually in the light of new knowledge.' Knowledge affects practice, but 'practice wisdom' is also a part of that knowledge, and this study has looked at the ways in which the average local authority social worker uses knowledge and practice wisdom in the service he offers to children at risk and their families.

Many aspects of social policy and social work were touched upon in the review of the literature and the analysis of cases, but fundamental to them all is the debate about 'the least detrimental alternative' (Goldstein et al., 1973; Solnit, 1977). What then, does this study contribute to this debate? First, it should not be read as stating that those children who were still at home had been unharmed by all that had happened to them. In that sense it confirms the point made earlier that it is more helpful in such cases to look for the least detrimental alternative than for the ideal. Even with this reservation it could be seen to present counter-arguments to those, most recently Barbara Tizard (1977), who argue for less emphasis to be placed on returning children to their natural families, and more on placing them with substitute, and preferably adoptive, families. But Tizard stresses that her study was of families where the children were mostly received into care as very young babies, and where most of the parents did not want to make a home for them. Over half of the parents had asked for adoption.

The children in this study had all lived at home for long enough to be seen as part of the family, however imperfect the relationship might have been; and, perhaps more importantly, the parents, except perhaps one, wanted them home, and would not have consented to adoption. This book therefore has nothing to contribute to the debate about adoptive or foster placements for infants whose parents do not wish to make a home for them, or are clearly unable to do so. However, most children coming into care do not fall into that category, and happily it is now more possible to place such children quickly in adoptive homes if the parents ask for this. Most children do have bonds, however fragile, with their parents, and most parents do have some hope, however unrealistic, of resuming their care. It is therefore argued that this study, although principally about children who went home, has also implications for some children who remain in care for long periods.

In the analysis of why these particular children went home it was suggested that the attitudes of the social workers towards maintenance of a child's birth identify, and the rights of parents, where possible, to care for their children, influenced the outcome for the child by influencing the nature of the social work help offered. Thus, although the major influence on whether children went home seemed to be the determination of the families to stay together as a unit, it is suggested that social workers were an important influence on whether the parents' determination petered out, or carried them through the pain and effort involved in retaining bonds and making return home a possibility. This may be particularly the case when, on reception into care, the parents' reaction is one of depression and hopelessness as was more often the case in Thorpe's (1974b) study, rather than anger, as was more frequently the case in this study.

Some writers suggest that parents should not be pressed to visit and resume care of their children if they seem reluctant to do so, and some of the social workers interviewed and with whom the findings have been discussed were influenced by this view. However, if the thesis of 'filial deprivation' is accepted, it is an extremely skilled task to differentiate between reluctance and distress at parting with the child. In view of the evidence from Jenkins and Norman (1972), Aldgate (1978a) and others that frequency of visiting is correlated with successful return home, to adopt a 'let's wait and see if they are really interested' approach to parental visiting may mean in many cases that the option of the child's going home will be effectively closed. Several parents in this study confirmed how easy it would have been for them to give up the struggle to retain a relationship with children placed away from home.

Contrary to Howells's (1974) and Tizard's (1977) suggestions, the evidence of lack of skilled work with parents in the early days after reception into care in this and other studies suggests that many social workers do adopt a 'wait and see' policy; they are either unaware of the research findings on filial deprivation or agree with those who believe that the least detrimental alternative for the child in care will often be a new start in a substitute family. It seems, therefore, that in the present climate of conflicting theories the possibility of a child returning home will be influenced substantially by the personal or professional values, or competence, of individual social workers and their immediate seniors. However, the thesis that social workers put too much weight on the blood tie is an over-simplification.

Whatever the view taken by the social worker about the respective merits of return home or placement in a new family, an early assessment of the relationships within the family, and the ability of the parents to meet the child's needs, is essential. All social workers interviewed saw the likely provision of good enough care as being the paramount factor in deciding about return home. Much work has been done in recent years in order to help those involved in assessing

the strengths and weaknesses in families, especially by Michael Rutter (1975b). Sula Wolff (1978) stresses the importance not only of observations of the situation at the time, but of taking a full case history, and this point is also made by those working specifically in the field of child abuse. (2) Welcome though this research is, there is a danger that the problem of assessing whether children should go home will be over-simplified. As Wolff puts it:
> Research findings tell us about probabilities. They provide broad guidelines, but can act as a firm base only for decisions about groups of clients, rarely for individual cases (Wolff, 1978, p.103).

The guides to practice produced by the Association of British Adoption and Fostering Agencies are to be welcomed in that they translate the research findings into case material which is most easily absorbed by busy social workers. There is, however, a risk that a 'check list' approach will convey the impression that there is a right answer which can be ascertained by knowing enough facts about a case:
> Where there are more than two stress factors, e.g., marital problems, bad housing, physical ill health, alcoholism, etc., the risks are even greater. It is therefore important to make an accurate assessment of the numbers of problems in the family before embarking on plans for rehabilitation (ABAFA, 1977a, p.9).

Several of the children in this study would not have gone home if the problems at the time of reception into care had been used as indicating what the situation would be in the future. The writers of the introduction to 'Good Enough Parenting' (CCETSW, 1978) stress the importance of deciding not only whether parenting is good enough at the time, but also whether it can be made good enough by whatever means are at the disposal of the social services. Gill Gorrell Barnes's (1978) case history, and Jacqueline Roberts (1978), talking of the work of the Park Hospital, give examples of this positive approach. This attitude was echoed by those workers in the study who said they were concerned to know not only whether bonds existed between parents and children, but also whether there was the potential in the parents, especially step-parents, to make bonds, and who made considerable efforts to improve the emotional and material circumstances of the parents. If, as the research of Kadushin and Tizard seems to show, children can be placed successfully in substitute homes, it is at least possible that they can be successfully placed back with one or both parents if circumstances have improved. Rutter (1972; 1975b) has shown that the capacity to get over the trauma of parting and make new relationships is related to the stresses to which a person is subjected.

These two questions of bonds and the stresses placed on children lead on to the question of the placement of the children if they leave home. Where preventive social work is being undertaken before removal from home becomes necessary, the knowledge of family strengths and interactions might allow for the appropriate placement, though even here the reaction of the child and his family to separation is difficult to predict. In most cases, if there is to be any possibility of a return home a full assessment of the family requires a placement where bonds can be maintained. This can be in a foster home where foster parents are able to encourage parental visiting; in residential care; or in units such as that provided at the Park Hospital for the whole family.

One of the most depressing aspects of this study was that such placements were rarely available, and only in about a third of the cases was the placement the one which the social worker would ideally have chosen. Such assessment placements, which are particularly valuable if there is flexibility about the length of stay, have the disadvantage that another move will most likely be necessary if it becomes apparent that the parents cannot resume care of the children. However, the distress caused to some of the children in this study placed initially in long-term foster care when there was a possibility of their returning home, suggests that the harm done by a move, if carefully prepared, is less likely to be permanently damaging than being subjected to a 'tug-of-love' situation. The social workers interviewed were also of the opinion that some children in the study, and some of their siblings, remained in long-term care because they were wrongly placed initially.

One of the major decisions about these children was not only whether they should go home, but when. There are important arguments in favour of a quick decision, as outlined in 'Good Enough Parenting' by Phillida Sawbridge and Madeline Carriline (1978) and in the ABAFA Practice Guides (1976, 1977). However, time must be allowed to work through the sense of numbness felt by the parents at the loss of the children, and to alleviate the effects of whatever stressful situation led to care. A parent living on his or her own or with a new partner may have a distinctly improved ability to be an adequate parent, as was the case with Mr Smith. In the study the original plan was changed in over a third of the cases. This may well be because insufficient care was put into making the plan in the first place, but it may also be because circumstances changed. The case of Jim Peters seems to show that if foster parents are able to give affection and good care to a young child, and yet accept the need for his parents to visit and help him to transfer his attachments back to them, he need not be seriously damaged by the change. On the other hand, Eve Smith's placement in a home where the foster parents could not accept parental involvement placed her in a stressful situation, and arguably made her return home more difficult and more damaging than it need have been. The point being made is that stressful situations can, and frequently do, result from wrong placements in care, as well as from problems in the child's own home. Thus, when weighing up the difficulties likely to arise for a child if long-term plans are delayed, the nature of the current placement is of considerable importance, and once more the vital significance of the initial decision about where to place the child is emphasised.

Some of the cases in this study support the view of several of the social workers interviewed that children can maintain bonds with natural parents whilst being given loving care by foster parents or residential workers. Some foster parents and residential workers are able to go beyond this already difficult task and offer an environment for children and visiting parents in which bonds which are tenuous or distorted can be repaired. The social worker involved with the Dunns thought that if this sort of foster home had been available when Carol first came into care, and had been able to give short-term care at times of stress, as relatives are able to in most families, Carol would not have been so hurt by her parents' behaviour and they might have been enabled to play a more positive role in her life.

The decision about the right time for children to return home tends to be seen in terms of the child, or the placement in care, and to be essentially a social work or case conference decision. Several of the parents in this study complained of their lack of real involvement in this decision, and their comments suggest that more weight should be placed on their own views about the right time for them to have the children home, in terms of their own emotional readiness. Their views must obviously be balanced against the need to protect the child and the strength of relationships, but there were indications that the attempt to eliminate all risks resulted in some children being placed at greater risk by delays. Having decided that return home had a reasonable chance of providing the least detrimental alternative for the child despite adverse factors, social workers, and more frequently managers and case conferences, seemed to demand a pattern of behaviour and level of frustration tolerance which many more emotionally stable families would have had difficulty in tolerating.

All the writers on abusing parents stress their lack of self-confidence and reluctance to trust, especially those in authority, but this did not seem to be sufficiently allowed for in assessing their reactions to delay. In retrospect, it seems clear that Jim Peters would have been less 'at risk' if he had gone home three months earlier when his mother felt emotionally ready for him, and if other more positive measures such as the provision of day care or a family aide been taken to minimise the degree of risk. The relationship of trust between the social worker and the parents in the early days when the child returns home is of such importance that what parents see as 'dithering around' unnecessarily at the last minute should be avoided wherever possible. The feeling of some of the parents that the social workers had little say in decision-making, which was reinforced by such delays, was one factor which prevented some parents from being honest with them when the children returned home.

Some cases where children have gone home have had tragic outcomes, and these have been the ones which have attracted attention. On the other hand, studies of children in care listed in Chapter 1 have shown that children separated permanently from their parents risk becoming institutionalised or seriously damaged emotionally by foster or adoptive home breakdown. This study has shown that children can and do go home, and make satisfactory progress, whilst other studies have shown that children in similar circumstances can be satisfactorily placed with adoptive or foster parents.

In looking at ways in which return home can be made a satisfactory option I take the view that where parents wish to care for their children and can be helped to offer good enough care, they and their children have the right to such help. The 1975 Children Act requires the views of children to be ascertained when decisions are made about their future; and in 'Who Cares?' (Page and Clarke, 1977) young people in care make a moving and coherent plea for greater involvement in the decisions which affect their lives. It must be assumed (until it is shown not to be the case) that parents too care about their children, even if they are sometimes unable to meet their needs. The parents I interviewed certainly did and were prepared to share their own painful experiences in the hope that their comments would be of some help to others in similar positions in the future. The last word is left to a father, two of whose children were back with him, but one other had become so much a part of her foster family that he no longer hoped for her return.

'After the court, I was very bitter against the welfare. I think, now, they do good, but the way they do it is bad. I'm not blaming the welfare but I think there could have been more done to keep us together. I seem to get on better with this social worker, but that could be time. If she had been the first one on the case, that might have been the same for her. But I would say, I'm still against the welfare. I think there's a lot of children in care today who should be at home, if they had looked into the case properly. Naturally I think the welfare were right in some ways, what they did. But really speaking, my little girl who is still in care could be here now if the right thing had been done at the right time.'

'Children are easy enough to bring up and look after if you bring them up right. If I lost these two now, I would be that cut up. I think I am on trial, but I think, I might be wrong, that the welfare are satisfied. Fred misses his mum, though. He said to me the other day, "If I had £10,000 I would like my mum to come back." What's going to happen to Pam when she grows up? She knows I don't visit because of the mother and father bit, and that I want her home. When she gets older, she might go against the foster people for that, and she will be a strange person to me. But I don't want her to be put out on the road with no help from no one. Because kiddies today, they really want someone to put their minds to the right path.'

'I would say 80 per cent of people that are mixed up in the welfare are against them, because I think it's very hard when your children are in care to get them back again, especially if you are a man. I think myself, and I talk to other people and they say: "If they are in the care of the welfare you have no chance of getting them home." I think a lot of people go and see their children, and something gets in their mind, and that sort of fizzles out. They go every week at first, and then they speak to other people about having them home and there doesn't seem any chance. They go once a week, and they go once a month, and then they don't go at all, and I think that's where the welfare could do better in some way. And that is how I was getting. My mother and other people told me, you might as well pack up going.'

Appendix I

THE LEGAL FRAMEWORK

Most children who come into care in Britain do so at their parents' request under Section 1 of the 1948 Children Act. In 1976, of over 52,000 children coming into the care of the local authorities, approximately 40,000 did so voluntarily, and approximately 12,000 through the courts. Those who are committed to care through the courts tend to stay longer. Thus, although in 1975-6 only 23 per cent of children coming into care came via the courts, more than 50 per cent of the children actually in care on 31 March 1976 were there under a care order. It should also be noted that the number of children coming into care under care orders is increasing.

Care orders are usually made by Juvenile Courts under the provisions of the 1969 Children and Young Persons Act, although they can also be made if a child is found guilty of an offence under criminal law, or as a result of matrimonial proceedings (Matrimonial Proceedings Acts, 1958, 1960, and Matrimonial Causes Act, 1965). The original intention of the 1969 Act, at least for children under 16, was to diminish the need to prosecute juvenile offenders, and instead to take steps to ensure their welfare by use of the special provisions of the Act. For this reason the committing of an offence is just one of the several reasons for the making of a care order. The Act stated:

If the court before which a child or young person is brought under this section is of opinion that any of the following conditions is satisfied with respect of him, that is to say -
a) his proper development is being avoidably prevented or neglected, or his health is being avoidably impaired or neglected or he is being ill-treated; or
b) it is probable that the condition set out in the preceding paragraph will be satisfied in his case (because a court has found it so in the case of another juvenile member of the same household); or
c) he is exposed to moral danger; or
d) he is beyond the control of his parent or guardian; or
e) he is of compulsory school age and is not receiving efficient full-time education suitable to his age, ability and aptitude; or
f) he is guilty of an offence, excluding homicide,
and also that he is in need of care or control which he is unlikely

to receive unless the court makes an order in respect of him – the court may, if it thinks fit, make such an order.

It should be noted, however, the act has never been fully implemented, and children over 10 years are still often prosecuted under criminal law, and care orders made on a simple proof of guilt without the need to prove the final clause, i.e. that an order is necessary. For a fuller discussion of the Act and general discussion of social policy aspects of child care legislation see Packman (1975). The orders which the court can make are:

a) an order requiring his parent or guardian to enter into a recognisance to take proper care of him or exercise proper control over him; or
b) a supervision order; or
c) a care order; or
d) a hospital order within the terms of Part 5 of the Mental Health Act, 1959; or
e) a guardianship order under the provisions of that Act.

The most usual decision is for a care order or a supervision order. A court can also write in conditions under a supervision order, requiring a child to be involved in 'intermediate treatment', or requiring the parents to give social workers or others access to the child. Intermediate treatment involves the offering to the child of constructive experiences, and he may, under such an order, be placed away from home for a period not exceeding three months at any one time. It should be noted that under care proceedings the court does not have to apportion blame. It has to be satisfied, for example, that a child has been neglected, but does not have to show that any one person has done the neglecting. Parents may, however, be prosecuted for an offence against a child, either under the terms of the 1933 Children and Young Persons Act and its amendments, or under the criminal law of assault. The decision about whether to prosecute lies with the police, though consultation with the social services department and others through the machinery of the area review committee is advised, whereas the decision about whether to initiate care proceedings lies with the local authority social services department, though again consultation with the area review committee is strongly advised in cases of children at risk.

Ever since the passing of the 1948 Children Act the social workers have been required to avoid receiving a child into care, or to work towards his return home, wherever 'it appears to them consistent with the welfare of the child so to do'. Section 1 of the 1963 Children and Young Persons Act requires the local authority to give aid, including financial aid, to diminish the need to receive children into care, or to prevent them coming before a court, and also to enable children in care to go home. It will also be noted that the 1969 Act is broadly sympathetic to parents, and to the aims of prevention and rehabilitation. The court has to be satisfied that a child's proper development is being avoidably neglected. It could be argued that the housing conditions in which some families live would make some degree of neglect unavoidable. It has also been argued, in a recent case referred to the local government 'ombudsman', that a child was wrongly retained in statutory care because the local authority had not fulfilled its duties under Section 1 of the 1963 Act to help the parents in the first place to avoid the need for a care order, and subsequently to assist them to improve their circumstances so that the child could return home.

The 1969 Act also places emphasis on voluntary help, and an order should only be made if the family is unlikely to accept help unless an order is made. There is evidence that many courts fail to satisfy themselves in respect of this clause, and hence make care orders which are neither necessary nor in keeping with the spirit of the law. This seems to happen frequently in cases of school non-attendance.

One further legal provision is of relevance to this study. A child received into care under Section 1 of the 1948 Act may subsequently be the subject of a resolution of the social services committee under Section 2 of that Act (as amended by the 1975 Children Act), whereby that committee assumes parental rights over the child. This, in fact, means that unless the parent objects, there is no court hearing. Parents may consent in writing to the passing of such a resolution, and must be informed in writing if parental rights are assumed by the committee, and the grounds for this action. If they object the case must be heard by a Juvenile Court within fourteen days, or the resolution lapses. The grounds on which parental rights over a child may be assumed are:

1 that his parents are dead, and that he has no guardian or custodian;
2 that the whereabouts of the parent or guardian have been unknown for not less than twelve months;
3 that a parent suffers from some permanent disability rendering him incapable of caring for the child;
4 that a parent or guardian suffers from a mental disorder which renders him unfit to have the care of a child;
5 that a parent is of such habits and mode of life as to be unfit to have the care of the child;
6 that the parent or guardian has so persistently failed without reasonable cause to discharge the obligations of a parent or guardian as to be unfit to have the care of the child;
7 that a parent whose parental rights have been assumed under 3, 4, 5 and 6 comes to live with the child and his other parent;
8 that the child has been in the care of the local authority or voluntary society for the previous three years.

The effect of a resolution under Section 2 of the 1948 Children Act is similar to that of a care order. Unless the care order is revoked by a court, or the Section 2 resolution by the committee or a court, the parental rights and duties over the child remain with the local authority until he is 18. Once a care order has been made, the decision about where the child should be placed lies with the social services department, although young people over 15 found guilty of an offence can be sentenced for Borstal training by a Crown Court. The laws require that the progress of all children in care should be reviewed at least at six-monthly intervals. Table A.1 shows the placements of the 400 or so children coming into care in 1975-6 in the county where the study took place, and compares the placements of the 130 children who were the subjects of care orders.

TABLE A.1 First placement of children coming into care in study county

	Care order children %	Total children %
Boarded out	20	58
Observation and assessment centres	18	8
Community homes	13	17
At home 'on trial'	36	10
Other (e.g. hospital)	13	7

It will be noted that those coming into care on care orders are more likely to be placed in observation and assessment centres than those coming into care voluntarily, and also that the largest number of those in care on care orders was placed initially at home. The above figures relate to children admitted to care during the year. As mentioned above, if one looks at the children in care at any one time, the proportion of children who are the subjects of care orders is higher. In the county studied some 800 children were in care at the end of the year, and of the 400 children on care orders 30 per cent (approximately 130) were living at home.

Because of the wide discretion given by legislation to the social services department to decide about the placement of children in its care, the administrative provisions of these departments are of some importance. Of particular relevance to this study are case conferences and other arrangements for making decisions about placements, and the special procedures resulting from the DHSS Memoranda dated 1974 and 1976 for cases of actual or suspected non-accidental injury to children or failure to thrive. Under these procedures area review committees have been set up to co-ordinate the work of all those agencies who may become involved with cases of child abuse, and case conferences are held to discuss individual cases. (See Carter (1976), Franklin (1973), Desborough and Stevenson (1977) for fuller discussions of these procedures and of case conferences.)

Appendix II

INTRODUCTORY LETTER FROM THE DIRECTOR OF SOCIAL SERVICES

Dear

I am writing to ask if you would be prepared to take part in a study of the social work services which are offered to families whose children have been in care or appeared before the Juvenile Court. The study is being undertaken by Mrs J. Thoburn of the University of ————— and the aim is to look at ways in which the service we offer to families can be improved.

Mrs Thoburn would like to talk to parents, and ask their views about the help they and their children have been offered. The interview will take approximately one hour, and a small fee (£1.50) will be paid for the time and effort taken. Although the study will be taking place in ———shire, nothing of what is said in interview will be passed on to any member of my staff, so I hope if you take part you will feel able to talk freely, knowing that your comments will be treated as strictly confidential.

I hope you will be able to help but will quite understand if you prefer not to. So that I can know if you are willing to be interviewed or whether you would prefer to talk about the study with Mrs Thoburn, could you please fill in the tear-off slip below and return it as soon as possible within the next 2 weeks in the reply-paid envelope. I will then pass this information on to Mrs Thoburn who will, if you wish to take part, arrange a time to come and see you.

   Yours sincerely

Director of Social Services

Please tear-off and return within 2 weeks in the enclosed reply-paid envelope.

                                              Please tick one only

a. I would like to take part in the study

b. I would like to speak to Mrs Thoburn about the study in more detail

c. I do not wish to take part in the study

If a, or b, the most convenient times for Mrs Thoburn to call would be:

                Days _____
                     am   pm   evening

                Name _____

                Address _____
                         _____
                         _____

NOTES

CHAPTER 1   THE THEORETICAL FRAMEWORK

1   For a further discussion of this concept see Goldstein et al., 1973, pp.53-64.
2   This term is used throughout the book in the sense explored extensively by Winnicott (1965, 1971). It implies that 'perfect' care is not available and that, for each child, what is 'good enough' will vary with individual personalities and circumstances.
3   The importance of the 'blood tie' is discussed in Chapter 7. It is not a term much in evidence in social work literature, and is perhaps accepted more widely by the legal than the social work profession and by parents themselves.
4   In the debate on the 1975 Act Dr David Owen laid great stress on parental duties as opposed to parental rights.

CHAPTER 2   OUTLINE OF THE STUDY AND METHODS USED

1   Nevertheless, there are reasons (discussed below) for believing that the systematic biases in the sample were slight, and the sample (30 per cent) was fairly large in relation to the population of families in the study area with children home on trial (over a half of those in the relevant age-range).
2   For an explanation of child care legislation, and a fuller discussion of numbers of children in care, see Appendix I.
3   For a discussion of possible reasons for variations in numbers of children in care see Packman (1968).
4   Because of methods of recording changes of placement it was difficult to be sure that all children who had been home and returned to care were included.
5   All except two of the children initially on supervision orders subsequently came into care on care orders. Two younger children were initially in care on interim care orders.

CHAPTER 3 SOME ILLUSTRATIVE CASE STUDIES

1 In this case home placement was by choice, but in others teenagers went home after court because there was no vacancy at an observation and assessment centre. It is a debatable point as to whether such placements should be described as 'home on trial' placements at all, but they appear as such in the statistics. If this situation goes on for more than a week or so, and particularly if behaviour at home is satisfactory, it can be difficult for the child and his parents to accept the need for him to go away.

The preference for working with a child on a care order but placed at home, rather than on a supervision order, which was fairly common amongst the social workers interviewed, may explain why, since the passing of the 1969 Children and Young Persons Act, more care orders are being made at an earlier stage than prior to the Act. There is evidence that the increased availability of resources for intermediate treatment will lead to social workers viewing more favourably supervision orders with conditions for intermediate treatment.

CHAPTER 4 PARENTS AND CHILDREN

1 See especially Aldgate (1978a), Thorpe (1974a, b), Wilson and Herbert (1978), Gray and Parr (1957), Packman (1968), Holman (1973a; 1976), George (1970).

CHAPTER 5 THE PROCESS OF CARE: ITS IMPACT ON PARENTS AND CHILDREN

1 See Thorpe (1974a, b), Weinstein (1960), Aldgate (1978a), Jenkins and Norman (1972) for fuller discussions of the importance of parental contact and its relationship with whether the child returns home.
2 See especially Roberts (1978), Jones (1978) and the proceedings of the Second International Congress on Child Abuse and Neglect (forthcoming).

CHAPTER 6 THE SOCIAL WORKERS AND THE HELP THEY OFFERED

1 See Sainsbury (1975) for a much fuller analysis of the clients' views of the casework relationship.
2 For a discussion of empathy in child care cases see Berry and Mann (1978).
3 See Mayer and Timms (1970) for a fuller discussion of the clients' reactions to casework.
4 Organisational issues and the availability of resources are discussed in Chapter 7.

CHAPTER 7 DECISION-MAKING AND PLACEMENT POLICY

1 See Howells (1974), Reports of Committees of Inquiry after the deaths of Maria Colwell (DHSS, 1974), John Auckland (DHSS, 1975), and Wayne Brewer (Somerset County Council, 1977).
2 Thorpe (1974a, b) and Rowe and Lambert (1973) and other writers on children in care suggest that indifferent social work at the early stages of care results in placements becoming long-term unnecessarily.
3 Parsloe (in Stevenson and Parsloe, 1978), in discussing the implications for the training of social workers of the findings of the recent DHSS study, commented on the fact that there were few examples of 'conscious use of practice theory'.
4 Although these issues have been discussed with some residential social workers and managers, it should be noted that in discussing residential care the study does not adequately represent their views. 'A Roof Over Their Heads?' (Newman and Mackintosh, 1975) provides a very full discussion of the provision of residential care for children.
5 For a detailed study of these procedures see 'The Central Child Abuse Register' (BASW, 1978).

CHAPTER 8 WHO GOES HOME? SOME CONCLUSIONS AND SUGGESTIONS FOR AN IMPROVED SERVICE

1 Four major research projects on children in care sponsored by the DHSS are currently being undertaken by Lydia Lambert and David Fruin at the National Children's Bureau, Jean Packman at Exeter University, and Spencer Milham at Dartington Social Research Unit.
2 See particularly Gorell Barnes (1978) and Lynch and Roberts (1978).

BIBLIOGRAPHY

ADAMSON, G. (1973), 'The Care-takers', Bristol, Bookstall Publications.
ALDGATE, J. (1976a), The Child in Care and his Parents, 'Adoption and Fostering', no.2, pp.29-40.
ALDGATE, J. (1976b), 'Returning Home: Working with Parents and Children', address to BASW Family Care Conference, Birmingham, BASW Publications.
ALDGATE, J. (1978a), A Study of Factors which Influence the Stay of Children in the Care of Two Local Authorities in Scotland, PhD thesis, University of Edinburgh.
ALDGATE, J. (1978b), Advantages of Residential Care, 'Adoption and Fostering', no.92, pp.29-33.
ALDGATE, J. (1980), Identification of Factors Influencing Length of Stay in Care, in J.P. Triseliotis, 'New Developments in Foster Care and Adoption', Routledge & Kegan Paul, London.
Association of British Adoption and Fostering Agencies (1976), 'Practice Guide to the Children Act 1975', London, ABAFA.
Association of British Adoption and Fostering Agencies (1977a), 'Assumption of Parental Rights and Duties', London, ABAFA.
Association of British Adoption and Fostering Agencies (1977b), 'Planning for Children in Long-Term Care', London, ABAFA.
BAHER, E., HYMAN, C., JONES, C., JONES, R., KERR, A. and MITCHELL, R. (1977), 'At Risk', London, Routledge & Kegan Paul.
BERRY, J. (1975), 'Daily Experience in Residential Life', London, Routledge & Kegan Paul.
BERRY, J. and MANN, P. (1978), Empathy and Parental Fitness, 'Adoption and Fostering', no.92, pp.48-54.
BOWLBY, J. (1951), 'Maternal Care and Mental Health', Geneva, World Health Organisation.
BOWLBY, J. (1971), 'Attachment and Loss', London, Penguin.
British Association of Social Workers (1972), 'Social Action and Social Work', Birmingham, BASW Publications.
British Association of Social Workers (1975a), The Children Bill, 'Social Work Today', vol.5, no.25, pp.777-9.
British Association of Social Workers (1975b), Code of Practice for Social Work with Children at Risk, 'Social Work Today', vol.6, no.11, pp.345-50.

British Association of Social Workers (1975c), 'A Code of Ethics for Social Work', Birmingham, BASW Publications.
British Association of Social Workers (1978), 'The Central Child Abuse Register', Birmingham, BASW Publications.
BROWNE, E. (1978), Social Work Activities, in 'Social Service Teams - The Practitioner's View', O. Stevenson and P. Parsloe (eds), London, HMSO.
CARTER, J. (1976), Co-ordination and Child Abuse, 'Social Work Service', April, pp.22-8.
CARVER, V. (ed.) (1978), 'Child Abuse: A Study Text', Milton Keynes, Open University Press.
Central Council for Education and Training in Social Work (1978), 'Good Enough Parenting', London, CCETSW.
CLARKE, A.M. and A.D. (1976), 'Early Experiences: Myth and Evidence', London, Open Books.
COOPER, J. (1978), 'Patterns of Family Placement', London, National Children's Bureau.
CRELLIN, E., PRINGLE, M.L.K. and WEST, P. (1971), 'Born Illegitimate', London, National Foundation for Educational Research.
DAVIES, M. (1974), 'Social Work in the Environment', Home Office Research Studies, London, HMSO.
Department of Health and Social Security (1974), Report of the Committee of Inquiry into the Care and Supervision Provided in Relation to Maria Colwell, London, HMSO.
Department of Health and Social Security (1974; 1976), 'Non-Accidental Injury to Children', LASSL(74)13, LASSL(76)2, London, HMSO.
Department of Health and Social Security (1975), Report of the Committee of Inquiry into the Provision and Co-ordination of Services to the Family of John George Auckland, London, HMSO.
Department of Health and Social Security (1976), 'Foster Care: A Guide to Practice', London, HMSO.
DESBOROUGH, C. and STEVENSON, O. (1977), 'Case Conferences: A Study of Interprofessional Communication Concerning Children at Risk', University of Keele.
DINNAGE, R. and PRINGLE, M.L.K. (1967a), 'Residential Child Care: Facts and Fallacies', London, Longman.
DINNAGE, R. and PRINGLE, M.L.K. (1967b), 'Foster Home Care: Facts and Fallacies', London, Longman.
FANSHEL, D. (1971), The Exit of Children from Foster Care: An Interim Research Report, in 'Child Welfare', New York, no.50, pp.65-80.
FANSHEL, D. and SHINN, E.B. (1978), 'Children in Foster Care - A Longitudinal Investigation', Columbia University Press, New York.
FOLKARD, M.S., SMITH, D.E. and SMITH, D.D. (1974; 1976), 'Intensive Matched Probation and After-Care Treatment', Home Office Research Studies, 24 and 26, London, HMSO.
FRANKLIN, A.W. (ed.) (1973), 'Tunbridge Wells Study Group on Non-Accidental Injury to Children', London, Spastics Society.
GEORGE, V. (1970), 'Foster Care', London, Routledge & Kegan Paul.
GEORGE, V. and WILDING, P. (1972), 'Motherless Families', London, Routledge & Kegan Paul.
GLAMPSON, A. and GOLDBERG, E.M. (1976), The Consumer's Viewpoint, 'Social Work Today', vol.8, no.6, pp.7-12.

GOLDBERG, E.M. (1970), 'Helping the Aged', London, Allen & Unwin.
GOLDBERG, E.M. and FRUIN, D.S. (1976), 'Towards Accountability in Social Work', 'British Journal of Social Work', vol.6, no.1, pp.3-19.
GOLDBERG, E.M., WARBURTON, R.W., LYONS, L. and WILLMOTT, R.R. (1978), Towards Accountability in Social Work: Long-Term Social Work in an Area Office, 'British Journal of Social Work', vol.8, no.3, pp.253-87.
GOLDBERG, E.M., WARBURTON, R.W., McGUINNESS, B. and ROWLANDS, J.H. (1977), Towards Accountability in Social Work: One Year's Intake in an Area Office, 'British Journal of Social Work', vol.7, no.3, pp.257-83.
GOLDSTEIN, J., FREUD, A. and SOLNIT, A. (1973), 'Beyond the Best Interests of the Child', New York, Free Press.
GORRELL BARNES, G. (1978), Non-Accidental Injury: A Case Example, in 'Good Enough Parenting', London, Central Council for Education and Training in Social Work, pp.60-79.
GRAY, P.G. and PARR, E.A. (1957), 'Children in Care and the Recruitment of Foster Parents', London, HMSO Social Survey.
HAZEL, N., COX, R. and ASHLEY-MUDIE, P. (1977), Second Report of the Special Family Project, Canterbury, Kent Social Services Department.
Her Majesty's Stationary Office (1974), 'Report of the Committee on One-Parent Families', London, Cmnd 5629-1.
HEYWOOD, J.S. and ALLEN, B.K. (1971), 'Financial Help in Social Work', Manchester University Press.
HILL, M. (1978), Resources, in 'Social Services Teams - The Practitioner's View', O. Stevenson and P. Parsloe (eds), London, HMSO.
HOLMAN, R. (1973a), 'Socially Deprived Families in Britain', London, Bedford Square Press.
HOLMAN, R. (1973b), 'Trading in Children', London, Routledge & Kegan Paul.
HOLMAN, R. (1975), The Place of Fostering in Social Work, 'British Journal of Social Work', vol.5, no.1, pp.3-29.
HOLMAN, R. (1976), 'Inequality in Child Care', London, Child Poverty Action Group.
HOWELLS, J. (1974), 'Remember Maria', London, Butterworth.
HOWELLS, J. (1975), Children are not Meant to Die, in 'Whose Children', Birmingham, BASW Publications.
HYMAN, C.A. (1978), Some Characteristics of Abusing Families Reported to the NSPCC Special Units, 'British Journal of Social Work', vol.8, no.2, pp.171-9.
JENKINS, S. and NORMAN, E. (1972), 'Filial Deprivation and Foster Care', New York, Columbia University Press.
JONES, C. (1978), The Predicament of. Abused Children, in 'Child Abuse', C. Lee (ed.), Milton Keynes, Open University Press.
JORDAN, B. (1974), 'Poor Parents', London, Routledge & Kegan Paul.
JORDAN, B. (1976), 'Freedom and the Welfare State', London, Routledge & Kegan Paul.
JOSEPH, K. (1972), The Cycle of Deprivation, in 'Social Welfare in Modern Britain', E. Butterworth and R. Holman (eds), London, Fontana.
KADUSHIN, A. (1970), 'Adopting Older Children', New York, Columbia University Press.

KENYON, J. and GOULD, T. (1972), 'Stories From the Dole Queue', London, Temple Smith.
LEE, C.M. (ed.) (1978), 'Child Abuse: A Reader and Sourcebook', Milton Keynes, Open University Press.
LEONARD, P., (1975), 'Poverty Consciousness and Action', Birmingham, BASW Publications.
LISTER, R. and EMMETT, T. (1976), 'Under the Safety Net', London, Child Poverty Action Group.
LYNCH, M. and ROBERTS, J. (1978), Predisposing Factors within the Family, in V. Carver (ed.), 'Child Abuse', Milton Keynes, Open University Press.
MARSDEN, D. (1969), 'Mothers Alone', London, Penguin.
MARSDEN, D. and DUFF, E. (1975), 'Workless', London, Penguin.
MAYER, J. and TIMMS, N. (1970), 'The Client Speaks', London, Routledge & Kegan Paul.
McWHINNIE, A. (1978), Professional Fostering, 'Adoption and Fostering', no.93, pp.32-40.
MORGAN, P. (1975), 'Child Care: Sense and Fable', London, Temple Smith.
National Society for the Prevention of Cruelty to Children (1974), 'Yo-Yo Children', London, NSPCC Publications.
NEILL, J., FRUIN, D., GOLDBERG, E.M. and WARBURTON, W. (1973), Reactions to Integration, 'Social Work Today', vol.4, no.15, pp.458-64.
NEWMAN, N. (ed.) (1975), 'In Cash or Kind', University of Edinburgh.
NEWMAN, N. and MACKINTOSH, H. (1975), 'A Roof Over Their Heads?' University of Edinburgh.
NEWSON, J. and E. (1963), 'Infant Care in an Urban Community', London, Allen & Unwin.
NEWSON, J. and E. (1968), 'Four Years Old in an Urban Community', London, Allen & Unwin.
PACKMAN, J. (1968), 'Child Care: Needs and Numbers', London, Allen & Unwin.
PACKMAN, J. (1975), 'The Child's Generation', Oxford, Blackwell.
PAGE, R. and CLARKE, G. (1977), 'Who Cares?' London, National Children's Bureau.
PARKER, R.A. (1966), 'Decision in Child Care', London, Allen & Unwin.
PARKER, R.A. (1971), 'Planning for Deprived Children', London, National Children's Home.
PARKER, R.A. (1978), Foster Care in Context, 'Adoption and Fostering', no.93, pp.27-32.
Portsmouth Social Services Department (1973), Fostering Study.
PRINGLE, M.L.K. (1974), 'The Needs of Children', London, Hutchinson.
PROSSER, H. (1978a), 'Perspectives in Foster Care', London, National Foundation for Educational Research.
PROSSER, H. (1978b), 'Perspectives on Residential Child Care', London, National Foundation for Educational Research.
REID, W.J. and SHYNE, A.W. (1969), 'Brief and Extended Casework', New York, Columbia University Press.
REINER, B. and KAUFMANN, I. (1959), 'Character Disorders in Parents of Delinquents', New York, Family Service Association of America.

ROBERTS, J. (1978), There's More to Child Abuse than Spotting Bruises, 'Community Care', London, no.219, pp.20-31.
ROBERTS, J., LYNCH, M. and DUFF, P. (1978), Abused Children and their Siblings - A Teacher's View, 'Therapeutic Education', no.6, no.1, pp.25-31.
ROBERTSON, J. and J. (1967; 1968), 'Young Children in Brief Separation', London, Tavistock Child Development Research Unit.
ROWE, J. (1977), Fostering in the Seventies and Beyond, 'Adoption and Fostering', no.90, pp.15-20.
ROWE, J. and LAMBERT, L. (1973), 'Children Who Wait', London, Association of British Adoption and Fostering Agencies.
RUTTER, M. (1972), 'Maternal Deprivation Reassessed', London, Penguin.
RUTTER, M. (1975a), 'Helping Troubled Children', London, Penguin.
RUTTER, M. (1975b), Attainment and Adjustment in Two Geographical Areas, 'British Journal of Psychiatry', no.126, pp.493-509.
RUTTER, M. and GRAHAM, P. (1968), The Reliability and Validity of the Psychiatric Assessment of the Child, 'British Journal of Psychiatry', no.114, pp.581-92.
RUTTER, M. and MADGE, N. (eds) (1976), 'Cycles of Disadvantage', London, Heinemann.
RUTTER, M., TIZARD, J. and WHITMORE, K. (eds) (1970), 'Education, Health and Behaviour', London, Longman.
SAINSBURY, E. (1975), 'Social Work with Families', London, Routledge & Kegan Paul.
SAWBRIDGE, P. and CARRILINE, M. (1978), Social Work Tasks in Relation to Placing Children in New Families, in 'Good Enough Parenting', London, CCETSW.
SCHAFFER, H. and E. (1968), 'Child Care and the Family', London, Bell.
Second International Congress on Child Abuse and Neglect: Report on Proceedings (1979), Oxford, Pergamon.
SHAW, I. (1975), Consumer Opinion and Social Policy, 'Journal of Social Policy, vol.5, no.1, pp.19-32.
SHAW, M. (1974), 'Social Work in Prison', Home Office Research Studies no.22, London, HMSO.
SHAW, M. and LEBENS, K. (1976), Children Between Families, 'Adoption and Fostering', no.2, pp.17-27.
SINFIELD, A. (1969), 'Which Way for Social Work?' London, Fabian Tract, no.393.
Somerset County Council (1977), Report of the Circumstances Surrounding the Death of Wayne Brewer, Taunton.
SOLNIT, A. (1977), Least Harmful to Children, 'Adoption and Fostering', no.87, pp.30-4.
SPECHT, H. and VICARY, A. (eds) (1977), 'Integrating Social Work Methods', London, Allen & Unwin.
STEVENSON, O. (1968), Reception into Care: Its Meaning for All Concerned, in 'Children in Care', R.J.N. Tod (ed.), London, Longman.
STEVENSON, O. (1974), Narrative and Comment on the Period from Maria's Birth, in March 1965, up to the Revocation of the Fit Person Order by the Hove Juvenile Court on 17th November, 1971, in the 'Report of the Committee of Inquiry into the Care and Supervision Provided in Relation to Maria Colwell, London, HMSO.

STEVENSON, O. (1975), The Social Worker's Responsibility to the Child, in 'Whose Children?' Birmingham, BASW Publications.
STEVENSON, O. (1976), 'From the General to the Specific', University of Keele.
STEVENSON, O. (1977), 'Someone Else's Child', London, Routledge & Kegan Paul, revised edition.
STEVENSON, O. and PARSLOE, P. (1978), 'Social Service Teams: The Practitioner's View', London, HMSO.
THOBURN, J. (1977), 'Who Goes Home?' unpublished report to the Central Council for Education and Training in Social Work, London, CCETSW.
THORPE, R. (1974a), Mum and Mrs So and So, 'Social Work Today', vol.4, no.22, pp.691-5.
THORPE, R. (1974b), The Social and Psychological Situation of the Long-Term Foster Child with Regard to his Natural Parents, PhD thesis, University of Nottingham.
TIMMS, R. and N. (1977), 'Perspectives in Social Work', London, Routledge & Kegan Paul.
TIZARD, B. (1977), 'Adoption, a Second Chance', London, Open Books.
TIZARD, J. and B. (1971), The Social Development of Two-Year-Old Children in Residential Nurseries, in 'The Origins of Human Social Relations', H. Schaffer (ed.), London, Academic Press.
TOD, R.J.N. (ed.) (1968), 'Children in Care', London, Longman.
TOD, R.J.N. (ed.) (1973), 'Social Work and Foster Care', London, Longman.
WEDGE, P. and PROSSER, H. (1973), 'Born to Fail?' London, Arrow Books.
WEINSTEIN, E. (1960), 'The Self-Image of the Foster Child', New York, Russell Sage.
WIER, S. (1975), 'The Children Bill: Rescue or Prevention?' London, Child Poverty Action Group.
WILDING, P. and GEORGE, V. (1975), Social Values and Social Policy, 'Journal of Social Policy', vol.4, no.4, pp.375-90.
WILSON, H. (1974), Parenting in Poverty, 'British Journal of Social Work', vol.4, no.3, pp.241-54.
WILSON, H. (1976), Some Observations on the Relevance of the Environment, address to BASW Child Care Conference, Birmingham, BASW.
WILSON, H. and HERBERT, G.W. (1978), 'Parents and Children in the Inner City', London, Routledge & Kegan Paul.
WINNICOTT, C. (1970), 'Child Care and Social Work', Bristol, Bookstall Publications.
WINNICOTT, D.W. (1965), 'The Family and Individual Development', London, Tavistock.
WINNICOTT, D.W. (1971), 'Playing and Reality', London, Tavistock.
WOLFF, S. (1978), The Case History in Child Care, in 'Good Enough Parenting', London, CCETSW.
WOLKIND, S. (1974), The Components of Affectionless Psychopathy in Institutionalised Children, 'Journal of Child Psychology and Psychiatry', vol.15, p.215.
WOLKIND, S. and RUTTER, M. (1973), Children Who Have Been in Care, An Epidemiological Study, 'Journal of Child Psychology and Psychiatry', vol.14, pp.97-105.

WOOTTON, B. (1959a) 'Social Science and Social Pathology', London, Allen & Unwin.
WOOTTON, B. (1959b), Daddy Knows Best, 'Twentieth Century', no.166.

INDEX

Adamson, G., 7
adoption, 3, 4, 33, 76, 126, 138, 140, 155, 167, 175-6, 179; adopted children, 49, 53; adoptive parents, 121
alcohol, abuse of, 42
Aldgate, J., 5, 7, 8, 11, 33, 53, 54, 55, 57, 59, 60, 66, 136, 169, 176, 188n
Allen, B.K., 102
area review committee, 161, 182, 184
assessment, 133, 135, 153, 176, 177; observation and assessment centres, 54, 141, 173, 188n, see also residential care
Association of British Adoption and Fostering Agencies, 118, 124, 175, 177, 178
attachments, see bonds
Auckland, John, 1, 71, 189n

Baher, E., 9, 11, 44, 91, 107, 143
battered women, 41; hostels for, 88, 131, 132, 133, 171
Berkshire Social Services Department, 136
Berry, J., 8, 66, 188n
best interests of child, see child, welfare of
blood-tie, 3, 60, 119-22, 125, 126, 176, 187n; see also child, sense of identity of; bonds

bonds, 4, 60, 119, 122-3, 169, 170, 178, see also blood-tie; with parents, 2, 136, 174; with substitute caretakers, 2, 129
Bowlby, J., 3
Brewer, Wayne, 95, 189n
British Association of Social Workers, 1, 5, 6, 102, 189n
Browne, E., 11, 116

care order, ix, 5, 59, 92, 141, 152-6, 172, 181, 182, 183; length of, 53; reasons for, 13, 46, 53, 104, 126, 127, 150, 151; revocation of, 15, 65, 104, 152, 155
Carriline, M., 178
Carter, J., 184
Carver, V., 11
case conferences, 72, 133, 136, 161, 163-6, 170, 173, 174, 179, 184
casework, 78, 80, 86-9; with children, 106, 108; see also social work
Central Council for Education and Training in Social Work, ix, 2, 118, 124, 177
child guidance service, 74, 75
Child Poverty Action Group, 4, 5
children: abuse of, 1, 37, 51, 65, 91; ages of, 51; attitudes

towards placement of, 126, 177; behaviour of, 62, 66; in care, ix, 2, 5, 7, 9, 13, 15, 177; concept of time of, 3; delinquency of, 49, 51, 66; divided loyalties of, 9, 58, 131, 173; health of, 36, 37; illegitimate, 4; legal status of, 52; mental health of, 47; needs of, 2, 124; neglect of, 1, 65, 153; problems of, 47-50, 51; proper growth and development of, 2, 3, 8, 9, 123-6, 176; protection of, 11, 95, 97; relationships with parents, 3; relationships with caretakers, 129; rights of, 7, 126; at risk, 1, 2, 11, 123, 143; sense of identity of, 7, 68, 119, 122-4, 126, 176; separation from parents, 8; theories of development of, 3; welfare of, ix, 2, 7, 14, 18, 56, 66, 119, 122, 126
Children Act 1948, 2, 181, 182, see also voluntary care; section 2 of, 5, 15, 52, 59, 83, 150, 152, 156-8, 183
Children Act 1975, xi, 2, 5, 8, 55, 125, 152, 168, 171, 179, 183, 187n
Children and Young Persons Act 1933, 182
Children and Young Persons Act 1963, 2, 5, 6, 76, 102, 104, 113, 172, 182-3
Children and Young Persons Act 1969, 50, 181-3, 188n; see also care order
children's homes, see residential care; assessment
Clarke, A.M. and A.D., 4
Clarke, G., 179
client: captive, ix; choice of, ix; satisfied or dissatisfied, ix, 10; see also parents, children
Colwell, Maria, 1, 9, 167, 168, 189n
consumer: consumer studies, ix, 9-10, 15; see also client
Cooper, J., 8, 136

Courts, 13, 35, 90, 96, 99, 118, 127, 141, 150-2, 157, 164, 170, 172, 173, 181-3; Family, 172; Juvenile, 5, 52, 181, 183; Magistrate's, 52; parents' reactions to, 158-61
Crellin, E., 4

Dartington Social Research Unit, 189n
Davies, M., 9
day care, 4, 5, 13, 101, 102, 110, 131, 132, 171, 173, 174, 179
Department of Health and Social Security, xi, 11, 104, 116, 145, 161, 184, 189n
deprivation: cycle of, 4, 6, 46; filial, 7, 55, 59, 176; material, 4, 36; maternal, 3, 4, 8, 46
Desborough, C., 184
Dinnage, R., 8
Drabble, M., 90
Duff, E., 9, 13

education welfare officer, 74
Emmett, T., 102
employment/unemployment, 9, 35, 170
environment, 5, 43, 46, 170; see also parents, material circumstances of

failure to thrive, see child, neglect of
family: extended, 40, 121, 146, 148, 150, 174; see also parents
family aide, see home help
family service unit, 86
Fanshel, D., 7
fathers, 101, 171; see also marriage; parents; single-parent families
financial problems, 35, 100; see also poverty
Finer Committee, 171
Folkard, M.S., 9

foster parents, 38, 16, 54, 62, 63, 64, 89, 122, 126, 128, 130, 134, 135-40, 173-4; attitudes towards parents, 106, 135, 138, 145, 177-9; 'professional', 8, 9, 56, 135, 173, 177-8; as substitute parents, 8, 9, 138-40, 173, 176, 180
Franklin, A.W., 184
Fruin, D., 10, 115, 189n

General Practitioners, 37, 38, 74, 75
George, V., 5, 7, 9, 37, 42, 54, 55, 66, 188n
Glampson, A., 113, 114
Goldberg, E.M., 9, 10, 11, 113, 114, 115
Goldstein, J., 2, 121, 175, 187n
good enough care, see child, proper development of
Gorrell Barnes, G., 177, 189n
Gould, T., 9
Graham, P., 67
Gray, P.G., 188n
group work, 78, 89, 110, 133, 175
guardian ad litem, 152, 171

Hazel, N., 136
health visitors, 74, 75
Herbert, G.W., 4, 43, 188n
Heywood, J.S., 102
Hill, M., 11, 102
Holman, R., 1, 4, 5, 7, 8, 32, 36, 55, 66, 132, 135, 188n
home help, 101, 102, 103, 131, 171, 174, 179
housing, 33-5, 100, 128, 170; council, 33; housing departments, 99; lack of, 5, 13, 126, 171
Howells, J., 1, 73, 119, 161, 176, 189n
Hyman, C.A., 116

inequality, 5
institutional care, see residential care

intermediate treatment, 110, 133, 153, 155-6, 172, 174, 182, 188n; see also supervision orders

Jenkins, S., 7, 55, 59, 60, 176, 188n
Jones, C.O., 8, 188n
Jordan, B., 4, 11, 102, 103
Joseph, K., 4

Kadushin, A., 4, 66
Kaufmann, I., 11
Kent Family Placement Scheme, 136
Kenyon, J., 9

Lambert, L., 7, 54, 55, 68, 175, 189n
lawyers, 99, 127, 155, 159, 172
least detrimental alternative, see child, welfare of; placement
Lebens, K., 7, 8, 135
Lee, C.M., 11
Leonard, P., 6, 7
Lister, R., 102
Lynch, M., 11, 91, 189n

Mackintosh, H., 189
McWhinnie, A., 136
Madge, N., 4
magistrates, 159, 171, 172; see also Courts
management, 161, 170, 172, 179; accountability of, 162, 173; attitude of parents to, 162
Mann, P., 188n
marriage/marital problems, 32, 41-2, 125, 132, 171; see also parents; single-parent families
Marsden, D., 9, 13, 42
Matrimonial Proceedings Acts, 181
Mayer, J., ix, 9, 10, 11, 98, 113, 188n
member of parliament, 101, 128, 167
Meurs, Steven, 1, 71, 167
Milham, S., 189n

Mind Campaign, 4
Morgan, E., 4
mothers, see parents; single-parent families

National Association for the Welfare of Children in Hospital, 90
National Children's Bureau, 8
National Society for the Prevention of Cruelty to Children, 9, 11, 74, 75, 116
Newman, N., 12, 102, 189n
Newson, J. and E., 2, 43
non-accidental injury: procedures for, 72, 161, 165, 184; register, 119, 161; see also child, abuse of
Norman, E., 7, 55, 59, 61, 176, 188n

Open University, 11
Owen, D., 187n

Packman, J., 5, 182, 187n, 188n 189n
Page, R., 179
parental rights resolution, see Children Act 1948
parents, see also single-parent families; adoptive, 7, see also adoption; anger of, 59, 90-2; attitudes to care orders, 155, 158-61; attitudes to child placement, 3, 55, 59-61, 125, 129, 143, 169-70, 174, 176, 177, 178, see also deprivation, filial; attitudes to children, 43-5, 122-4, 141, 179-80; attitudes to substitute care-takers, 62, 138-40, 143, 146-8; attitudes to social workers, 84, 85, 95, 197; child care practices of, 36, 45-7; childhood experiences of, 39-40; delinquency of, 40-1; duties of, 5; financial contributions to children in care, 104-5; health of, 13, 36, 126, 171; inadequacy of, 4, 5; income of, 35-6, 171; intelligence of, 38; mental health of, 37-9, 120, 171; natural, 3, 4, 7, 8, 9; personalities of, 6, 38; problems of, 35, 46-7, 177, 179; psychological, 3, see also adoption, and foster parents; resources of, 5; rights of, 2, 5, 11, 126, 174, 183, see also Children Act, 1948, section 2; satisfaction with service of, 110, 112-13; social class of, 33; step-parents, 33, 43, 63, 64, 177; substitute, 3, 4, 13, see also adoption, foster parents
Park Hospital, Oxford, 11, 173, 177
Parker, R.A. 8, 66
Parr, E.A., 188n
Parsloe, P., 9, 10, 11, 163, 167, 189n
Place of Safety Order, 144, 151, 156
placement of child in care, 7-9, 13, 133-5, 171, 173, 177-9, 184; availability of, 127, 130, 134; change of, 54, 134; decisions about, 3, 4, 13, 18, 61, 118, 126-8, 134, 163; at home on trial, ix, 1, 7, 8, 13, 61, 64-9, 93, 119, 120, 125, 143, 164, 175, 179, 188n; in hospital, 8; initial, 53, 184; least detrimental alternative, 2, 13, 64, 175-9; planning for, 127; policies on, 3, 7-9; review of, 184; of siblings, 56; success or failure of, 14, 15-16, 64, 69, see also adoption; assessment; children; foster parents; residential care
police, 75, 99, 133, 150
Portsmouth Fostering Study, 136
poverty, 5, 6; see also financial problems
press, see publicity
prevention, 1, 3, 6, 77, 115, 116, 131-3, 177, 182; see also social work
Pringle, L.M.K., 1, 3, 8
probation order, 74, 75, 150, 151, 154

Prosser, H., 8
psychiatrists, 74, 75, 76, 158, 166; see also parents, mental health of
publicity, 157, 160, 167, 172

records, 97, 173; parents' attitudes towards, 97, 124, 162
rehabilitation, see placement, at home on trial
Reid, W.J., 114
Reiner, B., 11
residential care, 3, 8, 16, 54, 57, 134, 135, 139, 140-2, 148-50, 172, 173, 177, 189n; see also assessment
resources, 5, 131-5, 151, 170-1, 172, 173
Roberts, J., 11, 91, 107, 116, 177, 188n, 189n
Robertson, J. and J., 3
Rowe, J., 7, 8, 9, 54, 55, 68, 136, 175, 189n
Rutter, M., 3, 4, 46, 67, 177

Sainsbury, E., ix, 9, 11, 98, 99, 110, 113, 114, 188n
Sawbridge, P., 178
Schaffer, H. and E., 5
schools, 49, 54, 66, 99, 109, 123, 133, 142, 183; community schools, 54, 141, see also residential care
senior social workers, 89, 162, 163, 172; see also management; social workers, supervision of
Shaw, I., 10
Shaw, Margaret, 9
Shaw, Martin, 7, 8, 135
Shelter, 4
Shyne, A.W., 114
Sinfield, A., 6, 100
single-parent families, 1, 5, 9, 33, 42-3, 102, 103, 125, 137, 171; see also marriage, parents
social security, 35, 41, 99, 132
social services departments: committees of, 13, 52, 150 reorganisation of, 10
social work, 6, 7, 9-12, 120, 173-6; authority in, x, 71, 83, 89-98, 109; with children, 105-10, 174; confidentiality in, 90, 96; contracts with clients, 87, 116; effectiveness of, 9, 11, 14; empathy in, 81, 114, 124, 175; function of, 6; goals of, 87; practical help in, 6, 11, 78, 100-5, 153, 174; and social action, 6; specialisms in, 10, 73, 115; supportive, 86-9, 115; task-centred, 115-16; theory of, 7, 11, 78, 114-15; and welfare rights, 6; see also casework; prevention; social workers
Social Work (Scotland) Act, 102, 172
social workers, 10-11; accountability of, 162, 164; anxiety of, 11, 167; attitudes of, 70, 119-22, 128, 170; changes of, 74, 124; characteristics of, 71-4, 76; ethics of, 6; honesty of, 83, 90; interviews with, 18; morale of, 10; need for consultation of, 86, 162, 164, 172; qualified or unqualified, 11, 71, 72, 161; relationships with children, 106-7; relationships with parents, 14, 80-6, 172, 179; residential, 88, 89, 143, 164, 174, 178, see also residential care; role of, 83-5, 128, 170, 174; satisfaction with service offered, 110-11; training of, 6, 174; values of, 81; see also social work; senior social workers
solicitors, see lawyers
Solnit, A., 175
Somerset County Council, 95, 189n
Specht, H., 116
statutory care, see care order
Stevenson, O., 8, 9, 10, 11, 62, 90, 119, 120, 163, 167, 175, 184, 189n
stigma, 5, 6
supervision orders, 15, 50, 52, 132, 133, 141, 150, 152-6, 163, 171, 172, 182; see also Courts; intermediate treatment

supplementary benefits, see poverty; social security

teachers, 74, 88, 89, 174; see also schools
Thorpe, R., 5, 7, 8, 11, 33, 55, 57, 59, 60, 66, 67, 143, 169, 170, 188n, 189n
Timms, N., ix, 9, 10, 11, 98, 99, 113, 188n
Tizard, B., 3, 175, 176
Tizard, J., 3, 66
Tod, R.J.N., 8
'tug-of-love', see child, divided loyalties of

Vickery, A., 116
visiting: children's reactions to, 55; of children to placement, 54, 174; of parents to placement, 7, 8, 54-5, 57, 59, 100, 134, 142-50, 170, 172, 176, 178; role of social worker with regard to, 136, 143, 144, 174; see also placement
voluntary care, 2, 53, 55, 76, 83, 102, 156, 175, 181, 183, 184; reasons for, 13; see also Children Act 1948

wardship, 160
Weinstein, E., 2, 7, 68, 188n
Wier, S., 5
Wilding, P., 5, 9, 37, 42
Wilson, H., 4, 5, 36, 43, 188n
Winnicott, C., 3
Winnicott, D.W., 3, 123, 187n
Wolff, S., 177
Wolkind, S., 3, 66, 67
Wootton, B., 6, 100

youth service, 174